Modern JavaScript for the Impatient

Modern JavaScript for the Impatient

Cay S. Horstmann

✦▾Addison-Wesley

Boston • Columbus • New York • San Francisco • Amsterdam • Cape Town
Dubai • London • Madrid • Milan • Munich • Paris • Montreal • Toronto • Delhi • Mexico City
São Paulo • Sydney • Hong Kong • Seoul • Singapore • Taipei • Tokyo

For information about buying this title in bulk quantities, or for special sales opportunities (which may include electronic versions; custom cover designs; and content particular to your business, training goals, marketing focus, or branding interests), please contact our corporate sales department at corpsales@pearsoned.com or (800) 382-3419.

For government sales inquiries, please contact governmentsales@pearsoned.com.

For questions about sales outside the United States, please contact intlcs@pearson.com.

Visit us on the Web: informit.com/aw

Library of Congress Control Number: 2020934310

Copyright © 2020 Pearson Education, Inc.

Cover illustration: Morphart Creation / Shutterstock

ISBN-13: 978-0-13-650214-2
ISBN-10: 0-13-650214-8

1 2020

To Chi—the most patient person in my life.

Contents

Preface

Experienced programmers familiar with languages such as Java, C#, C, and C++ often find themselves in a position where they need to work with JavaScript. User interfaces are increasingly web-based, and JavaScript is the *lingua franca* of the web browser. The Electron framework extends this capability to rich client applications, and there are multiple solutions for producing mobile JavaScript apps. Increasingly, JavaScript is used on the server side.

Many years ago, JavaScript was conceived as a language for "programming in the small," with a feature set that can be confusing and error-prone for larger programs. However, current standardization efforts and tool offerings go far beyond those humble beginnings.

Unfortunately, it is difficult to learn modern JavaScript without getting bogged down with obsolete JavaScript. Most books, courses, and blog posts are focused on transitioning from older JavaScript versions, which is not helpful for migrants from other languages.

That is the issue that this book addresses. I assume that you, the reader, are a competent programmer who understands branches and loops, functions, data structures, and the basics of object-oriented programming. I explain how to be productive with modern JavaScript, with only parenthetical remarks about obsolete features. You will learn how to put modern JavaScript to use, while avoiding pitfalls from the past.

JavaScript may not be perfect, but it has shown itself to be well-suited for user interface programming and many server-side tasks. As Jeff Atwood said presciently: "Any application that *can* be written in JavaScript, *will* eventually be written in JavaScript."

Work through this book, and learn how to produce the next version of your application in modern JavaScript!

Five Golden Rules

If you avoid a small number of "classic" features of JavaScript, you can greatly reduce the mental load of learning and using the language. These rules probably won't make sense to you right now, but I list them here for your future reference, and to reassure you that they are few in number.

1. Declare variables with let or const, not var.
2. Use strict mode.
3. Know your types and avoid automatic type conversion.
4. Understand prototypes, but use modern syntax for classes, constructors, and methods.
5. Don't use this outside constructors or methods.

And a meta-rule: *Avoid the Wat*—those snippets of confusing JavaScript code followed by a sarcastic "Wat?!" Some people find delight in demonstrating the supposed awfulness of JavaScript by dissecting obscure code. I have never learned anything useful from going down that rabbit hole. For example, what is the benefit of knowing that 2 * ['21'] is 42 but 2 + ['40'] is not, if the golden rule #3 tells you not to mess with type conversions? In general, when I run into a confusing situation, I ask myself how to avoid it, not how to explain its gory but useless details.

The Learning Paths

When I wrote the book, I was trying to put information where you can find it when you need it. But that's not necessarily the right place when you read the book for the first time. To help you customize your learning path, I tag each chapter with an icon that indicates its basic level. Sections that are more advanced than the chapter default get their own icons. You should absolutely skip those sections until you are ready for them.

Here are the icons:

The impatient rabbit denotes a **basic** topic that even the most impatient reader should not skip.

Alice indicates an **intermediate** topic that most programmers want to understand, but perhaps not on first reading.

The Cheshire cat points to an **advanced** topic that puts a smile on the face of a framework developer. Most application programmers can safely ignore these.

Finally, the mad hatter labels a **complex** and maddening topic, intended only for those with morbid curiosity.

A Tour of the Book

In **Chapter 1**, we get going with the basic concepts of JavaScript: values and their types, variables, and most importantly, object literals. **Chapter 2** covers control flow. You can probably skim over it quickly if you are familiar with Java, C#, or C++. In **Chapter 3**, you will learn about functions and functional programming, which is very important in JavaScript. JavaScript has an object model that is very different from class-based programming languages. **Chapter 4** goes into detail, with a focus on modern syntax. **Chapters 5** and **6** cover the library classes that you will most often use for working with numbers, dates, strings, and regular expressions. These chapters are largely at the basic level, with a sprinkling of more advanced sections.

The next four chapters cover intermediate level topics. In **Chapter 7**, you will see how to work with arrays and the other collections that the standard JavaScript library offers. If your programs interact with users from around the world, you will want to pay special attention to the coverage of internationalization in **Chapter 8**. **Chapter 9** on asynchronous programming is very important for all programmers. Asynchronous programming used to be quite complex in JavaScript, but it has become much simpler with the introduction of promises and the async and await keywords. JavaScript now has a standard module system that is the topic of **Chapter 10**. You will see how to use modules that other programmers have written, and to produce your own.

Chapter 11 covers metaprogramming at an advanced level. You will want to read this chapter if you need to create tools that analyze and transform arbitrary JavaScript objects. **Chapter 12** completes the coverage of JavaScript with another advanced topic: iterators and generators, which are powerful mechanisms for visiting and producing arbitrary sequences of values.

Finally, there is a bonus chapter, **Chapter 13**, on TypeScript. TypeScript is a superset of JavaScript that adds compile-time typing. It is not a part of standard JavaScript, but it is very popular. Read this chapter to decide whether you want to stick with plain JavaScript or use compile-time types.

The purpose of this book is to give you a firm grounding of the JavaScript *language* so that you can use it with confidence. However, you will need to turn elsewhere for the ever-changing landscape of tools and frameworks.

Why I Wrote This Book

JavaScript is one of the most used programming languages on the planet. Like so many programmers, I knew a bit of *pidgin* JavaScript, and one day, I had to learn serious JavaScript in a hurry. But how?

There are any number of books that teach a little bit of JavaScript for casual web developers, but I already knew that much JavaScript. Flanagan's *Rhino book*[1] was great in 1996, but now it burdens readers with too many accidents from the past. Crockford's *JavaScript: The Good Parts*[2] was a wake-up call in 2008, but much of its message has been internalized in subsequent changes to the language. There are many books that bring old-style JavaScript programmers into the world of modern standards, but they assume an amount of "classic" JavaScript that was out of my comfort zone.

Of course, the web is awash in JavaScript-themed blogs of varying quality—some accurate but many with a tenuous grasp of the facts. I did not find it effective to scour the web for blogs and gauge their levels of truthfulness.

Oddly enough, I could not find a book for the millions of programmers who know Java or a similar language and who want to learn JavaScript as it exists today, without the historical baggage.

So I had to write it.

---

1. David Flanagan, *JavaScript: The Definitive Guide, Sixth Edition* (O'Reilly Media, 2011).
2. Published by O'Reilly Media, 2008.

Acknowledgments

I would like to once again thank my editor Greg Doench for supporting this project, as well as Dmitry Kirsanov and Alina Kirsanova for copyediting and typesetting the book. My special gratitude goes to the reviewers Gail Anderson, Tom Austin, Scott Davis, Scott Good, Kito Mann, Bob Nicholson, Ron Mak, and Henri Tremblay, for diligently spotting errors and providing thoughtful suggestions for improvements.

Cay Horstmann
Berlin
March 2020

Register your copy of *Modern JavaScript for the Impatient* on the InformIT site for convenient access to updates and/or corrections as they become available. To start the registration process, go to informit.com/register and log in or create an account. Enter the product ISBN (9780136502142) and click Submit. Look on the Registered Products tab for an Access Bonus Content link next to this product, and follow that link to access any available bonus materials. If you would like to be notified of exclusive offers on new editions and updates, please check the box to receive email from us.

About the Author

Cay S. Horstmann is principal author of *Core Java*™, *Volumes I & II, Eleventh Edition* (Pearson, 2018), *Scala for the Impatient, Second Edition* (Addison-Wesley, 2016), and *Core Java SE 9 for the Impatient* (Addison-Wesley, 2017). Cay is a professor emeritus of computer science at San Jose State University, a Java Champion, and a frequent speaker at computer industry conferences.

Values and Variables

Chapter 1

In this chapter, you will learn about the data types that you can manipulate in a JavaScript program: numbers, strings, and other primitive types, as well as objects and arrays. You will see how to store these values in variables, how to convert values from one type to another, and how to combine values with operators.

Even the most enthusiastic JavaScript programmers will agree that some language constructs—meant to be helpful for writing short programs—can lead to unintuitive results and are best avoided. In this and the following chapters, I will point out these issues and provide simple rules for safe programming.

1.1 Running JavaScript

To run JavaScript programs as you read this book, you can use a number of different approaches.

JavaScript was originally intended to execute in a browser. You can embed JavaScript in an HTML file and invoke the `window.alert` method to display values. As an example, here is such a file:

```
<html>
  <head>
    <title>My First JavaScript Program</title>
    <script type="text/javascript">
        let a = 6
        let b = 7
        window.alert(a * b)
    </script>
  </head>
  <body>
  </body>
</html>
```

Simply open the file in your favorite web browser, and the result is displayed in a dialog box—see Figure 1-1.

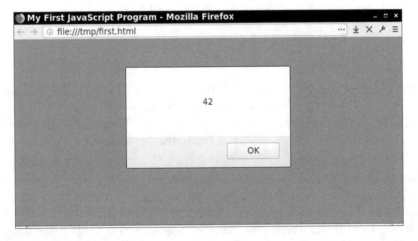

Figure 1-1 Running JavaScript code in a web browser

You can type short instruction sequences into the console that is part of the development tools of your browser. Find out the menu or keyboard shortcut to display the development tools (for many browsers, it is the F12 key, or the Ctrl+Alt+I, or, on the Mac, the Cmd+Alt+I key combination). Then pick the "Console" tab and type in your JavaScript code—see Figure 1-2.

Figure 1-2 Running JavaScript code in the development tools console

A third approach is to install Node.js from http://nodejs.org. Then, open a terminal and execute the `node` program which launches a JavaScript "read-eval-print loop," or REPL. Type commands and see their results, as shown in Figure 1-3.

Figure 1-3 Running JavaScript code with the Node.js REPL

For longer code sequences, put the instructions in a file and use the `console.log` method to produce output. For example, you can put these instructions into a file `first.js`:

```
let a = 6
let b = 7
console.log(a * b)
```

Then, run the command

```
node first.js
```

The output of the `console.log` command will be displayed in the terminal.

You can also use a development environment such as Visual Studio Code, Eclipse, Komodo, or WebStorm. These environments let you edit and execute JavaScript code, as shown in Figure 1-4.

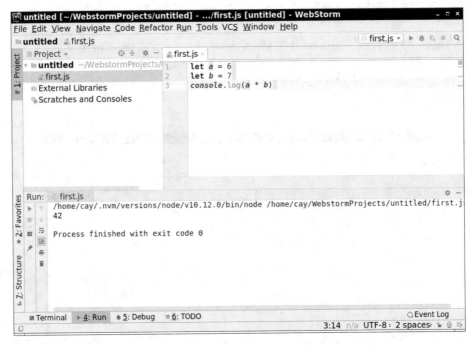

Figure 1-4 Executing JavaScript code in a development environment

1.2 Types and the typeof Operator

Every value in JavaScript is one of the following types:

- A number
- The Boolean values `false` and `true`
- The special values `null` and `undefined`
- A string
- A symbol
- An object

The non-object types are collectively called *primitive types*.

You will find out more about these types in the sections that follow, except for symbols that are discussed in Chapter 11.

Given a value, you can find its type with the `typeof` operator that returns a string `'number'`, `'boolean'`, `'undefined'`, `'object'`, `'string'`, `'symbol'`, or one of a small number of other strings. For example, `typeof 42` is the string `'number'`.

NOTE: Even though the null type is distinct from the object type, `typeof null` is the string `'object'`. This is a historical accident.

CAUTION: Similar to Java, you can construct objects that wrap numbers, Boolean values, and strings. For example, `typeof new Number(42)` and `typeof new String('Hello')` are `'object'`. However, in JavaScript, there is no good reason to construct such wrapper instances. Since they can be a cause of confusion, coding standards often forbid their use.

1.3 Comments

JavaScript has two kinds of comments. Single-line comments start with // and extend to the end of the line

```
// like this
```

Comments that are delimited by /* and */ can span multiple lines

```
/*
  like
  this
*/
```

In this book, I use a Roman font to make the comments easier to read. Of course, your text editor will likely use some kind of color coding instead.

 NOTE: Unlike Java, JavaScript does not have a special form of documentation comments. However, there are third party tools such as JSDoc (`http://usejsdoc.org`) that provide the same functionality.

1.4 Variable Declarations

You can store a value in a variable with the `let` statement:

```
let counter = 0
```

In JavaScript, variables do not have a type. You are free to store values of any type in any variable. For example, it is legal to replace the contents of `counter` with a string:

```
counter = 'zero'
```

It is almost certainly not a good idea to do this. Nevertheless, there are situations where having untyped variables makes it easy to write generic code that works with different types.

If you do not initialize a variable, it has the special value `undefined`:

```
let x // Declares x and sets it to undefined
```

 NOTE: You may have noticed that the statements above are not terminated by semicolons. In JavaScript, like in Python, semicolons are not required at the end of a line. In Python, it is considered "unpythonic" to add unnecessary semicolons. However, JavaScript programmers are split on that question. I will discuss the pros and cons in Chapter 2. Generally, I try not to take sides in unproductive discussions, but for this book, I have to pick one or the other. I use the "no semicolon" style for one simple reason: It doesn't look like Java or C++. You can see right away that a code snippet is JavaScript.

If you never change the value of a variable, you should declare it with a `const` statement:

```
const PI = 3.141592653589793
```

If you try to modify the value contained in a `const`, a run-time error occurs.

You can declare multiple variables with a single `const` or `let` statement:

```
const FREEZING = 0, BOILING = 100
let x, y
```

However, many programmers prefer to declare each variable with a separate statement.

 CAUTION: Avoid two obsolete forms of variable declarations, with the `var` keyword and with no keyword at all:

```
var counter = 0 // Obsolete
coutner = 1 // Note the misspelling—creates a new variable!
```

The `var` declaration has some serious deficiencies; you can read about them in Chapter 3. The "create upon first assignment" behavior is obviously dangerous. If you misspell a variable name, a new variable is created. For that reason, "create upon first assignment" is an error in *strict mode*, a mode that forbids certain outdated constructs. You will see in Chapter 3 how to turn on strict mode.

 TIP: In the preface, I list the five golden rules that, if followed, eliminate most of the confusion caused by "classic" JavaScript features. The first two golden rules are:

1. Declare variables with `let` or `const`, not `var`.

2. Use strict mode.

1.5 Identifiers

The name of a variable must follow the general syntax for *identifiers*. An identifier consists of Unicode letters, digits, and the _ and $ characters. The first character cannot be a digit. Names with $ characters are sometimes used in tools and libraries. Some programmers use identifiers starting or ending with underscores to indicate "private" features. With your own names, it is best to avoid $ as well as _ at the start or at the end. Internal _ are fine, but many JavaScript programmers prefer the `camelCase` format where uppercase letters are used for word boundaries.

You cannot use the following keywords as identifiers:

```
break case catch class const continue debugger default delete do
else enum export extends false finally for function if import in instanceof
new null return super switch this throw true try typeof var void while with
```

In strict mode, these keywords are also forbidden:

```
implements interface let package protected private public static
```

The following keywords are more recent additions to the language; you can use them as identifiers for backwards compatibility, but you shouldn't:

```
await as async from get of set target yield
```

> **NOTE:** You can use any Unicode letters or digits in identifiers, such as:
>
> ```
> const π = 3.141592653589793
> ```
>
> However, this is not common, probably because many programmers lack input methods for typing such characters.

1.6 Numbers

JavaScript has no explicit integer type. All numbers are double-precision floating-point numbers. Of course, you can use integer values; you simply don't worry about the difference between, say, 1 and 1.0. What about roundoff? Any integer numbers between Number.MIN_SAFE_INTEGER ($-2^{53} + 1$ or -9,007,199,254,740,991) and Number.MAX_SAFE_INTEGER ($2^{53} - 1$ or 9,007,199,254,740,991) are represented accurately. That's a larger range than integers in Java. As long as results stay within this range, arithmetic operations on integers are also accurate. Outside the range, you will encounter roundoff errors. For example, Number.MAX_SAFE_INTEGER * 10 evaluates to 90071992547409900.

> **NOTE:** If the integer range is insufficient, you can use "big integers," which can have an arbitrary number of digits. Big integers are described in Chapter 5.

As with floating-point numbers in any programming language, you cannot avoid roundoff errors with fractional values. For example, 0.1 + 0.2 evaluates to 0.30000000000000004, as it would in Java, C++, or Python. This is inevitable since decimal numbers such as 0.1, 0.2, and 0.3 do not have exact binary representations. If you need to compute with dollars and cents, you should represent all quantities as integer multiples of a penny.

See Chapter 5 for other forms of number literals such as hexadecimal numbers.

To convert a string to a number, you can use the parseFloat or parseInt functions:

```
const notQuitePi = parseFloat('3.14') // The number 3.14
const evenLessPi = parseInt('3') // The integer 3
```

The `toString` method converts a number back to a string:

```
const notQuitePiString = notQuitePi.toString() // The string '3.14'
const evenLessPiString = (3).toString() // The string '3'
```

 NOTE: JavaScript, like C++ but unlike Java, has both functions and methods. The `parseFloat` and `parseInt` functions are not methods, so you don't invoke them with the dot notation.

 NOTE: As you saw in the preceding code snippet, you can apply methods to number literals. However, you must enclose the number literal in parentheses so that the dot isn't interpreted as a decimal separator.

 CAUTION: What happens when you use a fractional number when an integer is expected? It depends on the situation. Suppose you extract a substring of a string. Then fractional positions are truncated to the next smaller integer:

```
'Hello'.substring(0, 2.5) // The string 'He'
```

But when you provide a fractional index, the result is `undefined`:

```
'Hello'[2.5] // undefined
```

It isn't worth figuring out when a fractional number happens to work as an integer. If you are in such a situation, make your intent explicit by calling `Math.trunc(x)` to discard the fractional part, or `Math.round(x)` to round to the nearest integer.

If you divide by zero, the result is `Infinity` or `-Infinity`. However, `0 / 0` is `NaN`, the "not a number" constant.

Some number-producing functions return `NaN` to indicate a faulty input. For example, `parseFloat('pie')` is `NaN`.

1.7 Arithmetic Operators

JavaScript has the usual operators `+ - * /` for addition, subtraction, multiplication, and division. Note that the `/` operator always yields a floating-point result, even if both operands are integers. For example, `1 / 2` is `0.5`, not `0` as it would be in Java or C++.

The % operator yields the remainder of the integer division for non-negative integer operands, just as it does in Java, C++, and Python. For example, if k is a non-negative integer, then k % 2 is 0 if k is even, 1 if k is odd.

If k and n are positive values, possibly fractional, then k % n is the value that is obtained by subtracting n from k until the result is less than n. For example, 3.5 % 1.2 is 1.1, the result of subtracting 1.2 twice. See Exercise 3 for negative operands.

The ** operator denotes "raising to a power," as it does in Python (and all the way back to Fortran). The value of 2 ** 10 is 1024, 2 ** -1 is 0.5, and 2 ** 0.5 is the square root of 2.

If an operand of any arithmetic operator is the "not a number" value NaN, the result is again NaN.

As in Java, C++, and Python, you can combine assignment and arithmetic operations:

```
counter += 10 // The same as counter = counter + 10
```

The ++ and -- operators increment and decrement a variable:

```
counter++ // The same as counter = counter + 1
```

 CAUTION: Just as Java and C++, JavaScript copies the C language where ++ can be applied either after or before a variable, yielding the pre-increment or post-increment value.

```
let counter = 0
let riddle = counter++
let enigma = ++counter
```

What are the values of riddle and enigma? If you don't happen to know, you can find out by carefully parsing the preceding description, or by trying it out, or by tapping the fount of wisdom that is the Internet. However, I urge you never to write code that depends on this knowledge.

Some programmers find the ++ and -- operators so reprehensible that they resolve never to use them. And there is no real need—after all, counter += 1 is not much longer than counter++. In this book, I will use the ++ and -- operators, but never in a situation where their value is captured.

As in Java, the + operator is also used for string concatenation. If s is a string and x a value of any type, then s + x and x + s are strings, obtained by turning x into a string and joining it with s.

For example,

```
let counter = 7
let agent = '00' + counter // The string '007'
```

 CAUTION: As you saw, the expression x + y is a number if both operands are numbers, and a string if at least one operand is a string. In all other cases, the rules get complex and the results are rarely useful. Either both operands are turned into strings and concatenated, or both are converted into numbers and added. For example, the expression null + undefined is evaluated as the numeric addition 0 + NaN, which results in NaN (see Table 1-1).

With the other arithmetic operators, only conversion to numbers is attempted. For example, the value of 6 * '7' is 42—the string '7' is converted to the number 7.

Table 1–1 Conversion to Numbers and Strings

Value	To Number	To String
A number	Itself	A string containing the digits of the number
A string containing the digits of a number	The number value	Itself
The empty string ''	0	''
Any other string	NaN	Itself
false	0	'false'
true	1	'true'
null	0	'null'
undefined	NaN	'undefined'
The empty array []	0	''
An array containing a single number	The number	A string containing the digits of the number
Other arrays	NaN	The elements converted to strings and joined by commas, such as '1,2,3'
Objects	By default, NaN, but can be customized	By default, '[object Object]', but can be customized

TIP: Don't rely on automatic type conversions with arithmetic operators. The rules are confusing and can lead to unintended results. If you want to process operands that are strings or single-element arrays, convert them explicitly.

 TIP: Prefer template literals (Section 1.11, "Template Literals," page 15) over string concatenation. This way, you don't have to remember what the + operator does to non-numeric operands.

1.8 Boolean Values

The Boolean type has two values, false and true. In a condition, values of any type will be converted to a Boolean value. The values 0, NaN, null, undefined, and the empty string are each converted to false, all others to true.

This sounds simple enough, but as you will see in the following chapter, it can lead to very confusing results. To minimize confusion, it is a good idea to use actual Boolean values for all conditions.

1.9 null and undefined

JavaScript has two ways to indicate the absence of a value. When a variable is declared but not initialized, its value is undefined. This commonly happens with functions. When you call a function and fail to provide a parameter, the parameter variable has the value undefined.

The null value is intended to denote the intentional absence of a value.

Is this a useful distinction? There are two schools of thought. Some programmers think that having two "bottom" values is error-prone and suggest that you only use one. In that case, you should use undefined. You can't avoid undefined in the JavaScript language, but you can (mostly) avoid null.

The opposing point of view is that you should never set values to undefined and never return undefined from a function, but always use null for missing values. Then, undefined may signal a serious problem.

 TIP: In any project, explicitly settle on one or the other approach: Use either undefined or null for indicating the intentional absence of a value. Otherwise, you end up with pointless philosophical discussions and unnecessary checks for both undefined and null.

CAUTION: Unlike `null`, `undefined` is *not* a reserved word. It is a variable in the global scope. In ancient times, you were able to assign a new value to the global `undefined` variable! This was clearly a terrible idea, and now `undefined` is a constant. However, you can still declare *local* variables called `undefined`. Of course, that's also a bad idea. Don't declare local variables `NaN` and `Infinity` either.

1.10 String Literals

String literals are enclosed in single or double quotes: `'Hello'` or `"Hello"`. In this book, I always use single quotes as delimiters.

If you use a quote inside a string that is delimited by the same quote type, escape it with a backslash. You should also escape backslashes and the control characters in Table 1-2.

For example, `'\\\'\'\\\n'` is a string of length 5, containing `\'\` followed by a newline.

Table 1-2 Escape Sequences for Special Characters

Escape Sequence	Name	Unicode Value
\b	Backspace	\u{0008}
\t	Tab	\u{0009}
\n	Linefeed	\u{000A}
\r	Carriage return	\u{000D}
\f	Form feed	\u{000C}
\v	Vertical tab	\u{000B}
\'	Single quote	\u{0027}
\"	Double quote	\u{0022}
\\	Backslash	\u{005C}

\newline	Continuation to the next line	Nothing—no newline is added:
		`"Hel\`
		`lo"`
		is the string `"Hello"`

To include arbitrary Unicode characters in a JavaScript string, you can just type or paste them, provided your source file uses an appropriate encoding (such as UTF-8):

```
let greeting = 'Hello 🌐'
```

If it is important to keep your files in ASCII, you can use the \u{*code point*} notation:

```
let greeting = 'Hello \u{1F310}'
```

Unfortunately, there is a nasty twist to Unicode in JavaScript. To understand the details, we have to delve into the history of Unicode. Before Unicode, there was a mix of incompatible character encodings where one sequence of bytes could mean very different things to readers in the USA, Russia, or China.

Unicode was designed to solve these problems. When the unification effort started in the 1980s, a 16-bit code was deemed more than sufficient to encode all characters used in all languages in the world, with room to spare for future expansion. In 1991, Unicode 1.0 was released, using slightly less than half of the available 65,536 code values. When JavaScript and Java were created in 1995, both embraced Unicode. In both languages, strings are sequences of 16-bit values.

Of course, over time, the inevitable happened. Unicode grew beyond 65,536 characters. Now, Unicode uses 21 bits, and everyone believes that is truly sufficient. But JavaScript is stuck with 16-bit values.

We need a bit of terminology to explain how this problem is resolved. A Unicode *code point* is a 21-bit value that is associated with a character. JavaScript uses the UTF-16 encoding which represents all Unicode code points with one or two 16-bit values called *code units*. Characters up to \u{FFFF} use one code unit. All others characters are encoded with two code units, taken from a reserved area that doesn't encode any characters. For example, \u{1F310} is encoded as the sequence 0xD83C 0xDF10. (See http://en.wikipedia.org/wiki/UTF-16 for a description of the encoding algorithm.)

You don't need to know the details of the encoding, but you do need to know that some characters require a single 16-bit code unit, and others require two.

For example, the string 'Hello 🌐' has "length" 8, even though it contains seven Unicode characters. (Note the space between Hello and 🌐.) You can use the bracket operator to access the code units of a string. The expression `greeting[0]` is a string consisting of a single letter `'H'`. But the bracket operator doesn't work with characters that require two code units. The code units for the ☺ character are at positions 6 and 7. The expressions `greeting[6]` and `greeting[7]` are strings of length 1, each containing a single code unit that doesn't encode a character. In other words, they are not proper Unicode strings.

TIP: In Chapter 2, you will see how you can visit the individual code points of a string with the `for of` loop.

NOTE: You can provide 16-bit code units in string literals. Then, omit the braces: `\uD83C\uDF10`. For code units up to `\u{0xFF}`, you can use "hex escapes"—for example, `\xA0` instead of `\u{00A0}`. I can think of no good reason to do either.

In Chapter 6, you will learn about the various methods for working with strings.

NOTE: JavaScript also has literals for regular expressions—see Chapter 6.

1.11 Template Literals

Template literals are strings that can contain expressions and span multiple lines. These strings are delimited by backticks (`` ` `` . . . `` ` ``). For example,

```
let destination = 'world' // A regular string
let greeting = `Hello, ${destination.toUpperCase()}!` // A template literal
```

The embedded expressions inside `${. . .}` are evaluated, converted to a string if necessary, and spliced into the template. In this case, the result is the string

```
Hello, WORLD!
```

You can nest template literals inside the `${. . .}` expressions:

```
greeting = `Hello, ${firstname.length > 0 ? `${firstname[0]}. ` : '' } ${lastname}`
```

Any newlines inside the template literal are included in the string. For example,

```
greeting = `<div>Hello</div>
<div>${destination}</div>
`
```

sets greeting to the string '<div>Hello</div>\n<div>World</div>\n' with a newline after each line. (Windows line endings \r\n in the source file are converted to Unix line endings \n in the resulting string.)

To include backticks, dollar signs, or backslashes in template literals, escape them with backslashes: `` `\`\$\\` `` is the string containing the three characters `` `$\ ``.

 NOTE: A *tagged template literal* is a template literal that is preceded by a function, like this:

```
html`<div>Hello, ${destination}</div>`
```

In this example, the html function is invoked with the template fragments '<div>Hello, ' and '</div>' and the value of the expression destination.

In Chapter 6, you will see how to write your own tag functions.

1.12 Objects

JavaScript objects are very different from those in class-based languages such as Java and C++. A JavaScript object is simply a set of name/value pairs or "properties," like this:

```
{ name: 'Harry Smith', age: 42 }
```

Such an object has only public data and neither encapsulation nor behavior. The object is not an instance of any particular class. In other words, it is nothing like an object in traditional object-oriented programming. As you will see in Chapter 4, it is possible to declare classes and methods, but the mechanisms are very different from most other languages.

Of course, you can store an object in a variable:

```
const harry = { name: 'Harry Smith', age: 42 }
```

Once you have such a variable, you can access the object properties with the usual dot notation:

```
let harrysAge = harry.age
```

You can modify existing properties or add new properties:

```
harry.age = 40
harry.salary = 90000
```

> **NOTE:** The `harry` variable was declared as `const`, but as you just saw, you can mutate the object to which it refers. However, you cannot assign a different value to a `const` variable.
>
> ```
> const sally = { name: 'Sally Lee' }
> sally.age = 28 // OK—mutates the object to which sally refers
> sally = { name: 'Sally Albright' }
>     // Error—cannot assign a different value to a const variable
> ```
>
> In other words, `const` is like `final` in Java and not at all like `const` in C++.

Use the `delete` operator to remove a property:

```
delete harry.salary
```

Accessing a nonexistent property yields `undefined`:

```
let boss = harry.supervisor // undefined
```

A property name can be computed. Then, use array brackets to access the property value:

```
let field = 'Age'
let harrysAge = harry[field.toLowerCase()]
```

1.13 Object Literal Syntax

This is the first of several intermediate-level sections in this chapter. Feel free to skip the sections with this icon if you are just starting to learn JavaScript.

An object literal can have a trailing comma. This makes it easy to add other properties as the code evolves:

```
let harry = {
  name: 'Harry Smith',
  age: 42, // Add more properties below
}
```

Quite often, when declaring an object literal, property values are stored in variables whose names are equal to the property names. For example,

```
let age = 43
let harry = { name: 'Harry Smith', age: age }
  // The 'age' property is set to the value of the age variable
```

There is a shortcut for this situation:

```
let harry = { name: 'Harry Smith', age } // The age property is now 43
```

Use brackets for the computed property names in object literals:

```
let harry = { name: 'Harry Smith', [field.toLowerCase()] : 42 }
```

A property name is always a string. If the name doesn't follow the rules of an identifier, quote it in an object literal:

```
let harry = { name: 'Harry Smith', 'favorite beer': 'IPA' }
```

To access such a property, you cannot use the dot notation. Use brackets instead:

```
harry['favorite beer'] = 'Lager'
```

Such property names are not common, but they can sometimes be convenient. For example, you can have an object whose property names are file names and whose property values are the contents of those files.

 CAUTION: There are parsing situations where an opening brace can indicate an object literal or a block statement. In those cases, the block statement takes precedence. For example, if you type

```
{} - 1
```

into the browser console or Node.js, the empty block is executed. Then, the expression - 1 is evaluated and displayed.

In contrast, in the expression

```
1 - {}
```

{} is an empty object that is converted to NaN. Then the result (also NaN) is displayed.

This ambiguity doesn't normally occur in practical programs. When you form an object literal, you usually store it in a variable, pass it as an argument, or return it as a result. In all those situations, the parser would not expect a block.

If you ever have a situation where an object literal is falsely parsed as a block, the remedy is simple: Enclose the object literal in parentheses. You will see an example in Section 1.16, "Destructuring" (page 21).

1.14 Arrays

In JavaScript, an array is simply an object whose property names are the strings '0', '1', '2', and so on. (Strings are used because numbers can't be property names.)

You can declare array literals by enclosing their elements in square brackets:

```
const numbers = [1, 2, 3, 'many']
```

This is an object with five properties: '0', '1', '2', '3', and 'length'.

The `length` property is one more than the highest index, converted to a number. The value of `numbers.length` is the number `4`.

You need to use the bracket notation to access the first four properties: `numbers['1']` is `2`. For your convenience, the argument inside the brackets is automatically converted to a string. You can use `numbers[1]` instead, which gives you the illusion of working with an array in a language such as Java or C++.

Note that the element types in an array don't need to match. The `numbers` array contains three numbers and a string.

An array can have missing elements:

```
const someNumbers = [ , 2, , 9] // No properties '0', '2'
```

As with any object, a nonexistent property has the value `undefined`. For example, `someNumbers[0]` and `someNumbers[6]` are `undefined`.

You can add new elements past the end:

```
someNumbers[6] = 11 // Now someNumbers has length 7
```

Note that, as with all objects, you can change the properties of an array that is referenced by a `const` variable.

 NOTE: A *trailing* comma does *not* indicate a missing element. For example, `[1, 2, 7, 9,]` has four elements, and the highest index is 3. As with object literals, trailing commas are intended for literals that may be expanded over time, such as:

```
const developers = [
  'Harry Smith',
  'Sally Lee',
  // Add more elements above
]
```

Since arrays are objects, you can add arbitrary properties:

```
numbers.lucky = true
```

This is not common, but it is perfectly valid JavaScript.

The `typeof` operator returns `'object'` for an array. To test whether an object is an array, call `Array.isArray(obj)`.

When an array needs to be converted to a string, all elements are turned into strings and joined with commas. For example,

```
'' + [1, 2, 3]
```

is the string `'1,2,3'`.

An array of length 0 becomes an empty string.

JavaScript, like Java, has no notion of multidimensional arrays, but you can simulate them with arrays of arrays. For example,

```
const melancholyMagicSquare = [
  [16, 3, 2, 13],
  [5, 10, 11, 8],
  [9, 6, 7, 12],
  [4, 15, 14, 1]
]
```

Then, use two bracket pairs to access an element:

```
melancholyMagicSquare[1][2] // 11
```

In Chapter 2, you will see how to visit all elements of an array. Turn to Chapter 7 for a complete discussion of all array methods.

1.15 JSON

The JavaScript Object Notation or JSON is a lightweight text format for exchanging object data between applications (which may or may not be implemented in JavaScript).

In a nutshell, JSON uses the JavaScript syntax for object and array literals, with a few restrictions:

- Values are object literals, array literals, strings, floating-point numbers, and the values true, false, and null.

- All strings are delimited by double quotes, not single quotes.

- All property names are delimited by double quotes.

- There are no trailing commas or skipped elements.

See www.json.org for a formal description of the notation.

An example of a JSON string is:

```
{ "name": "Harry Smith", "age": 42, "lucky numbers": [17, 29], "lucky": false }
```

The JSON.stringify method turns a JavaScript object into a JSON string, and JSON.parse parses a JSON string, yielding a JavaScript object. These methods are commonly used when communicating with a server via HTTP.

 CAUTION: JSON.stringify drops object properties whose value is undefined, and it turns array elements with undefined values to null. For example, JSON.stringify({ name: ['Harry', undefined, 'Smith'], age: undefined }) is the string '{"name":["Harry",null,"Smith"]}'.

Some programmers use the `JSON.stringify` method for logging. A logging command

```
console.log(`harry=${harry}`)
```

gives you a useless message

```
harry=[object Object]
```

A remedy is to call `JSON.stringify`:

```
console.log(`harry=${JSON.stringify(harry)}`)
```

Note that this problem only occurs with strings that contain objects. If you log an object by itself, the console displays it nicely. An easy alternative is to log the names and values separately:

```
console.log('harry=', harry, 'sally=', sally)
```

Or even easier, put them into an object:

```
console.log({harry, sally}) // Logs the object { harry: { . . . }, sally: { . . . } }
```

1.16 Destructuring

Destructuring is a convenient syntax for fetching the elements of an array or values of an object. As with the other intermediate-level topics in this chapter, feel free to skip this section until you are ready for it.

In this section, we start out with the basic syntax. The following section covers some of the finer points.

Let's look at arrays first. Suppose you have an array `pair` with two elements. Of course, you can get the elements like this:

```
let first = pair[0]
let second = pair[1]
```

With destructuring, this becomes:

```
let [first, second] = pair
```

This statement declares variables `first` and `second` and initializes them with `pair[0]` and `pair[1]`.

The left-hand side of a destructuring assignment is not actually an array literal. After all, `first` and `second` don't yet exist. Think of the left-hand side as a pattern that describes how the variables should be matched with the right-hand side.

Consider this more complex case and observe how the variables are matched with the array elements:

```
let [first, [second, third]] = [1, [2, 3]]
   // Sets first to 1, second to 2, and third to 3
```

The array on the right-hand side can be longer than the pattern on the left-hand side. The unmatched elements are simply ignored:

```
let [first, second] = [1, 2, 3]
```

If the array is shorter, the unmatched variables are set to undefined:

```
let [first, second] = [1]
  // Sets first to 1, second to undefined
```

If the variables first and second are already declared, you can use destructuring to set them to new values:

```
[first, second] = [4, 5]
```

 TIP: To swap the values of the variables x and y, simply use:

```
[x, y] = [y, x]
```

If you use destructuring for an assignment, the left-hand side doesn't have to consist of variables. You can use any *lvalues*—expressions that can be on the left-hand side of an assignment. For example, this is valid destructuring:

```
[numbers[0], harry.age] = [13, 42] // Same as numbers[0] = 13; harry.age = 42
```

Destructuring for objects is similar. Use property names instead of array positions:

```
let harry = { name: 'Harry', age: 42 }
let { name: harrysName, age: harrysAge } = harry
```

This code snippet declares two variables harrysName and harrysAge and initializes them with the name and age property values of the right-hand side object.

Keep in mind that the left-hand side is *not* an object literal. It is a pattern to show how the variables are matched with the right-hand side.

Destructuring with objects is most compelling when the property has the same name as the variable. In that case, you can omit the property name and colon. This statement declares two variables name and age and initializes them with the identically named properties of the object on the right-hand side:

```
let { name, age } = harry
```

That is the same as:

```
let { name: name, age: age } = harry
```

or, of course,

```
let name = harry.name
let age = harry.age
```

CAUTION: If you use object destructuring to set existing variables, you must enclose the assignment expression in parentheses:

```
({name, age} = sally)
```

Otherwise, the opening brace will be parsed as the start of a block statement.

1.17 Advanced Destructuring

In the preceding section, I focused on the easiest and most compelling parts of the destructuring syntax. In this advanced section, you will see additional features that are powerful but less intuitive. Feel free to skip this section and come back to it when you feel comfortable with the basics.

1.17.1 More about Object Destructuring

You can destructure nested objects:

```
let pat = { name: 'Pat', birthday: { day: 14, month: 3, year: 2000 } }
let { birthday: { year: patsBirthYear } } = pat
  // Declares the variable patsBirthYear and initializes it to 2000
```

Once again, note that the left-hand side of the second statement *is not an object*. It is a pattern for matching the variables with the right-hand side. The statement has the same effect as:

```
let patsBirthYear = pat.birthday.year
```

As with object literals, computed property names are supported:

```
let field = 'Age'
let { [field.toLowerCase()]: harrysAge } = harry
  // Sets value to harry[field.toLowerCase()]
```

1.17.2 Rest Declarations

When destructuring an array, you can capture any remaining elements into an array. Add a prefix ... before the variable name.

```
numbers = [1, 7, 2, 9]
let [first, second, ...others] = numbers
  // first is 1, second is 7, and others is [2, 9]
```

If the array on the right-hand side doesn't have sufficient elements, then the rest variable becomes an empty array:

```
let [first, second, ...others] = [42]
  // first is 42, second is undefined, and others is []
```

A rest declaration also works for objects:

```
let { name, ...allButName } = harry
  // allButName is { age: 42 }
```

The `allButName` variable is set to an object containing all properties other than the one with key `name`.

1.17.3 Defaults

For each variable, you can provide a default that is used if the desired value is not present in the object or array, or if the value is `undefined`. Put `=` and an expression after the variable name:

```
let [first, second = 0] = [42]
  // Sets first to 42, second to 0 since the right-hand side has
  // no matching element
let { nickname = 'None' } = harry
  // Sets nickname to 'None' since harry has no nickname property
```

The default expressions can make use of previously set variables:

```
let { name, nickname = name } = harry
  // Both name and nickname are set to harry.name
```

Here is a typical application of destructuring with defaults. Suppose you are given an object that describes certain processing details, for example formatting instructions. If a particular property is not provided, then you want to use a default:

```
let config = { separator: '; ' }
const { separator = ',', leftDelimiter = '[', rightDelimiter = ']' } = config
```

In the example, the `separator` variable is initialized with the custom separator, and the default delimiters are used because they are not supplied in the configuration. The destructuring syntax is quite a bit more concise than looking up each property, checking whether it is defined, and providing the default if it isn't.

In Chapter 3, you will see a similar use case where destructuring is used for function parameters.

Exercises

1. What happens when you add `0` to the values `NaN`, `Infinity`, `false`, `true`, `null`, and `undefined`? What happens when you concatenate the empty string with `NaN`, `Infinity`, `false`, `true`, `null`, and `undefined`? Guess first and then try it out.

2. What are [] + [], {} + [], [] + {}, {} + {}, [] - {}? Compare the results of evaluating the expressions at the command line and assigning them to a variable. Explain your findings.

3. As in Java and C++ (and unlike Python which follows many centuries of mathematical experience), n % 2 is -1 if n is a negative integer. Explore the behavior of the % operator for negative operands. Analyze integers and floating-point numbers.

4. Suppose angle is some angle in degrees that, after adding or subtracting other angles, has assumed an arbitrary value. You want to normalize it so that it is between 0 (inclusive) and 360 (exclusive). How do you do that with the % operator?

5. List as many different ways as you can to produce the string with two backslash characters \\ in JavaScript, using the mechanisms described in this chapter.

6. List as many different ways as you can to produce the string with the single character ⊕ in JavaScript.

7. Give a realistic example in which a template string has an embedded expression that contains another template string with an embedded expression.

8. Give three ways of producing an array with a "hole" in the index sequence.

9. Declare an array with elements at index positions 0, 0.5, 1, 1.5, and 2.

10. What happens when an array of arrays is converted to a string?

11. Make a couple of objects representing people and store them in variables harry and sally. To each person, add a property friends that contains an array with their best friends. Suppose harry is a friend of sally and sally is a friend of harry. What happens when you log each object? What happens when you call JSON.stringify?

Control Structures

Topics in This Chapter

Chapter 2

In this chapter, you will learn about the control structures of the JavaScript language: branches, loops, and catching exceptions. The chapter also gives an overview of JavaScript statements and describes the process of automatic semicolon insertion.

2.1 Expressions and Statements

JavaScript, like Java and C++, differentiates between expressions and statements. An expression has a value. For example, 6 * 7 is an expression with value 42. A method call such as Math.max(6, 7) is another example of an expression.

A statement never has a value. Instead, it is executed to achieve some effect.

For example,

```
let number = 6 * 7;
```

is a statement whose effect is to declare and initialize the number variable. Such a statement is called a variable declaration.

Apart from variable declarations, other common statement types are branches and loops. You will see those later in this chapter.

The simplest form of a statement is an *expression statement*. It consists of an expression, followed by a semicolon. Here is an example:

```
console.log(6 * 7);
```

The expression `console.log(6 * 7)` has a side effect—displaying `42` on the console. It also has a value, which happens to be `undefined`, since the `console.log` method has chosen not to return anything more interesting. Even if the expression had a more interesting value, it would not matter—the value of an expression statement is discarded.

Therefore, an expression statement is only useful for an expression that has a side effect. The expression statement

```
6 * 7;
```

is legal JavaScript, but it has no effect in a program.

It is useful to understand the difference between expressions and statements—but in JavaScript, it is a bit tricky to see the difference between an expression and an expression statement. As you will see in the next section, a semicolon is automatically added if you write a line containing a single expression, turning it into a statement. For that reason, you cannot observe an expression in a browser's JavaScript console or in Node.js.

For example, try typing `6 * 7`. The value of the expression is displayed:

```
6 * 7
42
```

That is what a read-eval-print loop, or REPL, does: It reads an expression, evaluates it, and prints the value.

Except, because of automatic semicolon insertion, the JavaScript REPL actually sees the *statement*

```
6 * 7;
```

Statements don't have values, but the JavaScript REPL displays values for them anyway.

Try typing in a variable declaration:

```
let number = 6 * 7;
undefined
```

As you just saw, for an expression statement, the REPL displays the value of the expression. For a variable declaration, the REPL displays `undefined`. Exercise 1 explores what is displayed for other statements.

When you run your own experiments with the REPL, it is important that you know how to interpret the output. For example, type in this expression statement and observe the response:

```
console.log(6 * 7);
42
undefined
```

The first line of output is the side effect of the `console.log` call. The second line is the return value of the method call. As already mentioned, the `console.log` method returns `undefined`.

2.2 Semicolon Insertion

In JavaScript, certain statements must be terminated with semicolons. The most common ones are variable declarations, expression statements, and nonlinear control flow (`break`, `continue`, `return`, `throw`). However, JavaScript will helpfully insert semicolons for you.

The basic rule is simple. When processing a statement, the parser includes every token until it encounters a semicolon or an "offending token"—something that could not be part of the statement. If the offending token is preceded by a line terminator, or is a }, or is the end of input, then the parser adds a semicolon.

Here is an example:

```
let a = x
  + someComplicatedFunctionCall()
let b = y
```

No semicolon is added after the first line. The `+` token at the start of the second line is not "offending."

But the `let` token at the start of the third line is offending. It could not have been a part of the first variable declaration. Because the offending token comes after a line terminator, a semicolon is inserted:

```
let a = x
  + someComplicatedFunctionCall();
let b = y
```

The "offending token" rule is simple, and it works well in almost all cases. However, it fails when a statement *starts* with a token that could have been a part of the preceding statement. Consider this example:

```
let x = a
(console.log(6 * 7))
```

No semicolon is inserted after `a`.

Syntactically,

```
a(console.log(6 * 7))
```

is valid JavaScript: It calls a function `a` with the value returned by the call to `console.log`. In other words, the `(` token on the second line was *not* an offending token.

Of course, this example is rather artificial. The parentheses around `console.log(6 * 7)` were not necessary. Here is another commonly cited example:

```
let a = x
[1, 2, 3].forEach(console.log)
```

Because a `[` can appear after `x`, no semicolon is inserted. In the unlikely case that you want to loop over an array literal in this way, store the array in a variable:

```
let a = x
const numbers = [1, 2, 3]
numbers.forEach(console.log)
```

 TIP: Never start a statement with `(` or `[`. Then you don't have to worry about the statement being considered a continuation of the previous line.

 NOTE: In the absence of a semicolon, a line starting with a template or regular expression literal can be merged with the preceding line, for example:

```
let a = x
`Fred`.toUpperCase()
```

Here, x`Fred` is parsed as a tagged template literal. But you would never write such code in practice. When you work with a string or regular expression, you want to use the result, and the literal won't be at the start of the statement.

The second semicolon rule can be more problematic. A semicolon is inserted after a nonlinear control flow statement (`break`, `continue`, `return`, `throw`, or `yield`) that is immediately followed by a line terminator. If you write

```
return
    x + someComplicatedExpression;
```

then a semicolon is automatically added:

```
return ;
    x + someComplicatedExpression;
```

The function returns without yielding any value. The second line is an expression statement that is never executed.

The remedy is trivial. Don't put a line break after return. Put at least one token of the return value expression in the same line:

```
return x +
  someComplicatedExpression;
```

You must pay attention to this rule *even if you faithfully put semicolons everywhere*.

Apart from the "offending token" and "nonlinear control flow" rules, there is another obscure rule. A semicolon is inserted if a ++ or -- is immediately preceded by a line terminator.

According to this rule,

```
x
++
y
```

means

```
x;
++y;
```

As long as you keep the ++ on the same line as its operand, you don't have to worry about this rule.

The automatic insertion rules are part of the language. They work tolerably well in practice. If you like semicolons, by all means, put them in. If you don't, omit them. *Either way*, you need to pay attention to a couple of corner cases.

NOTE: Semicolons are *only* inserted before a line terminator or a }. If you have multiple statements on the same line, you need to provide semicolons:

```
if (i < j) { i++; j-- }
```

Here, the semicolon is necessary to separate the i++ and j-- statements.

2.3 Branches

If you are familiar with C, C++, Java, or C#, you can safely skip this section.

The conditional statement in JavaScript has the form

```
if (condition) statement
```

The condition must be surrounded by parentheses.

TIP: In the condition, you should produce either `true` or `false`, even though JavaScript allows arbitrary values and converts them to Boolean values. As you will see in the next section, these conversions can be unintuitive and potentially dangerous. Follow the golden rule #3 from the preface:

- Know your types and avoid automatic type conversion.

You will often want to execute multiple statements when a condition is fulfilled. In this case, use a *block statement* that takes the form

```
{
    statement₁
    statement₂
    . . .
}
```

An optional `else` clause is executed when the condition is not fulfilled, for example:

```
if (yourSales > target) {
  performance = 'Good'
  bonus = 100
} else {
  performance = 'Mediocre'
  bonus = 0
}
```

 NOTE: This example shows the "one true brace style" in which the opening brace is placed at the end of the line preceding the first statement of the block. This style is commonly used with JavaScript.

If the `else` clause is another `if` statement, the following format is conventionally used:

```
if (yourSales > 2 * target) {
  performance = 'Excellent'
  bonus = 1000
} else if (yourSales > target) {
  performance = 'Good'
  bonus = 100
} else {
  performance = 'Mediocre'
  bonus = 0
}
```

Braces are not necessary around single statements:

```
if (yourSales > target)
  bonus = 100
```

 CAUTION: If you don't use braces, or if you use braces but not the "one true brace style" with an if/else statement, then you can write code that works in a program file but fails when pasting into a JavaScript console. Consider this example:

```
if (yourSales > target)
  bonus = 100
else
  bonus = 0
```

Some JavaScript consoles analyze the code one line at a time. Such a console will think that the if statement is complete before the else clause. To avoid this problem, use braces or place the entire if statement in a single line

```
if (yourSales > target) bonus = 100; else bonus = 0
```

It is sometimes convenient to have an expression analog to the if statement. Consider computing the larger of two values:

```
let max = undefined
if (x > y) max = x; else max = y
```

It would be nicer to initialize max with the larger of x and y. Since if is a statement, we cannot write:

```
let max = if (x > y) x else y // Error—if statement not expected
```

Instead, use the ? : operator, also called the "conditional" operator. The expression *condition* ? *first* : *second* evaluates to *first* if the condition is fulfilled, *second* otherwise. This solves our problem:

```
let max = x > y ? x : y
```

 NOTE: The expression x > y ? x : y is a convenient example to illustrate the conditional operator, but you should use the standard library method Math.max if you need the largest of two or more values.

2.4 Boolishness

This is a "mad hatter" section that describes a confusing feature of JavaScript in some detail. Feel free to skip the section if you follow the advice of the preceding section and only use Boolean values in conditions.

In JavaScript, conditions (such as the one in the `if` statement) need not be Boolean values. The "falsish" values `0`, `NaN`, `null`, `undefined`, and the empty string make the condition fail. All other values are "truish" and make the condition succeed. These are also often called "falsy" or "truthy." None of these is an official term in the language specification.

> **NOTE:** Boolishness also applies for loop conditions, the operands of the Boolean operators `&&`, `||`, and `!`, and the first operand of the `? :` operator. All these constructs are covered later in this chapter.

The Boolean conversion rule sounds reasonable at first glance. Suppose you have a variable `performance`, and you only want to use it if it isn't `undefined`. So you write:

```
if (performance) . . . // Danger
```

Sure, the test fails as expected if `performance` is `undefined`. As a freebie, it also fails if `performance` is `null`.

But what if `performance` is the empty string? Or the number zero? Do you really want to treat these values the same way as absent values? Sometimes you do, and sometimes you don't. Shouldn't your code clearly indicate what your intent is? Just write what you mean:

```
if (performance !== undefined) . . .
```

2.5 Comparison and Equality Testing

JavaScript has the usual assortment of comparison operators:

```
<  less than
<= less than or equal
>  greater than
>= greater than or equal
```

When used to compare numbers, these operators are unsurprising:

```
3 < 4 // true
3 >= 4 // false
```

Any comparison involving NaN yields false:

```
NaN < 4 // false
NaN >= 4 // false
NaN <= NaN // false
```

The same operators also compare strings, using lexicographic order.

```
'Hello' < 'Goodbye' // false—H comes after G
'Hello' < 'Hi' // true—e comes before i
```

When comparing values with <, <=, >, >=, be sure that both operands are numbers or both operands are strings. Convert operands explicitly if necessary. Otherwise, JavaScript will convert operands for you, sometimes with undesirable results—see the following section.

Use these operators to test for equality:

```
=== strictly equal to
!== not strictly equal to
```

The strict equality operators are straightforward. Operands of different types are never strictly equal. The undefined and null values are only strictly equal to themselves. Numbers, Boolean values, and strings are strictly equal if their values are equal.

```
'42' === 42 // false—different types
undefined === null // false
'42' === '4' + 2 // true—same string value '42'
```

There are also "loose equality" operators == and != that can compare values of different types. This is not generally useful—see the following section if you care about the details.

 CAUTION: You cannot use

```
x === NaN
```

to check whether x equals NaN. No two NaN values are considered to be equal to one another. Instead, call Number.isNaN(x).

 NOTE: Object.is(x, y) is almost the same as x === y, except that Object.is(+0, -0) is false and Object.is(NaN, NaN) is true.

As in Java and Python, equality of objects (including arrays) means that the two operands refer to the same object. References to different objects are never equal, even if both objects have the same contents.

```
let harry = { name: 'Harry Smith', age: 42 }
let harry2 = harry
harry === harry2 // true—two references to the same object
let harry3 = { name: 'Harry Smith', age: 42 }
harry === harry3 // false—different objects
```

2.6 Mixed Comparisons

This is another "mad hatter" section that describes potentially confusing features of JavaScript in some detail. By all means, skip the section if you follow the advice of the golden rule #3—to avoid mixed-type comparisons, and in particular the "weak equality" operators (== and !=).

Still here? Let's first look at mixed-type comparisons with the <, <=, >, >= operators.

If one operand is a number, the other operand is converted to a number. Suppose the other operand is a string. The conversion yields the numeric value if the string happens to contain a number, 0 if the string is empty, or NaN otherwise. Moreover, any comparison involving NaN is false—even NaN <= NaN.

```
'42' < 5 // false—'42' is converted to the number 42
'' < 5 // true—'' is converted to the number 0
'Hello' <= 5 // false—'Hello' is converted to NaN
5 <= 'Hello' // false—'Hello' is converted to NaN
```

Now suppose the other operand is an array:

```
[4] < 5 // true—[4] is converted to the number 4
[] < 5 // true—[] is converted to the number 0
[3, 4] < 5 // false—[3, 4] is converted to NaN
```

If neither operand is a number, both are converted to strings. These comparisons rarely yield meaningful outcomes:

```
[1, 2, 3] < {} // true—[1, 2, 3] is converted to '1,2,3', {} to '[object Object]'
```

Next, let us look at loose equality $x == y$ more closely. Here is how it works:

- If the two operands have the same type, compare them strictly.

- The values undefined and null are loosely equal to themselves *and each other* but not to any other values.

- If one operand is a number and the other a string, convert the string to a number and compare strictly.

- If one operand is a Boolean value, convert both to numbers and compare strictly.

- If one operand is an object but the other is not, convert the object to a primitive type (see Chapter 8), then compare loosely.

For example:

```
'' == 0 // true—'' is converted to 0
'0' == 0 // true—'0' is converted to 0
'0' == false // true—both are converted to 0
undefined == false // false—undefined is only equal to itself and null
```

Have another look at the strings `''` and `'0'`. They are both "equal to" `0`. But they are not "equal to" each other:

```
'' == '0' // false—no conversion since both operands are strings
```

As you can see, the loose comparison rules are not very useful and can easily lead to subtle errors. Avoid this quagmire by using strict equality operators (`===` and `!==`).

 NOTE: The loose comparison `x == null` actually tests whether `x` is `undefined` or `null`, and `x != null` tests whether `x` is neither. Some programmers who have resolved never to use loose equality make an exception for this case.

2.7 Boolean Operators

JavaScript has three operators to combine Boolean values:

```
&& and
|| or
!  not
```

The expression `x && y` is `true` if both `x` and `y` are `true`, and `x || y` is `true` if at least one of `x` and `y` are. The expression `!x` is `true` if `x` is `false`.

The `&&` and `||` operators are evaluated lazily. If the left operand decides the result (falsish for `&&`, truish for `||`), the right operand is not evaluated. This is often useful—for example:

```
if (i < a.length && a[i] > 0) // a[i] > 0 is not evaluated if i ≥ a.length
```

The `&&` and `||` operands have another curious twist if the operands are not Boolean values. They yield one of the operands as the expression value. If the left operand decides the result, it becomes the value of the expression, and the right operand is not evaluated. Otherwise, the expression value is the value of the right operand.

For example:

```
0 && 'Harry' // 0
0 || 'Harry' // 'Harry'
```

Some programmers try to take advantage of this behavior and write code such as the following:

```
let result = arg && arg.someMethod()
```

The intent is to check that arg isn't undefined or null before calling the method. If it is, then result is also undefined or null. This idiom breaks down if arg is zero, an empty string, or false.

Another use is to produce a default value when a method returns undefined or null:

```
let result = arg.someMethod() || defaultValue
```

Again, this breaks down if the method can return zero, an empty string, or false.

What is needed is a convenient way of using a value unless it is undefined or null. Two operators for this are, as of early 2020, in "proposal stage 3," which means they are likely to be adopted in a future version of JavaScript.

The expression x ?? y yields x if x is not undefined or null, and y otherwise. In the expression

```
let result = arg.someMethod() ?? defaultValue
```

the default value is used only when the method returns undefined or null.

The expression x?.*propertyName* yields the given property if x is not undefined or null, and undefined otherwise. Consider

```
let recipient = person?.name
```

If person is neither undefined nor null, then the right-hand side is exactly the same as person.name. But if person is undefined or null, then recipient is set to undefined. If you had used the . operator instead of ?., then an exception would have occurred.

You can chain the ?. operators:

```
let recipientLength = person?.name?.length
```

If person or person.name is undefined or null, then recipientLength is set to undefined.

NOTE: JavaScript also has bitwise operators & | ^ ~ that first truncate their operands to 32-bit integers and then combine their bits, exactly like their counterparts in Java or C++. There are shift operators << >> >>> that shift the bits, with the left operand truncated to a 32-bit integer and the right operand truncated to a 5-bit integer. If you need to fiddle with individual bits of 32-bit integers, go ahead and use these operators. Otherwise, stay away from them.

 CAUTION: Some programmers use the expression x | 0 to remove the fractional part of a number x. This produces incorrect results if $x \geq 2^{31}$. It is better to use Math.floor(x) instead.

2.8 The `switch` Statement

JavaScript has a `switch` statement that is just like the `switch` statement in C, C++, Java, and C#—warts and all. Skip this section if you are familiar with `switch`.

The `switch` statement compares an expression with many possible values. Here is an example:

```
let description = ''
switch (someExpression) {
  case 0:
    description = 'zero'
    break
  case false:
  case true:
    description = 'boolean'
    break
  case '':
    description = 'empty string' // See the "Caution" note below
  default:
    description = 'something else'
}
```

Execution starts at the `case` label that strictly equals the value of the expression and continues until the next `break` or the end of the `switch` statement. If none of the `case` labels match, then execution starts at the `default` label if it is present.

Since strict equality is used for matching, case labels should not be objects.

CAUTION: If you forget to add a break at the end of an alternative, execution falls through to the next alternative! This happens in the preceding example when value is the empty string. The description is first set to 'empty string', then to 'something else'. This "fall through" behavior is plainly dangerous and a common cause for errors. For that reason, some developers avoid the switch statement.

 TIP: In many cases, the difference in performance between a switch statement and the equivalent set of if statements is negligible. However, if you have a large number of cases, then the virtual machine can use a "jump table" for efficiently jumping to the appropriate case.

2.9 while and do Loops

This is another section that you can skip if you know C, C++, Java, or C#.

The while loop executes a statement (which may be a block statement) while a condition is fulfilled. The general form is

while (*condition*) *statement*

The following loop determines how long it will take to save a specific amount of money for your well-earned retirement, assuming you deposit the same amount of money per year and the money earns a specified interest rate.

```
let years = 0
while (balance < goal) {
  balance += paymentAmount
  let interest = balance * interestRate / 100
  balance += interest
  years++
}
console.log(`${years} years.`)
```

The while loop will never execute if the condition is false at the outset. If you want to make sure a block is executed at least once, you need to move the test to the bottom, using the do/while loop. Its syntax looks like this:

do *statement* while (*condition*)

This loop executes the statement (which is typically a block) and then tests the condition. If the condition is fulfilled, the statement and the test are repeated. Here is an example. Suppose we just processed s[i] and are now looking at the next space in the string:

```
do {
  i++
} while (i < s.length && s[i] != ' ')
```

When the loop ends, either i is past the end of the string, or s[i] is a space. The do loop is much less common than the while loop.

2.10 for Loops

The for loop is a general construct for iterating over elements. The following three sections discuss the variants that JavaScript offers.

2.10.1 The Classic for Loop

The classic form of the for loop works just like in C, C++, Java, or C#. It works with a counter or similar variable that is updated after every iteration. The following loop logs the numbers from 1 to 10:

```
for (let i = 1; i <= 10; i++)
  console.log(i)
```

The first slot of the for statement holds the counter initialization. The second slot gives the condition that will be tested before each new pass through the loop. The third slot specifies how to update the counter after each loop iteration.

The nature of the initialization, test, and update depends on the kind of traversal that you want. For example, this loop visits the elements of an array in reverse order:

```
for (let i = a.length - 1; i >= 0; i--)
  console.log(a[i])
```

 TIP: You can place arbitrary variable declarations or expressions in the first slot, and arbitrary expressions in the other slots of a for loop. However, it is an unwritten rule of good taste that you should initialize, test, and update the same variable.

 NOTE: It is possible to cram multiple update expressions into the third slot of a for loop by using the *comma operator*:

```
for (let i = 0, j = a.length - 1; i < j; i++, j--) {
  let temp = a[i]
  a[i] = a[j]
  a[j] = temp
}
```

In the expression i++, j--, the comma operator joins the two expressions i++ and j-- to a new expression. The value of a comma expression is the value of the second operand. In this situation, the value is unused—we only care about the side effects of incrementing and decrementing.

The comma operator is generally unloved because it can be confusing. For example, Math.max((9, 3)) is the maximum of the single value (9, 3)—that is, 3.

The comma in the declaration let i = 0, j = a.length - 1 is not a comma operator but a syntactical part of the let statement. This statement declares two variables i and j.

2.10.2 The for of Loop

The for of loop iterates over the elements of an *iterable object*, most commonly an array or string. (In Chapter 8, you will see how to make other objects iterable.)

Here is an example:

```
let arr = [, 2, , 4]
arr[9] = 100
for (const element of arr)
  console.log(element) // Prints undefined, 2, undefined, 4, undefined (5 times), 100
```

The loop visits all elements of the array from index 0 to arr.length − 1, in increasing order. The elements at indexes 0, 2, and 4 through 8 are reported as undefined.

The variable element is created in each loop iteration and initialized with the current element value. It is declared as const since it is not changed in the loop body.

The for of loop is a pleasant improvement over the classic for loop if you need to process all elements in a array. However, there are still plenty of opportunities to use the classic for loop. For example, you might not want to traverse the entire array, or you may need the index value inside the loop.

When the for of loop iterates over a string, it visits each *Unicode code point*. That is the behavior that you want. For example:

```
let greeting = 'Hello 🌐'
for (const c of greeting)
  console.log(c) // Prints H e l l o, a space, and 🌐
```

You need not worry about the fact that 🌐 uses two code units, stored in greeting[6] and greeting[7].

2.10.3 The for in Loop

You cannot use the for of loop to iterate over the property values of an arbitrary object, and you probably wouldn't want to—the property values are usually meaningless without the keys. Instead, visit the keys with the for in loop:

```
let obj = { name: 'Harry Smith', age: 42 }
for (const key in obj)
  console.log(`${key}: ${obj[key]}`)
```

This loop prints age: 42 and name: Harry Smith in some order.

The for in loop traverses the keys of the given object. As you will see in Chapters 4 and 8, "prototype" properties are included in the iteration, whereas certain "nonenumerable" properties are skipped. The order in which the keys are traversed depends on the implementation, so you should not rely on it.

NOTE: The for of loop in JavaScript is the same as the "generalized" for loop in Java, also called the "for each" loop. The for in loop in JavaScript has no Java equivalent.

You can use a for in loop to iterate over the property names of an array.

```
let numbers = [1, 2, , 4]
numbers[99] = 100
for (const i in numbers)
  console.log(`${i}: ${numbers[i]}`)
```

This loop sets i to '0', '1', '3', and '99'. Note that, as for all JavaScript objects, the property keys are strings. Even though common JavaScript implementations iterate over arrays in numerical order, it is best not to rely on that. If the iteration order matters to you, it is best to use a for of loop or a classic for loop.

CAUTION: Beware of expressions such as numbers[i + 1] in a for in loop. For example,

```
if (numbers[i] === numbers[i + 1]) // Error! i + 1 is '01', '11', and so on
```

The condition does *not* compare adjacent elements. Since i holds a string, the + operator *concatenates strings*. If i is '0', then i + 1 is '01'.

To fix this problem, convert the string i to a number:

```
if (numbers[i] === numbers[parseInt(i) + 1])
```

Or use a classic for loop.

Of course, if you add other properties to your array, they are also visited:

```
numbers.lucky = true
for (const i in numbers) // i is '0', '1', '3', '99', 'lucky'
  console.log(`${i}: ${numbers[i]}`)
```

As you will see in Chapter 4, it is possible for others to add enumerable properties to `Array.prototype` or `Object.prototype`. Those will show up in a `for in` loop. Therefore, modern JavaScript etiquette strongly discourages this practice. Nevertheless, some programmers warn against the `for in` loop because they worry about legacy libraries or colleagues who paste random code from the Internet.

 NOTE: In the next chapter, you will learn about another way of iterating over an array, using functional programming techniques. For example, you can log all array elements like this:

```
arr.forEach((element, key) => { console.log(`${key}: ${element}`) })
```

The provided function is called for all elements and index keys (as numbers 0 1 3 99, not strings).

 CAUTION: When the `for in` loop iterates over a string, it visits the indexes of each *Unicode code unit*. That is probably not what you want. For example:

```
let greeting = 'Hello 😀'
for (const i of greeting)
  console.log(greeting[i])
    // Prints H e l l o, a space, and two broken symbols
```

The indexes 6 and 7 for the two code units of the Unicode character 😀 are visited separately.

2.11 Breaking and Continuing

Sometimes, you want to exit a loop as soon as you reach a goal. Suppose you look for the position of the first negative element in an array:

```
let i = 0
while (i < arr.length) {
  if (arr[i] < 0) . . .
   . . .
}
```

Upon seeing a negative element, you just want to exit the loop, so that i stays at the position of the element. That is what the break statement accomplishes.

```
let i = 0
while (i < arr.length) {
  if (arr[i] < 0) break
  i++
}
// Get here after break or when the loop terminates normally
```

The break statement is never necessary. You can always add a Boolean variable to control the loop termination—often called something like done or found:

```
let i = 0
let found = false
while (!found && i < arr.length) {
  if (arr[i] < 0) {
    found = true
  } else {
    i++
  }
}
```

Like Java, JavaScript offers a *labeled break* statement that lets you break out of multiple nested loops. Suppose you want to find the location of the first negative element in a two-dimensional array. When you have found it, you need to break out of two loops. Add a label (that is, an identifier followed by a colon) *before* the outer loop. A labeled break jumps *after* the labeled loop:

```
let i = 0
let j = 0
outer:
while (i < arr.length) {
  while (j < arr[i].length) {
    if (arr[i][j] < 0) break outer
    j++
  }
  i++
  j = 0
}
// Get here after break outer or when both loops terminate normally
```

The label in a labeled break statement must be on the same line as the break keyword.

Labeled breaks are not common.

Finally, there is a continue statement that, like the break statement, breaks the regular flow of control. The continue statement transfers control to the end of the innermost enclosing loop. Here is an example—averaging the positive elements of an array:

```
let count = 0
let sum = 0
for (let i = 0; i < arr.length; i++) {
  if (arr[i] <= 0) continue
  count++
  sum += arr[i]
}
let avg = count === 0 ? 0 : sum / count
```

When an element is not positive, the continue statement jumps immediately to the loop header, skipping the remainder of *only the current* iteration.

If a continue statement is used in a for loop, it jumps to the "update" part of the for loop, as in this example.

There is also a labeled form of the continue statement that jumps to the end of the loop with the matching label. Such statements are very uncommon.

Many programmers find the break and continue statements confusing. They are easily avoided, and in this book, I will not use them.

2.12 Catching Exceptions

Some methods return an error value when they are invoked with invalid arguments. For example, parseFloat('') returns a NaN value.

However, it is not always a good idea to return an error value. There may be no obvious way of distinguishing valid and invalid values. The parseFloat method is a good example. The call parseFloat('NaN') returns NaN, just like parseFloat('Infinity') returns the Infinity value. When parseFloat returns NaN, you cannot tell whether it parsed a valid 'NaN' string or an invalid argument.

In JavaScript, a method can take an alternative exit path if it is unable to complete its task in the normal way. Instead of returning a value, a method can *throw an exception*. In that case, execution does not resume at the code that called the method. Instead, a *catch clause* is executed. If an exception is not caught anywhere, the program terminates.

To catch an exception, use a try statement. The simplest form of this statement is as follows:

```
try {
  code
  more code
  more code
} catch {
  handler
}
```

If any code inside the `try` block throws an exception, then the program skips the remainder of the code in the `try` block and executes the handler code inside the `catch` clause.

For example, suppose you receive a JSON string and parse it. The call to `JSON.parse` throws an exception if the argument is not valid JSON. Handle that situation in the `catch` clause:

```
let input = . . . // Read input from somewhere
try {
  let data = JSON.parse(input)
  // If execution continues here, input is valid
  // Process data
  . . .
} catch {
  // Deal with the fact that the input is invalid
  . . .
}
```

In the handler, you can log that information, or take some evasive action to deal with the fact that you were handed a bad JSON string.

In Chapter 3, you will see additional variations of the `try` statement that give you more control over the exception handling process. There, you will also see how to throw your own exceptions.

Exercises

1. Browser consoles and the Node.js REPL display values when you enter statements. What values are displayed for the following kinds of statements?

    - An expression statement

    - A variable declaration

    - A block statement with at least one statement inside

    - An empty block statement

    - A `while`, `do`, or `for` loop whose body is executed at least once

- A loop whose body is never executed
- An if statement
- A try statement that completes normally
- A try statement whose catch clause is executed

2. What is wrong with the statement

```
if (x === 0) console.log('zero') else console.log('nonzero')
```

How do you fix the problem?

3. Consider a statement

```
let x = a
```

Which tokens could start the next line that prevent a semicolon to be inserted? Which ones can realistically occur in an actual program?

4. What are the results of comparing undefined, null, 0, and '' values with the operators < <= ==? Why?

5. Is a || b always the same as a ? a : b, no matter what type a and b are? Why or why not? Can you express a && b in a similar way?

6. Use the three kinds of for loop for finding the largest value in an array of numbers.

7. Consider this code snippet:

```
let arr = [1, 2, 3, 4, 5, 6, 7, 8, 9, 10, 11, 12]
for (i in arr) { if (i + 1 === 10) console.log(a[i]) }
```

Why doesn't it print anything?

8. Implement a switch statement that converts digits 0 through 9 to their English names 'zero' through 'nine'. How can you do this easily without a switch? What about the reverse conversion?

9. Suppose n is a number between 0 and 7 and you are supposed to set the array elements arr[k] through arr[k + n - 1] to zero. Use a switch with fallthrough.

10. Rewrite the do loop in Section 2.9, "while and do Loops" (page 40), as a while loop.

11. Rewrite all for loops in Section 2.10, "for Loops" (page 41), as while loops.

12. Rewrite the labeled break example in Section 2.11, "Breaking and Continuing" (page 44), to use two nested for loops.

13. Rewrite the labeled `break` example in Section 2.11, "Breaking and Continuing" (page 44), without a `break` statement. Introduce a Boolean variable to control the termination of the nested loops.

14. Rewrite the `continue` example in Section 2.11, "Breaking and Continuing" (page 44), without a `continue` statement.

15. Consider the problem of finding the first position in which an array `b` occurs as a subsequence of an array `a`. Write two nested loops:

```
let result = undefined
for (let i = 0; i < a.length - b.length; i++) {
  for (let j = 0; j < b.length; j++) {
    if (a[i + j] != b[j]) . . .
  }
  . . .
}
```

Complete with labeled `break` and `continue` statements. Then rewrite without `break` or `continue`.

Functions and Functional Programming

Chapter 3

In this chapter, you will learn how to write functions in JavaScript. JavaScript is a "functional" programming language. Functions are "first-class" values, just like numbers or strings. Functions can consume and produce other functions. Mastering a functional programming style is essential for working with modern JavaScript.

This chapter also covers the JavaScript parameter passing and scope rules, as well as the details of throwing and catching exceptions.

3.1 Declaring Functions

In JavaScript, you declare a function by providing

1. The name of the function

2. The names of the parameters

3. The body of the function, which computes and returns the function result

You do not specify the types of the function parameters or result. Here is an example:

```
function average(x, y) {
  return (x + y) / 2
}
```

The `return` statement yields the value that the function returns.

To call this function, simply pass the desired arguments:

```
let result = average(6, 7) // result is set to 6.5
```

What if you pass something other than a number? Whatever happens, happens. For example:

```
result = average('6', '7') // result is set to 33.5
```

When you pass strings, the `+` in the function body concatenates them. The resulting string `'67'` is converted to a number before the division by 2.

That looks rather casual to a Java, C#, or C++ programmer who is used to compile-time type checking. Indeed, if you mess up argument types, you only find out when something strange happens at runtime. On the flip side, you can write functions that work with arguments of multiple types, which can be convenient.

The `return` statement returns immediately, abandoning the remainder of the function. Consider this example—an `indexOf` function that computes the index of a value in an array:

```
function indexOf(arr, value) {
  for (let i in arr) {
    if (arr[i] === value) return i
  }
  return -1
}
```

As soon as a match is found, the index is returned and the function terminates.

A function may choose not to specify a return value. If the function body exits without a `return` statement, or a `return` keyword isn't followed by an expression, the function returns the `undefined` value. This usually happens when a function is solely called for a side effect.

 TIP: If a function sometimes returns a result, and sometimes you don't want to return anything, be explicit:

```
return undefined
```

NOTE: As mentioned in Chapter 2, a `return` statement must always have at least one token before the end of the line, to avoid automatic semicolon insertion. For example, if a function returns an object, put at least the opening brace on the same line:

```
return {
    average: (x + y) / 2,
    max: Math.max(x, y),
    . . .
}
```

3.2 Higher-Order Functions

JavaScript is a functional programming language. Functions are values that you can store in variables, pass as arguments, or return as function results.

For example, we can store the `average` function in a variable:

```
let f = average
```

Then you can call the function:

```
let result = f(6, 7)
```

When the expression `f(6, 7)` is executed, the contents of `f` is found to be a function. That function is called with arguments `6` and `7`.

We can later put another function into the variable `f`:

```
f = Math.max
```

Now when you compute `f(6, 7)`, the answer becomes `7`, the result of calling `Math.max` with the provided arguments.

Here is an example of passing a function as an argument. If `arr` is an array, the method call

```
arr.map(someFunction)
```

applies the provided function to all elements, and returns an array of the collected results (without modifying the original array). For example,

```
result = [0, 1, 2, 4].map(Math.sqrt)
```

sets `result` to

```
[0, 1, 1.4142135623730951, 2]
```

The `map` method is sometimes called a *higher-order function*: a function that consumes another function.

3.3 Function Literals

Let us continue the example of the preceding section. Suppose we want to multiply all array elements by 10. Of course, we can write a function

```
function multiplyBy10(x) { return x * 10 }
```

Now we can call:

```
result = [0, 1, 2, 4].map(multiplyBy10)
```

But it seems a waste to declare a new function just to use it once.

It is better to use a *function literal*. JavaScript has two syntactical variants. Here is the first one:

```
result = [0, 1, 2, 4].map(function (x) { return 10 * x })
```

The syntax is straightforward. You use the same function syntax as before, but now you omit the name. The function literal is a value that denotes the function with the specified action. That value is passed to the map method.

By itself, the function literal doesn't have a name, just like the array literal [0, 1, 2, 4] doesn't have a name. If you want to give the function a name, do what you always do when you want to give something a name—store it in a variable:

```
const average = function (x, y) { return (x + y) / 2 }
```

 TIP: Think of anonymous function literals as the "normal" case. A named function is a shorthand for declaring a function literal and then giving it a name.

3.4 Arrow Functions

In the preceding section, you saw how to declare function literals with the function keyword. There is a second, more concise form that uses the => operator, usually called "arrow":

```
const average = (x, y) => (x + y) / 2
```

You provide the parameter variables to the left of the arrow and the return value to the right.

If there is a single parameter, you don't need to enclose it in parentheses:

```
const multiplyBy10 = x => x * 10
```

If the function has no parameters, use an empty set of parentheses:

```
const dieToss = () => Math.trunc(Math.random() * 6) + 1
```

Note that dieToss is a function, not a number. Each time you call dieToss(), you get a random integer between 1 and 6.

If an arrow function is more complex, place its body inside a block statement. Use the return keyword to return a value out of the block:

```
const indexOf = (arr, value) => {
    for (let i in arr) {
      if (arr[i] === value) return i
    }
    return -1
}
```

 TIP: The => token must be on the same line as the parameters:

```
const average = (x, y) => // OK
(x + y) / 2
const distance  = (x, y) // Error
    => Math.abs(x - y)
```

If you write an arrow function on more than one line, it is clearer to use braces:

```
const average = (x, y) => {
  return (x + y) / 2
}
```

 CAUTION: If an arrow function does nothing but returns an object literal, then you must enclose the object in parentheses:

```
const stats = (x, y) => ({
    average: (x + y) / 2,
    distance: Math.abs(x - y)
})
```

Otherwise, the braces would be parsed as a block.

 TIP: As you will see in Chapter 4, arrow functions have more regular behavior than functions declared with the function keyword. Many JavaScript programmers prefer to use the arrow syntax for anonymous and nested functions. Some programmers use the arrow syntax for all functions, while others prefer to declare top-level functions with function. This is purely a matter of taste.

3.5 Functional Array Processing

Instead of iterating over an array with a `for of` or `for in` loop, you can use the `forEach` method. Pass a function that processes the elements and index values:

```
arr.forEach((element, index) => { console.log(`${index}: ${element}`) })
```

The function is called for each array element, in increasing index order.

If you only care about the elements, you can pass a function with one parameter:

```
arr.forEach(element => { console.log(`${element}`) })
```

The `forEach` method will call this function with both the element and the index, but in this example, the index is ignored.

The `forEach` method doesn't produce a result. Instead, the function that you pass to it must have some side effect—printing a value or making an assignment. It is even better if you can avoid side effects altogether and use methods such as `map` and `filter` that transform arrays into their desired form.

In Section 3.2, "Higher-Order Functions" (page 53), you saw the `map` method that transforms an array, applying a function to each element. Here is a practical example. Suppose you want to build an HTML list of items in an array. You can first enclose each of the items in a `li` element:

```
const enclose = (tag, contents) => `<${tag}>${contents}</${tag}>`
const listItems = items.map(i => enclose('li', i))
```

Actually, it is safer to first escape & and < characters in the items. Let's suppose we have an `htmlEscape` function for this purpose. (You will find an implementation in the book's companion code.) Then we can first transform the items to make them safe, and then enclose them:

```
const listItems = items
  .map(htmlEscape)
  .map(i => enclose('li', i))
```

Now the result is an array of `li` elements. Next, we concatenate all strings with the `Array.join` method (see Chapter 7), and enclose the resulting string in a `ul` element:

```
const list = enclose('ul',
  items
  .map(htmlEscape)
  .map(i => enclose('li', i))
  .join(''))
```

Another useful array method is `filter`. It receives a *predicate* function—a function that returns a Boolean (or Boolish) value. The result is an array of all elements that fulfill the predicate. Continuing the preceding example, we don't want to include empty strings in the list. We can remove them like this:

```
const list = enclose('ul',
  items
  .filter(i => i.trim() !== '')
  .map(htmlEscape)
  .map(i => enclose('li', i))
  .join(''))
```

This processing pipeline is a good example of a high-level "what, not how" style of programming. What do we want? Throw away empty strings, escape HTML, enclose items in li elements, and join them. How is this done? Ultimately, by a sequence of loops and branches, but that is an implementation detail.

3.6 Closures

The setTimeout function takes two arguments: a function to execute later, when a timeout has elapsed, and the duration of the timeout in milliseconds. For example, this call says "Goodbye" in ten seconds:

```
setTimeout(() => console.log('Goodbye'), 10000)
```

Let's make this more flexible:

```
const sayLater = (text, when) => {
  let task = () => console.log(text)
  setTimeout(task, when)
}
```

Now we can call:

```
sayLater('Hello', 1000)
sayLater('Goodbye', 10000)
```

Look at the variable text inside the arrow function () => console.log(**text**). If you think about it, something nonobvious is going on. The code of the arrow function runs long after the call to sayLater has returned. How does the text variable stay around? And how can it be first 'Hello' and then 'Goodbye'?

To understand what is happening, we need to refine our understanding of a function. A function has three ingredients:

1. A block of code

2. Parameters

3. The free variables—that is, the variables that are used in the code but are not declared as parameters or local variables

A function with free variables is called a *closure*.

In our example, `text` is a free variable of the arrow function. The data structure representing the closure stores a reference to the variable when the function is created. We say that the variable is *captured*. That way, its value is available when the function is later called.

In fact, the arrow function `() => console.log(text)` also captures a second variable, namely `console`.

But how does `text` get to have two different values? Let's do this in slow motion. The first call to `sayLater` creates a closure that captures the `text` parameter variable holding the value `'Hello'`. When the `sayLater` method exits, that variable does not go away because it is still used by the closure. When `sayLater` is called again, a second closure is created that captures a different `text` parameter variable, this time holding `'Goodbye'`.

In JavaScript, a captured variable is a reference to another variable, not its current value. If you change the contents of the captured variable, the change is visible in the closure. Consider this case:

```
let text = 'Goodbye'
setTimeout(() => console.log(text), 10000)
text = 'Hello'
```

In ten seconds, the string `'Hello'` is printed, even though `text` contained `'Goodbye'` when the closure was created.

 NOTE: The lambda expressions and inner classes in Java can also capture variables from enclosing scopes. But in Java, a captured local variable must be effectively `final`—that is, its value can never change.

Capturing mutable variables complicates the implementation of closures in JavaScript. A JavaScript closure remembers not just the initial value but the location of the captured variable. And the captured variable is kept alive for as long as the closure exists—even if it is a local variable of a terminated method.

The fundamental idea of a closure is very simple: A free variable inside a function means exactly what it means outside. However, the consequences are profound. It is very useful to capture variables and have them accessible indefinitely. The next section provides a dramatic illustration, by implementing objects and methods entirely with closures.

3.7 Hard Objects

Let's say we want to implement bank account objects. Each bank account has a balance. We can deposit and withdraw money.

We want to keep the object state private, so that nobody can modify it except through methods that we provide. Here is an outline of a factory function:

```
const createAccount = () => {
  . . .
  return {
    deposit: amount => { . . . },
    withdraw: amount => { . . . },
    getBalance: () => . . .
  }
}
```

Then we can construct as many accounts as we like:

```
const harrysAccount = createAccount()
const sallysAccount = createAccount()
sallysAccount.deposit(500)
```

Note that an account object contains only methods, not data. After all, if we added the balance to the account object, anyone could modify it. There are no "private" properties in JavaScript.

Where do we store the data? It's simple—as local variables in the factory function:

```
const createAccount = () => {
  let balance = 0
  return {
    . . .
  }
}
```

We capture the local data in the methods:

```
const createAccount = () => {
  . . .
  return {
    deposit: amount => {
      balance += amount
    },
    withdraw: amount => {
      if (balance >= amount)
        balance -= amount
    },
    getBalance: () => balance
  }
}
```

Each account has *its own* captured balance variable, namely the one that was created when the factory function was called.

You can provide parameters in the factory function:

```
const createAccount = (initialBalance) => {
  let balance = initialBalance + 10 // Bonus for opening the account
  return {
    . . .
  }
}
```

You can even capture the parameter variable instead of a local variable:

```
const createAccount = (balance) => {
  balance += 10 // Bonus for opening the account
  return {
    deposit: amount => {
      balance += amount
    },
    . . .
  }
}
```

At first glance, this looks like an odd way of producing objects. But these objects have two significant advantages. The state, consisting solely of captured local variables of the factory function, is automatically encapsulated. And you avoid the this parameter, which, as you will see in Chapter 4, is not straightforward in JavaScript.

This technique is sometimes called the "closure pattern" or "factory class pattern," but I like the term that Douglas Crockford uses in his book *How JavaScript Works*. He calls them "hard objects."

 NOTE: To further harden the object, you can use the Object.freeze method that yields an object whose properties cannot be modified or removed, and to which no new properties can be added.

```
const createAccount = (balance) => {
  return Object.freeze({
    deposit: amount => {
      balance += amount
    },
    . . .
  })
}
```

3.8 Strict Mode

As you have seen, JavaScript has its share of unusual features, some of which have proven to be poorly suited for large-scale software development. *Strict mode* outlaws some of these features. You should always use strict mode.

To enable strict mode, place the line

```
'use strict'
```

as the first non-comment line in your file. (Double quotes instead of single quotes are OK, as is a semicolon.)

If you want to force strict mode in the Node.js REPL, start it with

```
node --use-strict
```

 NOTE: In a browser console, you need to prefix each line that you want to execute in strict mode with `'use strict'`; or `'use strict'` followed by Shift+Enter. That is not very convenient.

You can apply strict mode to individual functions:

```
function strictInASeaOfSloppy() {
  'use strict'
  . . .
}
```

There is no good reason to use per-function strict mode with modern code. Apply strict mode to the entire file.

Finally, strict mode is enabled inside classes (see Chapter 4) and ECMAScript modules (see Chapter 10).

For the record, here are the key features of strict mode:

- Assigning a value to a previously undeclared variable is an error and does not create a global variable. You must use `let`, `const`, or `var` for all variable declarations.

- You cannot assign a new value to a read-only global property such as `NaN` or `undefined`. (Sadly, you can still declare local variables that shadow them.)

- Functions can only be declared at the top level of a script or function, not in a nested block.

- The `delete` operator cannot be applied to "unqualified identifiers." For example, `delete parseInt` is a syntax error. Trying to `delete` a property that is not "configurable" (such as `delete 'Hello'.length`) causes a runtime error.

- You cannot have duplicate function parameters (`function average(x, x)`). Of course, you never wanted those, but they are legal in the "sloppy" (non-strict) mode.

- You cannot use octal literals with a `0` prefix: `010` is a syntax error, not an octal 10 (which is 8 in decimal). If you want octal, use `0o10`.

- The `with` statement (which is not discussed in this book) is prohibited.

 NOTE: In strict mode, reading the value of an undeclared variable throws a `ReferenceError`. If you need to find out whether a variable has been declared (and initialized), you can't check

```
possiblyUndefinedVariable !== undefined
```

Instead, use the condition

```
typeof possiblyUndefinedVariable !== 'undefined'
```

3.9 Testing Argument Types

In JavaScript, you do not specify the types of function arguments. Therefore, you can allow callers to supply an argument of one type or another, and handle that argument according to its actual type.

As a somewhat contrived example, the `average` function may accept either numbers or arrays.

```
const average = (x, y) => {
  let sum = 0
  let n = 0
  if (Array.isArray(x)) {
    for (const value of x) { sum += value; n++ }
  } else {
    sum = x; n = 1
  }
  if (Array.isArray(y)) {
    for (const value of y) { sum += value }
  } else {
    sum += y; n++
  }
  return n === 0 ? 0 : sum / n
}
```

Now you can call:

```
result = average(1, 2)
result = average([1, 2, 3], 4)
result = average(1, [2, 3, 4])
result = average([1, 2], [3, 4, 5])
```

Table 3-1 shows how to test whether an argument x conforms to a given type.

Table 3-1 Type Tests

Type	Test	Notes
String	`typeof x === 'string' ||` `x instanceof String`	x might be constructed as `new String(. . .)`
Regular expression	`x instanceof RegExp`	
Number	`typeof x === 'number' ||` `x instanceof Number`	x might be constructed as `new Number(. . .)`
Anything that can be converted to a number	`typeof +x === 'number'`	Obtain the numeric value as `+x`
Array	`Array.isArray(x)`	
Function	`typeof x === 'function'`	

NOTE: Some programmers write functions that turn any argument values into numbers, such as

```
const average = (x, y) => {
  return (+x + +y) / 2
}
```

Then one can call

```
average('3', [4])
```

Is that degree of flexibility useful, harmless, or a harbinger of trouble? I don't recommend it.

3.10 Supplying More or Fewer Arguments

Suppose a function is declared with a particular number of parameters, for example:

```
const average = (x, y) => (x + y) / 2
```

It appears as if you must supply two arguments when you call the function. However, that is not the JavaScript way. You can call the function with more arguments—they are silently ignored:

```
let result = average(3, 4, 5) // 3.5—the last argument is ignored
```

Conversely, if you supply fewer arguments, then the missing ones are set to undefined. For example, average(3) is (3 + undefined) / 2, or NaN. If you want to support that call with a meaningful result, you can:

```
const average = (x, y) => y === undefined ? x : (x + y) / 2
```

3.11 Default Arguments

In the preceding section, you saw how to implement a function that is called with fewer arguments than parameters. Instead of manually checking for undefined argument values, you can provide default arguments in the function declaration. After the parameter, put an = and an expression for the default—that is, the value that should be used if no argument was passed.

Here is another way of making the average function work with one argument:

```
const average = (x, y = x) => (x + y) / 2
```

If you call average(3), then y is set to x—that is, 3—and the correct return value is computed.

You can provide multiple default values:

```
const average = (x = 0, y = x) => (x + y) / 2
```

Now average() returns zero.

You can even provide a default for the first parameter and not the others:

```
const average = (x = 0, y) => y === undefined ? x : (x + y) / 2
```

If no argument (or an explicit undefined) is supplied, the parameter is set to the default or, if none is provided, to undefined:

```
average(3) // average(3, undefined)
average() // average(0, undefined)
average(undefined, 3) // average(0, 3)
```

3.12 Rest Parameters and the Spread Operator

As you have seen, you can call a JavaScript function with any number of arguments. To process them all, declare the last parameter of the function as a "rest" parameter by prefixing it with the ... token:

```
const average = (first = 0, ...following) => {
  let sum = first
  for (const value of following) { sum += value }
  return sum / (1 + following.length)
}
```

When the function is called, the `following` parameter is an array that holds all arguments that have not been used to initialize the preceding parameters. For example, consider the call:

```
average(1, 7, 2, 9)
```

Then `first` is `1` and `following` is the array `[7, 2, 9]`.

Many functions and methods accept variable arguments. For example, the `Math.max` method yields the largest of its arguments, no matter how many:

```
let result = Math.max(3, 1, 4, 1, 5, 9, 2, 6) // Sets result to 9
```

What if the values are already in an array?

```
let numbers = [1, 7, 2, 9]
result = Math.max(numbers) // Yields NaN
```

That doesn't work. The `Math.max` method receives an array with one element—the array `[1, 7, 2, 9]`.

Instead, use the "spread" operator—the ... token placed before an array *argument*:

```
result = Math.max(...numbers) // Yields 9
```

The spread operator spreads out the elements as if they had been provided separately in the call.

 NOTE: Even though the spread operator and rest declaration look the same, their actions are the exact opposites of each other.

First, note that the spread operator is used with an argument, and the rest syntax applies to a variable declaration.

```
Math.max(...numbers) // Spread operator—argument in function call
const max = (...values) => { /* body */}
     // Rest declaration of parameter variable
```

The spread operator turns an array (or, in fact, any iterable) into a sequence of values. The rest declaration causes a sequence of values to be placed into an array.

Note that you can use the spread operator even if the function that you call doesn't have any rest parameters. For example, consider the `average` function of the preceding section that has two parameters. If you call

```
result = average(...numbers)
```

then all elements of `numbers` are passed as arguments to the function. The function uses the first two arguments and ignores the others.

NOTE: You can also use the spread operator in an array initializer:

```
let moreNumbers = [1, 2, 3, ...numbers] // Spread operator
```

Don't confuse this with the rest declaration used with destructuring. The rest declaration applies to a variable:

```
let [first, ...following] = numbers // Rest declaration
```

 TIP: Since strings are iterable, you can use the spread operator with a string:

```
let greeting = 'Hello 😀'
let characters = [...greeting]
```

The `characters` array contains the strings `'H'`, `'e'`, `'l'`, `'l'`, `'o'`, `' '`, and `'😀'`.

The syntax for default arguments and rest parameters are equally applicable to the `function` syntax:

```
function average(first = 0, ...following) { . . . }
```

3.13 Simulating Named Arguments with Destructuring

JavaScript has no "named argument" feature where you provide the parameter names in the call. But you can easily simulate named arguments by passing an object literal:

```
const result = mkString(values, { leftDelimiter: '(', rightDelimiter: ')' })
```

That is easy enough for the caller of the function. Now, let's turn to the function implementation. You can look up the object properties and supply defaults for missing values.

```
const mkString = (array, config) => {
  let separator = config.separator === undefined ? ',' : config.separator
  . . .
}
```

However, that is tedious. It is easier to use destructured parameters with defaults. (See Chapter 1 for the destructuring syntax.)

```
const mkString = (array, {
   separator = ',',
   leftDelimiter = '[',
   rightDelimiter = ']'
}) => {
   . . .
}
```

The destructuring syntax { **separator** = ',', **leftDelimiter** = '[', **rightDelimiter** = ']' } declares three parameter variables separator, leftDelimiter, and rightDelimiter that are initialized from the properties with the same names. The defaults are used if the properties are absent or have undefined values.

It is a good idea to provide a default {} for the configuration object:

```
const mkString = (array, {
   separator = ',',
   leftDelimiter = '[',
   rightDelimiter = ']'
} = {}) => {
   . . .
}
```

Now the function can be called without any configuration object:

```
const result = mkString(values) // The second argument defaults to {}
```

3.14 Hoisting

In this "mad hatter" section, we take up another complex subject that you can easily avoid by following three simple rules. They are:

- Don't use var
- Use strict mode
- Declare variables and functions before using them

If you want to understand what happens when you don't follow these rules, read on.

JavaScript has an unusual mechanism for determining the *scope* of a variable—that is, is the region of a program where the variable can be accessed. Consider a local variable, declared inside a function. In programming languages such as Java, C#, or C++, the scope extends from the point where the variable is declared until the end of the enclosing block. In JavaScript, a local variable declared with let appears to have the same behavior:

```
function doStuff() { // Start of block
  . . . // Attempting to access someVariable throws a ReferenceError
  let someVariable // Scope starts here
  . . . // Can access someVariable, value is undefined
  someVariable = 42
  . . . // Can access someVariable, value is 42
} // End of block, scope ends here
```

However, it is not quite so simple. You *can* access local variables in functions whose declarations precede the variable declaration:

```
function doStuff() {
  function localWork() {
    console.log(someVariable) // OK to access variable
    . . .
  }
  let someVariable = 42

  localWork() // Prints 42
}
```

In JavaScript, every declaration is *hoisted* to the top of its scope. That is, the variable or function is known to exist even before its declaration, and space is reserved to hold its value.

Inside a nested function, you can reference hoisted variables or functions. Consider the localWork function in the preceding example. The function knows the location of someVariable because it is hoisted to the top of the body of doStuff, even though that variable is declared after the function.

Of course, it can then happen that you access a variable before executing the statement that declares it. With let and const declarations, accessing a variable before it is declared throws a ReferenceError. The variable is in the "temporal dead zone" until its declaration is executed.

However, if a variable is declared with the archaic var keyword, then its value is simply undefined until the variable is initialized.

 TIP: Do not use var. It declares variables whose scope is the entire function, not the enclosing block. That is too broad:

```
function someFunction(arr) {
  // i, element already in scope but undefined
  for (var i = 0; i < arr.length; i++) {
    var element = arr[i]
    . . .
  }
  // i, element still in scope
}
```

Moreover, var doesn't play well with closures—see Exercise 10.

Since functions are hoisted, you can call a function before it is declared. In particularly, you can declare mutually recursive functions:

```
function isEven(n) { return n === 0 ? true : isOdd(n -1) }
function isOdd(n) { return n === 0 ? false : isEven(n -1) }
```

 NOTE: In strict mode, named functions can only be declared at the top level of a script or function, not inside a nested block. In non-strict mode, nested named functions are hoisted to the top of their enclosing function. Exercise 12 shows why this is a bad idea.

As long as you use strict mode and avoid var declarations, the hoisting behavior is unlikely to result in programming errors. However, it is a good idea to structure your code so that you declare variables and functions before they are used.

 NOTE: In ancient times, JavaScript programmers used "immediately invoked functions" to limit the scope of var declarations and functions:

```
(function () {
  var someVariable = 42
  function someFunction(. . .) { . . . }
  . . .
})() // Function is called here—note the ()
// someVariable, someFunction no longer in scope
```

After the anonymous function is called, it is never used again. The sole purpose is to encapsulate the declarations.

This device is no longer necessary. Simply use:

```
{
  let someVariable = 42
  const someFunction = (. . .) => { . . . }
  . . .
}
```

The declarations are confined to the block.

3.15 Throwing Exceptions

If a function is unable to compute a result, it can throw an exception. Depending on the kind of failure, this can be a better strategy than returning an error value such as NaN or undefined.

Use a `throw` statement to throw an exception:

```
throw value
```

The exception value can be a value of any type, but it is conventional to throw an error object. The `Error` function produces such an object with a given string describing the reason.

```
let reason = `Element ${elem} not found`
throw Error(reason)
```

When the `throw` statement executes, the function is terminated immediately. No return value is produced, not even `undefined`. Execution does not continue in the function call but instead in the nearest `catch` or `finally` clause, as described in the following sections.

 TIP: Exception handling is a good mechanism for unpredictable situations that the caller might not be able to handle. It is not so suitable for situations where failure is expected. Consider parsing user input. It is exceedingly likely that some users provide unsuitable input. In JavaScript, it is easy to return a "bottom" value such as `undefined`, `null`, or `NaN` (provided, of course, those could not be valid inputs). Or you can return an object that describes success or failure. For example, in Chapter 9, you will see a method that yields objects of the form { `status: 'fulfilled'`, `value:` *result* } or { `status: 'rejected'`, `reason:` *exception* }.

3.16 Catching Exceptions

To catch an exception, use a `try` statement. In Chapter 2, you saw how to catch an exception if you are not interested in the exception value. If you want to examine the exception value, add a variable to the `catch` clause:

```
try {
  // Do work
  . . .
} catch (e) {
  // Handle exceptions
  . . .
}
```

The variable in the catch clause (here, e) contains the exception value. As you saw in the preceding section, an exception value is conventionally an error object. Such an object has two properties: name and message. For example, if you call

```
JSON.parse('{ age: 42 }')
```

an exception is thrown with the name 'SyntaxError' and message 'Unexpected token a in JSON at position 2'. (The string in this example is invalid JSON because the age key is not enclosed in double quotes.)

The name of an object produced with the Error function is 'Error'. The JavaScript virtual machine throws errors with names 'SyntaxError', 'TypeError', 'RangeError', 'ReferenceError', 'URIError', or 'InternalError'.

In the handler, you can record that information in a suitable place. However, in JavaScript it is not usually productive to analyze the error object in detail, as you might in languages such as Java or C++.

When you log an error object on the console, JavaScript execution environments typically display the *stack trace*—the function and method calls between the throw and catch points. Unfortunately, there is no standard way of accessing the stack trace for logging it elsewhere.

NOTE: In Java and C++, you can catch exceptions by their type. Then you can handle errors of certain types at a low level and others at a higher level. Such strategies are not easily implemented in JavaScript. A catch clause catches *all* exceptions, and the exception objects carry limited information. In JavaScript, exception handlers typically carry out generic recovery or cleanup, without trying to analyze the cause of failure.

When the catch clause is entered, the exception is deemed to be handled. Processing resumes normally, executing the statements in the catch clause. The catch clause can exit with a return or break statement, or it can be completed by executing its last statement. In that case, execution moves to the next statement after the catch clause.

If you log exceptions at one level of your code but deal with failure at a higher level, then you want to *rethrow* the exception after logging it:

```
try {
  // Do work
  . . .
} catch (e) {
  console.log(e)
  throw e // Rethrow to a handler that deals with the failure
}
```

3.17 The finally Clause

A try statement can optionally have a finally clause. The code in the finally clause executes whether or not an exception occurred.

Let us first look at the simplest case: a try statement with a finally clause but no catch clause:

```
try {
  // Acquire resources
  . . .
  // Do work
  . . .
} finally {
  // Relinquish resources
  . . .
}
```

The finally clause is executed in all of the following cases:

• If all statements in the try clause completed without throwing an exception

• If a return or break statement was executed in the try clause

• If an exception occurred in any of the statements of the try clause

You can also have a try statement with catch and finally clauses:

```
try {
  . . .
} catch (e) {
  . . .
} finally {
  . . .
}
```

Now there is an additional pathway. If an exception occurs in the try clause, the catch clause is executed. No matter how the catch clause exits (normally or through a return/break/throw), the finally clause is executed afterwards.

The purpose of the finally clause is to have a single location for relinquishing resources (such as file handles or database connections) that were acquired in the try clause, whether or not an exception occurred.

CAUTION: It is legal, but confusing, to have `return/break/throw` statements in the `finally` clause. These statements take precedence over any statements in the `try` and `catch` clauses. For example:

```
try {
    // Do work
    . . .
    return true
} finally {
    . . .
    return false
}
```

If the `try` block is successful and `return true` is executed, the `finally` clause follows. Its `return false` masks the prior `return` statement.

Exercises

1. What does the `indexOf` function of Section 3.1, "Declaring Functions" (page 51), do when an object is passed instead of an array?

2. Rewrite the `indexOf` function of Section 3.1, "Declaring Functions" (page 51), so that it has a single return at the end.

3. Write a function `values(f, low, high)` that yields an array of function values `[f(low), f(low + 1), . . ., f(high)]`.

4. The `sort` method for arrays can take an argument that is a comparison function with two parameters—say, x and y. The function returns a negative integer if x should come before y, zero if x and y are indistinguishable, and a positive integer if x should come after y. Write calls, using arrow functions, that sort:

   • An array of positive integers by decreasing order

   • An array of people by increasing age

   • An array of strings by increasing length

5. Using the "hard objects" technique of Section 3.7, "Hard Objects" (page 59), implement a `constructCounter` method that produces counter objects whose `count` method increments a counter and yields the new value. The initial value and an optional increment are passed as parameters. (The default increment is 1.)

```
const myFirstCounter = constructCounter(0, 2)
console.log(myFirstCounter.count()) // 0
console.log(myFirstCounter.count()) // 2
```

6. A programmer thinks that "named parameters are almost implemented in JavaScript, but order still has precedence," offering the following "evidence" in the browser console:

```
function f(a=1, b=2){ console.log(`a=${a}, b=${b}`) }
f() // a=1, b=2
f(a=5) // a=5, b=2
f(a=7, b=10) // a=7, b=10
f(b=10, a=7) // Order is required: a=10, b=7
```

What is actually going on? (Hint: It has nothing to do with named parameters. Try it in strict mode.)

7. Write a function average that computes the average of an arbitrary sequence of numbers, using a rest parameter.

8. What happens when you pass a string argument to a rest parameter ...str? Come up with a useful example to take advantage of your observation.

9. Complete the mkString function of Section 3.13, "Simulating Named Arguments with Destructuring" (page 66).

10. The archaic var keyword interacts poorly with closures. Consider this example:

```
for (var i = 0; i < 10; i++) {
  setTimeout(() => console.log(i), 1000 * i)
}
```

What does this code snippet print? Why? (Hint: What is the scope of the variable i?) What simple change can you make to the code to print the numbers 0, 1, 2, . . . , 9 instead?

11. Consider this declaration of the factorial function:

```
const fac = n => n > 1 ? n * fac(n - 1) : 1
```

Explain why this only works because of variable hoisting.

12. In sloppy (non-strict) mode, functions can be declared inside a nested block, and they are hoisted to the enclosing function or script. Try out the following example a few times:

```
if (Math.random() < 0.5) {
  say('Hello')
  function say(greeting) { console.log(`${greeting}!`) }
}
say('Goodbye')
```

Depending on the result of Math.random, what is the outcome? What is the scope of say? When is it initialized? What happens when you activate strict mode?

13. Implement an average function that throws an exception if any of its arguments is not a number.

14. Some programmers are confused by statements that contain all three of try/catch/finally because there are so many possible pathways of control. Show how you can always rewrite such a statement using a try/catch statement and a try/finally statement.

Object-Oriented Programming

Topics in This Chapter

Chapter 4

As you know, JavaScript has objects, but they don't look like the objects you have seen in object-oriented programming languages such as Java or C++. In a JavaScript object, all properties are public, and they don't seem to belong to any class other than Object. It is not obvious how you might have methods or classes or inheritance.

You *can* have all that in JavaScript, and this chapter shows you how. Current versions of JavaScript provide syntax for declaring classes that looks very similar to Java, but the underlying mechanism is completely different. You really need to understand what goes on under the hood. For that reason, I first show you how to declare methods and constructor functions by hand, and then you will see how those constructs map to the class syntax.

4.1 Methods

JavaScript, unlike most object-oriented programming languages, lets you work with objects without first having to declare classes. You have already seen how to produce objects:

```
let harry = { name: 'Harry Smith', salary: 90000 }
```

According to the classic definition, an object has identity, state, and behavior. The object that you just saw certainly has identity—it is different from any other object. The object's state is provided by the properties. Let's add behavior in the form of a "method"—that is, a function-valued property:

```
harry = {
  name: 'Harry Smith',
  salary: 90000,
  raiseSalary: function(percent) {
    this.salary *= 1 + percent / 100
  }
}
```

Now we can raise the employee's salary with the familiar dot notation:

```
harry.raiseSalary(10)
```

Note that `raiseSalary` is a function declared in the `harry` object. That function looks like an ordinary function, except for one twist: In the body, we refer to `this.salary`. When the function is called, `this` refers to the object to the left of the dot operator.

There is a shortcut syntax for declaring methods. Simply omit the colon and the `function` keyword:

```
harry = {
  name: 'Harry Smith',
  salary: 90000,
  raiseSalary(percent) {
    this.salary *= 1 + percent / 100
  }
}
```

This looks similar to a method declaration in Java or C++, but it is just "syntactic sugar" for a function-valued property.

 CAUTION: The `this` reference only works in functions declared with `function` or the shortcut syntax that omits `function`, *not* with arrow functions. See Section 4.12, "The `this` Reference" (page 92), for more details.

4.2 Prototypes

Suppose you have many employee objects similar to the one in the preceding section. Then you need to make a `raiseSalary` property for each of them. You can write a factory function to automate that task:

```
function createEmployee(name, salary) {
  return {
    name: name,
    salary: salary,
    raiseSalary: function(percent) {
      this.salary *= 1 + percent / 100
    }
  }
}
```

Still, each employee object has its own `raiseSalary` property, even though the property value is the same function for all employees (see Figure 4-1). It would be better if all employees could share one function.

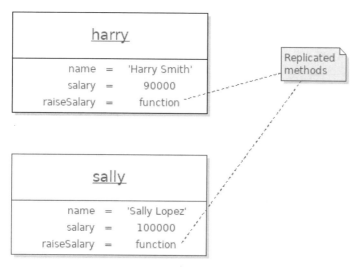

Figure 4-1 Objects with replicated methods

That is where *prototypes* come in. A prototype collects properties that are common to multiple objects. Here is a prototype object that holds the shared methods:

```
const employeePrototype = {
  raiseSalary: function(percent) {
    this.salary *= 1 + percent / 100
  }
}
```

When creating an employee object, we set its prototype. The prototype is an "internal slot" of the object. That is the technical term used in the ECMAScript language specification to denote an attribute of an object that is manipulated internally without being exposed to JavaScript programmers as a property. You can read and write the [[Property]] internal slot (as it is called in the specification) with the methods `Object.getPrototypeOf` and `Object.setPrototypeOf`. This function creates an employee object and sets the prototype:

```
function createEmployee(name, salary) {
  const result = { name, salary }
  Object.setPrototypeOf(result, employeePrototype)
  return result
}
```

Figure 4-2 shows the result of creating multiple employee objects that share the same prototype. In the figure, the prototype slot is denoted [[Prototype]], as in the ECMAScript specification.

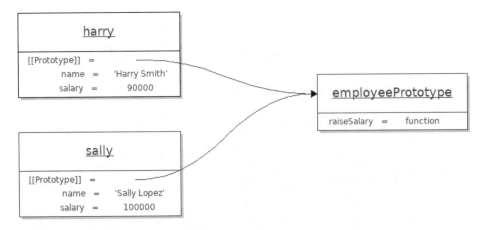

Figure 4-2 Objects with the same prototype

 CAUTION: In many JavaScript implementations, you can access the prototype of an object as `obj.__proto__`. This is not a standard notation, and you should use the `Object.getPrototypeOf` and `Object.setPrototypeOf` methods instead.

Now consider a method call

```
harry.raiseSalary(5)
```

When looking up `harry.raiseSalary`, no match is found in the `harry` object itself. Therefore, the property is searched in the prototype. Since `harry.[[Prototype]]` has a `raiseSalary` property, its value is the value of `harry.raiseSalary`.

As you will see later in this chapter, prototypes can be chained. If the prototype doesn't have a property, its prototype is searched, until the prototype chain ends.

The prototype lookup mechanism is completely general. Here, we used it to look up a method, but it works for any property. If a property isn't found in an object, then the prototype chain is searched, and the first match is the property value.

Prototype lookup is a simple concept which it is very important in JavaScript. Prototypes are used to implement classes and inheritance, and to modify the behavior of objects after they have been instantiated.

 NOTE: Lookup in the prototype chain is only used for *reading* property values. If you write to a property, the value is always updated in the object itself.

For example, suppose you change the `harry.raiseSalary` method:

```
harry.raiseSalary = function(rate) { this.salary = Number.MAX_VALUE }
```

This adds a new property directly to the `harry` object. It does not modify the prototype. All other employees retain the original `raiseSalary` property.

4.3 Constructors

In the preceding section, you saw how to write a factory function that creates new object instances with a shared prototype. There is special syntax for invoking such functions, using the `new` operator.

By convention, functions that construct objects are named after what would be the class in a class-based language. In our example, let's call the function `Employee`, as follows:

```
function Employee(name, salary) {
  this.name = name
  this.salary = salary
}
```

When you call

```
new Employee('Harry Smith', 90000)
```

the `new` operator creates a new empty object and then calls the constructor function. The `this` parameter points to that newly created object. The body of the `Employee` function sets the object properties by using the `this` parameter. The newly created object becomes the value of the `new` expression.

CAUTION: Do not return any result from a constructor function. Otherwise the value of the `new` expression is that returned value, not the newly created object.

In addition to invoking the constructor function, the `new` expression carries out another important step: It sets the object's [[Prototype]] internal slot.

The [[Prototype]] internal slot is set to a specific object, which is attached to the constructor function. Recall that a function is an object, so it can have properties. Each JavaScript *function* has a `prototype` property whose value is an object.

That object gives you a ready-made place for adding methods, like this:

```
Employee.prototype.raiseSalary = function(percent) {
    this.salary *= 1 + percent / 100
}
```

As you can see, there is a lot going on. Let us have another look at the call:

```
const harry = new Employee('Harry Smith', 90000)
```

Here are the steps in detail:

1. The `new` operator creates a new object.

2. The [[Prototype]] internal slot of that object is set to the `Employee.prototype` object.

3. The `new` operator calls the constructor function with three parameters: `this` (pointing to the newly created object), `name`, and `salary`.

4. The body of the `Employee` function sets the object properties by using the `this` parameter.

5. The constructor returns, and the value of the `new` operator is the now fully initialized object.

6. The variable `harry` is initialized with the object reference. Figure 4-3 shows the result.

As you can see in Figure 4-3, the `Employee.prototype` object has as its prototype the `Object.prototype` object which contributes the `toString` method and a few other methods.

The upshot of all this magic is that the `new` operator looks just like a constructor call in Java, C#, or C++. However, `Employee` isn't a class. It's just a function.

Then again, what is a class? In the textbook definition, a class is a set of objects with the same behavior, as provided by the methods. All objects that are obtained by calling `new Employee(. . .)` have the same set of methods. In

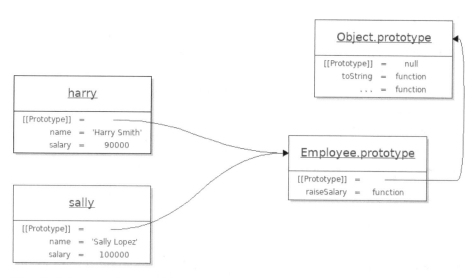

Figure 4-3 Objects created with a constructor

JavaScript, constructor functions are the equivalent of classes in class-based programming languages.

You won't often need to worry about the difference between traditional classes and the prototype-based system of JavaScript. As you will see in the following section, modern JavaScript syntax closely follows the conventions of class-based languages. However, every once in a while, you should remind yourself that a JavaScript class is nothing more than a constructor function, and that the common behavior is achieved with prototypes.

4.4 The Class Syntax

Nowadays, JavaScript has a class syntax that bundles up a constructor function and prototype methods in a familiar form. Here is the class syntax for the example of the preceding section:

```
class Employee {
  constructor(name, salary) {
    this.name = name
    this.salary = salary
  }
  raiseSalary(percent) {
    this.salary *= 1 + percent / 100
  }
}
```

This syntax does *exactly* the same as that of the preceding section. There still is no actual class. Behind the scenes, the `class` declaration merely declares a constructor function `Employee`. The `constructor` keyword declares the body of the `Employee` constructor function. The `raiseSalary` method is added to `Employee.prototype`.

As in the preceding section, you construct an object by calling the constructor function with the `new` operator:

```
const harry = new Employee('Harry Smith', 90000)
```

 NOTE: As mentioned in the preceding sections, the `constructor` should not return any value. However, if it does, it is ignored, and the `new` expression still returns the newly created object.

You should definitely use the `class` syntax. (This is the golden rule #4 in the preface.) The syntax gets a number of fiddly details right that you do not want to manage manually. Just realize that a JavaScript `class` is syntactic sugar for a constructor function and a prototype object holding the methods.

 NOTE: A class can have at most one `constructor`.

If you declare a class without a `constructor`, it automatically gets a constructor function with an empty body.

 CAUTION: Unlike in an object literal, in a `class` declaration you do not use commas to separate the method declarations.

 NOTE: Classes, unlike functions, are not hoisted. You need to declare a class before you can construct an instance.

 NOTE: The body of a class is executed in strict mode.

4.5 Getters and Setters

A *getter* is a method with no parameters that is declared with the keyword `get`:

```
class Person {
  constructor(last, first) {
    this.last = last;
    this.first = first
  }
  get fullName() { return `${this.last}, ${this.first}` }
}
```

You call the getter without parentheses, as if you accessed a property value:

```
const harry = new Person('Smith', 'Harry')
const harrysName = harry.fullName // 'Smith, Harry'
```

The `harry` object does not have a `fullName` property, but the getter method is invoked. You can think of a getter as a dynamically computed property.

You can also provide a *setter*, a method with one parameter:

```
class Person {
  . . .
  set fullName(value) {
    const parts = value.split(/,\s*/)
    this.last = parts[0]
    this.first = parts[1]
  }
}
```

The setter is invoked when assigning to `fullName`:

```
harry.fullName = 'Smith, Harold'
```

When you provide getters and setters, users of your class have the illusion of using properties, but you control the property values and any attempts to modify them.

4.6 Instance Fields and Private Methods

You can dynamically set an object property in the constructor or any method by assigning to `this.propertyName`. These properties work the same way as instance fields in a class-based language.

```
class BankAccount {
  constructor() { this.balance = 0 }
  deposit(amount) { this.balance += amount }
  . . .
}
```

Three proposals for alternative notations are in stage 3 in early 2020. You can list the names and initial values of the fields in the class declaration, like this:

```
class BankAccount {
  balance = 0
  deposit(amount) { this.balance += amount }
  . . .
}
```

A field is *private* (that is, inaccessible outside the methods of the class) when its name starts with #:

```
class BankAccount {
  #balance = 0
  deposit(amount) { this.#balance += amount }
  . . .
}
```

A method is private if its name starts with a #.

4.7 Static Methods and Fields

In a class declaration, you can declare a method as static. Such a method does not operate on any object. It is a plain function that is a property of the class. Here is an example:

```
class BankAccount {
  . . .
  static percentOf(amount, rate) { return amount * rate / 100 }
  . . .
  addInterest(rate) {
    this.balance += BankAccount.percentOf(this.balance, rate)
  }
}
```

To call a static method, whether inside or outside the class, add the class name, as in the example above.

Behind the scenes, the static method is a property of the constructor. In the olden days, one had to do that by hand:

```
BankAccount.percentOf = function(amount, rate) {
  return amount * rate / 100
}
```

In the same way, you can define the equivalent of static fields:

```
BankAccount.OVERDRAFT_FEE = 30
```

In early 2020, a class-based syntax for static fields is in proposal stage 3:

```
class BankAccount {
  static OVERDRAFT_FEE = 30
  . . .
  withdraw(amount) {
    if (this.balance < amount) {
      this.balance -= BankAccount.OVERDRAFT_FEE
    }
    . . .
  }
}
```

A static field simply becomes a property of the constructor function. As with static methods, you access the field through the class name, as BankAccount.OVERDRAFT_FEE.

Private static fields and methods (prefixed with #) are also currently in proposal stage 3.

You can declare getters and setters as static methods. As always, the setter can do error checking:

```
class BankAccount {
  . . .
  static get OVERDRAFT_FEE() {
    return this.#OVERDRAFT_FEE // In a static method, this is the constructor function
  }
  static set OVERDRAFT_FEE(newValue) {
    if (newValue > this.#OVERDRAFT_FEE) {
      this.#OVERDRAFT_FEE = newValue
    }
  }
}
```

4.8 Subclasses

A key concept in object-oriented programming is inheritance. A class specifies behavior for its instances. You can form a subclass of a given class (called the superclass) whose instances behave differently in some respect, while inheriting other behavior from the superclass.

A standard teaching example is an inheritance hierarchy with a superclass Employee and a subclass Manager. While employees are expected to complete their assigned tasks in return for receiving their salary, managers get bonuses on top of their base salary if they actually achieve what they are supposed to do.

In JavaScript, as in Java, you use the extends keyword to express this relationship among the Employee and Manager classes:

```
class Employee {
  constructor(name, salary) { . . . }
  raiseSalary(percent) { . . . }
  . . .
}

class Manager extends Employee {
  getSalary() { return this.salary + this.bonus }
  . . .
}
```

Behind the scenes, a prototype chain is established—see Figure 4-4. The prototype of Manager.prototype is set to Employee.prototype. That way, any method that is not declared in the subclass is looked up in the superclass.

For example, you can call the raiseSalary on a manager object:

```
const boss = new Manager(. . .)
boss.raiseSalary(10) // Calls Employee.prototype.raiseSalary
```

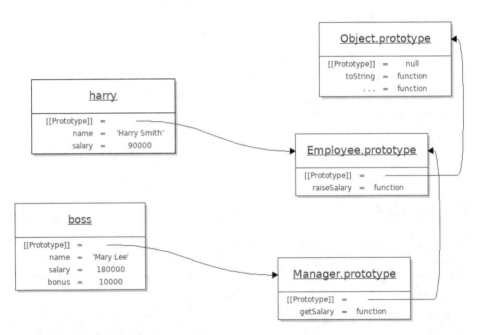

Figure 4-4 Prototype chain for inheritance

Prior to the extends syntax, JavaScript programmers had to establish such a prototype chain themselves.

The `instanceof` operator checks whether an object belongs to a class or one of its subclasses. Technically, the operator visits the prototype chain of an object and checks whether it contains the prototype of a given constructor function. For example,

```
boss instanceof Employee
```

is `true` since `Employee.prototype` is in the prototype chain of `boss`.

NOTE: In Java, the `extends` keyword is used to extend a fixed class. In JavaScript, `extends` is more dynamic. The right hand side of `extends` can be any expression that yields a function (or `null` to produce a class that doesn't extend `Object`). Section 4.11, "Class Expressions" (page 91), has an example.

NOTE: In Java and C++, it is common to define abstract superclasses or interfaces so that you can invoke methods that will be defined in subclasses. In JavaScript, there is no compile-time checking for method applications, and therefore, there is no need for abstract methods.

For example, suppose you model employees and contractors, and need to get salaries from objects of both classes. In a statically typed language, you would introduce a `Salaried` superclass or interface with an abstract `getSalary` method. In JavaScript, you simply call `person.getSalary()`.

4.9 Overriding Methods

Suppose both the superclass and the subclass have a `getSalary` method:

```
class Employee {
  . . .
  getSalary() { return this.salary }
}

class Manager extends Employee {
  . . .
  getSalary() { return this.salary + this.bonus }
}
```

Now consider a method call:

```
const empl = . . .
const salary = empl.getSalary()
```

If `empl` is a reference to a lowly employee, then the `Employee.prototype.getSalary` method is called. If, on the other hand, `empl` refers to a manager, the

`Manager.prototype.getSalary` method is invoked. This phenomenon—where the invoked method depends on the actual object that is being referenced—is called *polymorphism*. In JavaScript, polymorphism is a simple consequence of prototype chain lookup.

In this situation, we say that the `getSalary` method in the `Manager` class *overrides* the `getSalary` method of the `Employee` class.

Sometimes, you want to invoke the superclass method from the subclass. For example:

```
class Manager extends Employee {
  . . .
  getSalary() { return super.getSalary() + this.bonus }
}
```

In a method, `super` starts the lookup with the parent of the prototype object in which the method was declared. In our example, the call `super.getSalary` bypasses `Manager.prototype`, which is just as well because otherwise there would be an infinite recursion. Instead, the `getSalary` method in `Employee.prototype` is invoked.

 NOTE: In this section, we used the `getSalary` method as an example for method overriding. You can also override getters and setters:

```
class Manager extends Employee {
  . . .
  get salary() { return super.salary + this.bonus }
}
```

4.10 Subclass Construction

In a subclass constructor, you *must* invoke the superclass constructor. Use the syntax `super(. . .)`, just like in Java. Inside the parentheses, place the arguments that you want to pass to the superclass constructor:

```
class Manager extends Employee {
  constructor(name, salary, bonus) {
    super(name, salary) // Must call superclass constructor
    this.bonus = bonus // Afterwards, this is valid
  }
  . . .
}
```

You can only use the `this` reference after the call to `super`.

However, if you do not supply a subclass constructor, a constructor is automatically provided. That automatically provided constructor passes all arguments to the superclass constructor. (This is much more useful than in Java or C++, where the no-argument constructor of the superclass is called.)

```
class Manager extends Employee {
  // No constructor
  getSalary() { . . . }
}
```

```
const boss = new Manager('Mary Lee', 180000) // Calls Employee('Mary Lee', 180000)
```

Before the `extends` and `super` keywords were added to JavaScript, it was quite a bit more challenging to implement a subclass constructors that invokes the superclass constructor. This process—which is no longer necessary—requires advanced tools that are introduced in Chapter 11.

 NOTE: As you know, JavaScript doesn't really have classes. A class is just a constructor function. A subclass is a constructor function that calls a superclass constructor.

4.11 Class Expressions

You can declare anonymous classes, just like you can declare anonymous functions:

```
const Employee = class {
  constructor(name, salary) {
    this.name = name
    this.salary = salary
  }
  raiseSalary(percent) {
    this.salary *= 1 + percent / 100
  }
}
```

Recall that `class` yields a constructor function. This function is now stored in the variable `Employee`. In this example, there is no benefit over the named class notation `class Employee { . . . }`.

Here is a more useful application. You can provide methods that "mix in" a capability into an existing class:

```
const withToString = base =>
  class extends base {
    toString() {
      let result = '{'
      for (const key in this) {
        if (result !== '{') result += ', '
        result += `${key}=${this[key]}`
```

```
    }
    return result + '}'
  }
}
```

Call this function with a class (that is, a constructor function) in order to obtain an augmented class:

```
const PrettyPrintingEmployee = withToString(Employee) // A new class
e = new PrettyPrintingEmployee('Harry Smith', 90000) // An instance of the new class
console.log(e.toString())
  // Prints {name=Harry Smith, salary=90000}, not [object Object]
```

4.12 The this Reference

In this "mad hatter" section, we will have a closer look at the this reference. You can safely skip the section if you only use this in constructors, methods, and arrow functions, not inside named functions.

To see where this can be troublesome, first consider the new operator. What happens if you call a constructor function without new? If you make a call such as

```
let e = Employee('Harry Smith', 90000) // Forgot new
```

in strict mode, then the this variable is set to undefined.

Fortunately, this problem only arises with an old-style constructor function declaration. If you use the class syntax, it is illegal to call the constructor without new.

 CAUTION: If you don't use the class syntax, it is possible to declare constructor functions so that they do double duty, working with or without new. An example is the Number function:

```
const price = Number('19.95')
  // Parses the string and returns a primitive number, not an object
const aZeroUnlikeAnyOther = new Number(0)
  // Constructs a new object
```

Calling a constructor without new is not common in modern JavaScript usage.

Here is another potential problem. It is possible to invoke a method without an object. In that case, this is undefined:

```
const doLater = (what, arg) => { setTimeout(() => what(arg), 1000) }
doLater(BankAccount.prototype.deposit, 500) // Error
```

When the expression `what(arg)` is evaluated after one second, the `deposit` method is invoked. The method fails when accessing `this.balance` since `this` is `undefined`.

If you want to deposit money in a specific account, just provide the account:

```
doLater(amount => harrysAccount.deposit(amount), 500)
```

Next, consider nested functions. Inside a nested function that is declared with the `function` keyword, `this` is `undefined`. You can run into grief when you use `this` in a callback function:

```
class BankAccount {
  . . .
  spreadTheWealth(accounts) {
    accounts.forEach(function(account) {
      account.deposit(this.balance / accounts.length)
        // Error—this is undefined inside the nested function
    })
    this.balance = 0
  }
}
```

Here, `this.balance` does *not* refer to the balance of the bank account. It is `undefined` since it occurs in a nested function.

The best remedy is to use an arrow function for the callback:

```
class BankAccount {
  . . .
  spreadTheWealth(accounts) {
    accounts.forEach(account => {
      account.deposit(this.balance / accounts.length) // this correctly bound
    })
    this.balance = 0
  }
}
```

In an arrow function, `this` is statically bound to whatever `this` means outside the arrow function—in the example, to the `BankAccount` object invoking the `spreadTheWealth` method.

 NOTE: Before there were arrow functions, JavaScript programmers used a workaround—they initialized another variable with `this`:

```
spreadTheWealth(accounts) {
  const that = this
  accounts.forEach(function(account) {
    account.deposit(that.balance / accounts.length)
  })
  this.balance = 0
}
```

Here is another obscure example. Any method call `obj.method(args)` can also be written as `obj['method'](args)`. For that reason, `this` is set to `obj` if you make a call `obj[index](args)`, where `obj[index]` is a function, even though there is no dot operator in sight.

Let us construct such a situation, with an array of callbacks:

```
class BankAccount {
  constructor() {
    this.balance = 0
    this.observers = []
  }
  addObserver(f) {
    this.observers.push(f)
  }
  notifyObservers() {
    for (let i = 0; i < this.observers.length; i++) {
      this.observers[i]()
    }
  }
  deposit(amount) {
    this.balance += amount
    this.notifyObservers()
  }
  . . .
}
```

Now suppose you have a bank account:

```
const acct = new BankAccount()
```

And you add an observer:

```
class UserInterface {
  log(message) {
    . . .
  }
  start() {
    acct.addObserver(function() { this.log('More money!') })
    acct.deposit(1000)
  }
}
```

What is `this` when the function passed to `addObserver` is called? It is *the array of observers!* That's what it was set to in the call `this.observers[i]()`. Since the array has no `log` method, a runtime error occurs. Again, the remedy is to use an arrow function:

```
acct.addObserver(() => { this.log('More money!') })
```

TIP: Having `this` dynamically set, subject to an arcane set of rules, is problematic. To avoid trouble, don't use `this` inside functions defined with `function`. It is safe to use `this` in methods and constructors, and in arrow functions that are defined inside methods and constructors. That is the golden rule #5.

Exercises

1. Implement a function `createPoint` that creates a point in the plane with a given x and y coordinates. Provide methods `getX`, `getY`, `translate`, and `scale`. The `translate` method moves the point by a given amount in x and y direction. The scale method scales both coordinates by a given factor. Use only the techniques of Section 4.1, "Methods" (page 77).

2. Repeat the preceding exercise, but now implement a constructor function and use prototypes, as in Section 4.2, "Prototypes" (page 78).

3. Repeat the preceding exercise, but now use the `class` syntax.

4. Repeat the preceding exercise, but provide getters and setters for the x and y coordinates. In the setter, make sure the argument is a number.

5. Consider this function that makes a string "greetable" by adding a `greet` method:

    ```
    function createGreetable(str) {
      const result = new String(str)
      result.greet = function(greeting) { return `${greeting}, ${this}!` }
      return result
    }
    ```

    Typical usage:

    ```
    const g = createGreetable('World')
    console.log(g.greet('Hello'))
    ```

    This function has a drawback: each greetable string has its own copy of the `greet` method. Have `createGreetable` yield an object whose prototype contains the `greet` method. Make sure that you can still invoke all string methods.

6. Provide a method `withGreeter` that adds the `greet` method to any *class*, yielding a new class:

    ```
    const GreetableEmployee = withGreeter(Employee)
    const e = new GreetableEmployee('Harry Smith', 90000)
    console.log(e.greet('Hello'))
    ```

    Hint: Section 4.11, "Class Expressions" (page 91).

7. Rewrite the Employee class using private instance fields, as shown in Section 4.6, "Instance Fields and Private Methods" (page 85).

8. A classic example for an abstract class is a tree node. There are two kinds of nodes: those with children (parents) and those without (leaves).

```
class Node {
  depth() { throw Error("abstract method") }
}
class Parent extends Node {
  constructor(value, children) { . . . }
  depth() { return 1 + Math.max(...children.map(n => n.depth())) }
}
class Leaf extends Node {
  constructor(value) { . . . }
  depth() { return 1 }
}
```

This is how you would model tree nodes in Java or C++. But in JavaScript, you don't need an abstract class to be able to invoke n.depth(). Rewrite the classes without inheritance and provide a test program.

9. Provide a class Random with static methods

```
Random.nextDouble(low, high)
Random.nextInt(low, high)
Random.nextElement(array)
```

that produce a random number between low (inclusive) and high (exclusive), or a random element from the given array.

10. Provide a class BankAccount and subclasses SavingsAccount and CheckingAccount. A savings account has an instance field for the interest and an addInterest method that adds it. A checking account charges a fee for each withdrawal. Do not manipulate the superclass state directly but use the superclass methods.

11. Draw a diagram of SavingsAccount and CheckingAccount objects from the preceding exercise, similar to Figure 4-4.

12. Harry tries this code to toggle a CSS class when a button is clicked:

```
const button = document.getElementById('button1')
button.addEventListener('click', function () {
  this.classList.toggle('clicked')
})
```

It doesn't work. Why?

Sally, after searching the wisdom of the Internet, suggests:

```
button.addEventListener('click', event => {
  event.target.classList.toggle('clicked')
})
```

This works, but Harry feels it is cheating a bit. What if the listener hadn't produced the button as `event.target`? Fix the code so that you use neither `this` nor the `event` parameter.

13. In Section 4.12, "The `this` Reference" (page 92), you saw that the following doesn't work:

```
const action = BankAccount.prototype.deposit
action(1000)
```

Can you make it work by getting the action method from an instance, like this:

```
const harrysAccount = new BankAccount()
const action = harrysAccount.deposit
action(1000)
```

Why or why not?

14. In the preceding exercise, we defined an `action` function that deposits money into `harrysAccount`. It seemed a bit pointless, so let's add some context. The function below invokes a given function after a delay, passing the delay as an argument.

```
function invokeLater(f, delay) {
  setTimeout(() => f(delay), delay)
}
```

That's perfect for Harry to earn $1000 after 1000 milliseconds:

```
invokeLater(amount => harrysAccount.deposit(amount), 1000)
```

But what about Sally? Make a general function `depositInto` so that one can call

```
invokeLater(depositInto(sallysAccount), 1000)
```

Numbers and Dates

Chapter 5

In this short chapter, we will look at the JavaScript API for working with numbers and big integers. We will then turn to operations with dates. As you will see, JavaScript dates can be converted to numbers—a count of milliseconds. That conversion isn't actually useful, but it's an excuse for grouping both topics into this chapter instead of having two even shorter ones.

5.1 Number Literals

All JavaScript numbers are "double precision" values in the IEEE 754 floating-point standard, with a binary representation that occupies eight bytes.

Integer literals can be written in decimal, hexadecimal, octal, or binary:

```
42
0x2A
0o52
0b101010
```

 NOTE: The archaic octal notation with a leading zero and no o (such as 052) is disallowed in strict mode.

Floating-point literals can use exponential notation:

```
4.2e-3
```

The letters e x o b can be written in lowercase or uppercase: 4.2E-3 or 0X2A are OK.

 NOTE: C++ and Java allow hexadecimal floating-point literals such as 0x1.0p-10 = 2^{-10} = 0.0009765625. This notation is not supported in JavaScript.

Underscores in number literals are a stage 3 proposal in 2020. You can place underscores anywhere between digits to make the number more legible. The underscores are only for human readers—they are removed when the number is parsed. For example,

```
const speedOfLight = 299_792_458 // same as 299792458
```

The global variables Infinity and NaN denote the "infinity" and "not a number" values. For example, 1 / 0 is Infinity and 0 / 0 is NaN.

5.2 Number Formatting

To format an integer in a given number base between 2 and 36, use the toString method:

```
const n = 3735928559
n.toString(16) // 'deadbeef'
n.toString(8) // '33653337357'
n.toString(2) // '11011110101011011011111011101111'
```

You can also format floating-point numbers to a base other than 10:

```
const almostPi = 3.14
almostPi.toString(16) // 3.23d70a3d70a3e
```

The toFixed method formats a floating-point number in fixed format with a given number of digits after the decimal point. The call x.toExponential(p) uses exponential format with one digit before and p – 1 digits after the decimal point, and x.toPrecision(p) shows p significant digits:

```
const x = 1 / 600 // 0.0016666666666666668
x.toFixed(4) // '0.0017'
x.toExponential(4) // '1.667e-3'
x.toPrecision(4) // '0.001667'
```

The toPrecision method switches to exponential format if it would otherwise produce too many significant digits or zeroes—see Exercise 3.

NOTE: The JavaScript standard library has no equivalent to the C `printf` function, but there are third-party implementations such as `https://github.com/alexei/sprintf.js`.

The `console.log` method supports `printf`-style placeholders %d, %f, %s, but not width, fill, or precision modifiers.

5.3 Number Parsing

In Chapter 1, you saw how to parse strings containing numbers:

```
const notQuitePi = parseFloat('3.14') // The number 3.14
const evenLessPi = parseInt('3') // The integer 3
```

These functions ignore whitespace prefixes and non-numeric suffixes. For example, `parseInt(' 3A')` is also 3.

The result is `NaN` if there is no number after the optional whitespace. For example, `parseInt(' A3')` is `NaN`.

The `parseInt` function accepts hexadecimal notation: `parseInt('0x3A')` is 58.

Sometimes you want to accept only strings that actually represent decimal numbers in JavaScript format, without leading spaces or suffixes. In this case, your best bet is to use a regular expression:

```
const intRegex = /^[+-]?[0-9]+$/
if (intRegex.test(str)) value = parseInt(str)
```

For floating-point numbers, the regular expression is more complex:

```
const floatRegex = /^[+-]?((0|[1-9][0-9]*)(\.[0-9]*)?|\.[0-9]+)([eE][+-]?[0-9]+)?$/
if (floatRegex.test(str)) value = parseFloat(str)
```

See Chapter 6 for more information about regular expressions.

 CAUTION: The Internet is replete with almost correct recipes for recognizing strings that represent JavaScript numbers, but the devil is in the details. The regular expressions above accept exactly the decimal number literals from the JavaScript standard, optionally preceded by a sign. However, embedded underscores (such as `1_000_000`) are not supported.

To parse integers in a base other than 10, supply a base between 2 and 36 as the second argument.

```
parseInt('deadbeef', 16) // 3735928559
```

5.4 Number Functions and Constants

The functions `Number.parseInt` and `Number.parseFloat` are identical to the global `parseInt` and `parseFloat` functions.

The call `Number.isNaN(x)` checks whether x is `NaN`, the special "not a number" value. (You cannot check x `===` `NaN` because no two `NaN` values are considered to be equal to one another.)

To check that a value x is a number other than `Infinity`, `-Infinity`, or `NaN`, call `Number.isFinite(x)`.

 CAUTION: Do not use the global `isNaN` and `isFinite` functions—they first convert non-numeric arguments, which does not yield useful results:

```
isNaN('Hello') // true
isFinite([0]) // true
```

The static methods `Number.isInteger` and `Number.isSafeInteger` check whether the argument is an integer, or an integer in the safe range where no roundoff occurs.

That range extends from `Number.MIN_SAFE_INTEGER` ($-2^{53} + 1$ or $-9,007,199,254,740,991$) to `Number.MAX_SAFE_INTEGER` ($2^{53} - 1$ or $9,007,199,254,740,991$).

The largest number is `Number.MAX_VALUE` (($2 - 2^{-52}$) × 2^{1023} or about 1.8×10^{308}). The smallest positive number is `Number.MIN_VALUE` (2^{-1074} or about 5×10^{-324}). `Number.EPSILON` (2^{-52} or about 2.2×10^{-16}) is the gap between 1 and the next representable number greater than 1.

Finally, `Number.NaN`, `Number.POSITIVE_INFINITY`, and `Number.NEGATIVE_INFINITY` are the same as the global `NaN`, `Infinity`, and `-Infinity`. You can use those values if you are nervous about someone defining local variables named `NaN` and `Infinity`.

Table 5-1 shows the most useful features of the `Number` class.

Table 5-1 Useful Functions, Methods, and Constants of the Number Class

Name	Description
Functions	
isNaN(x)	true if x is NaN. Note that you cannot use === since x === NaN is always false.
isFinite(x)	true if x is not ±Infinity, NaN
isSafeInteger(x)	true if x is an integer in the "safe" range defined below
Methods	
toString(base)	The number in the given base (between 2 and 36). (200).toString(16) is 'c8'.
toFixed(digitsAfterDecimalPoint), toExponential(significantDigits), toPrecision(significantDigits)	The number in fixed or exponential format, or the more convenient of the two. Formatting 0.001666 with four digits yields '0.**0017**', '**1.667**e-3', '0.00**1667**'.
Constants	
MIN_SAFE_INTEGER, MAX_SAFE_INTEGER	The range of "safe" integers that can be represented as floating-point numbers without roundoff
MIN_VALUE, MAX_VALUE	The range of all floating-point numbers

5.5 Mathematical Functions and Constants

The Math class defines a number of functions and constants for mathematical computations—logarithms, trigonometry, and the like. Table 5-2 contains a complete list. Most of the functions are quite specialized.

Here are a few mathematical functions that are of general interest.

The max and min functions yield the largest and smallest of any number of arguments:

```
Math.max(x, y) // The larger of x and y
Math.min(...values) // The smallest element of the array values
```

The `Math.round` function rounds to the nearest integer, rounding up for positive numbers with fractional part ≥ 0.5 and negative numbers with fractional part > 0.5.

`Math.trunc` simply truncates the fractional part.

```
Math.round(2.5) // 3
Math.round(-2.5) // -2
Math.trunc(2.5) // 2
```

The call `Math.random()` yields a floating-point number between 0 (inclusive) and 1 (exclusive). To obtain a random floating-point number or integer between a (inclusive) and b (exclusive), call:

```
const randomDouble = a + (b - a) * Math.random()
const randomInt = a + Math.trunc((b - a) * Math.random()) // where a, b are integers
```

Table 5-2 Functions and Constants in the `Math` class

Name	Description
Functions	
`min(values. . .)`, `max(values)`	These functions can be called with any number of arguments
`abs(x)`, `sign(x)`	Absolute value and sign (1, 0, –1)
`random()`	Random number $0 \leq r < 1$
`round(x)`, `trunc(x)`, `floor(x)`, `ceil(x)`	Round to the nearest integer, to integer obtained by truncating the fractional part, to the next smaller or larger integer
`fround(x)`, `ftrunc(x)`, `ffloor(x)`, `fceil(x)`	Round to 32-bit floating-point number
`pow(x, y)`, `exp(x)`, `expm1(x)`, `log(x)`, `log2(x)`, `log10(x)`, `log1p(x)`	x^y, e^x, $e^x - 1$, $\ln(x)$, $\log_2(x)$, $\log_{10}(x)$, $\ln(1 + x)$
`sqrt(x)`, `cbrt(x)`, `hypot(x, y)`	$\sqrt{x}$, $\sqrt[3]{x}$, $\sqrt{x^2 + y^2}$
`sin(x)`, `cos(x)`, `tan(x)`, `asin(x)`, `acos(x)`, `atan(x)`, `atan2(y, x)`	Trigonometric functions
`sinh(x)`, `cosh(x)`, `tanh(x)`, `asinh(x)`, `acosh(x)`, `atanh`	Hyperbolic functions
Constants	
`E`, `PI`, `SQRT2`, `SQRT1_2`, `LN2`, `LN10`, `LOG2E`, `LOG10E`	e, π, $\sqrt{2}$, $\sqrt{1/2}$, $\ln(2)$, $\ln(10)$, $\log_2(e)$, $\log_{10}(e)$

5.6 Big Integers

A *big integer* is an integer with an arbitrary number of digits. A big integer literal has a suffix n, such as 8159152832478977343456112695961158942720000000000n. Alternatively, you can convert any integer-valued expression into a big integer as BigInt(expr).

The typeof operator returns 'bigint' when applied to a big integer.

Arithmetic operators combine big integers to a new big integer result:

```
let result = 8159152832478977343456112695961158942720000000000n * BigInt(41)
  // Sets result to 334525266131638071081700620534407516651520000000000n
```

> **CAUTION:** You cannot combine a big integer and a value of another type with an arithmetic operator. For example, 8159152832478977343456112695961158942720000000000n * 41 is an error.

When combining big integer values, the / operator yields a big integer result, discarding the remainder. For example, 100n / 3n is 33n.

The BigInt class has just two functions that are rather technical. The calls BigInt.asIntN(bits, n) and BigInt.asUintN(bits, n) reduce n modulo 2^{bits} into the interval $[-2^{bits-1} \ldots 2^{bits-1} - 1]$ or $[0 \ldots 2^{bits} - 1]$.

5.7 Constructing Dates

Before getting into the JavaScript API for dates, let us review a couple of concepts about measuring time on our planet.

Historically, the fundamental time unit—the second—was derived from Earth's rotation around its axis. There are 24 hours or $24 \times 60 \times 60 = 86400$ seconds in a full revolution, so it seems just a question of astronomical measurements to precisely define a second. Unfortunately, Earth wobbles slightly, and a more precise definition was needed. In 1967, a new definition of a second, matching the historical definition, was derived from an intrinsic property of atoms of caesium-133. Since then, a network of atomic clocks keeps the official time.

Ever so often, the official time keepers synchronize the absolute time with the rotation of Earth. At first, the official seconds were slightly adjusted, but starting in 1972, occasional "leap seconds" were inserted as needed. (In theory, a second might need to be removed once in a while, but that has not yet happened.) Clearly, leap seconds are a pain, and many computer systems instead use "smoothing" where time is artificially slowed down or sped up just before the leap second, keeping 86,400 seconds per day. This works because the local time on a computer isn't all that precise, and computers are used to synchronizing themselves with an external time service.

Because humans everywhere on the globe prefer to have midnight correspond to a point that is more or less in the middle of the night, there are varying local times. But to compare times, there needs to be a common point of reference. This is, for historical reasons, the time at the meridian that passes through the Royal Observatory in Greenwich (not adjusted for daylight savings time). This time is known as "Coordinated Universal Time," or UTC. The acronym is a compromise between the aforementioned English and the French "Temps Universel Coordiné," having the distinction of being incorrect in either language.

For representing time in a computer, it is convenient to have a fixed origin from which to count forward or backward. This is the "epoch": midnight UTC on Thursday, January 1, 1970.

In JavaScript, time is measured in smoothed milliseconds from the epoch, with a valid range of ±100,000,000 days in either direction.

JavaScript uses the standard ISO 8601 format for a point in time: `YYYY-MM-DDTHH:mm:ss.sssZ`, with four digits for the year, two digits for the month, day, hours, minutes, and seconds, and three digits for the milliseconds. The letter `T` separates the day and the hours, and the `Z` suffix denotes a zero offset from UTC.

For example, the epoch is:

```
1970-01-01T00:00:00.000Z
```

 NOTE: You may be wondering how that format works with a day that is 100,000,000 days—close to 274,000 years—away from the epoch. And what about dates before the "common era"?

For those dates, the year is specified with six digits and a sign, as ±YYYYYY. The largest valid JavaScript date is

```
+275760-09-13T00:00:00.000Z
```

The year before 0001 is 0000, and the year before that is -000001.

In JavaScript, a point in time is represented by an instance of the Date class. Calling the class Time would have been a splendid idea, but the class takes the name and a number of flaws from the Java Date class, and then adds its own idiosyncrasies.

Table 5-3 Useful Constructors, Functions, and Methods of the `Date` Class

Name	Description
Constructors	
`new Date(iso8601String)`	Constructs a `Date` from an ISO 8601 string such as `'1969-07-20T20:17:40.000Z'`
`new Date()`	Constructs a `Date` representing the current time
`new Date(millisecondsFromEpoch)`	
`new Date(year, zeroBasedMonth, day, hours, minutes, seconds, milliseconds)`	Uses the *local time zone*. At least two arguments are required.
Functions	
`UTC(year, zeroBasedMonth, day, hours, minutes, seconds, milliseconds)`	Yields milliseconds from the epoch, not a `Date` object
Methods	
`getUTCFullYear()`, `getUTCMonth()`, `getUTCDate()`, `getUTCHours()`, `getUTCMinutes()`, `getUTCSeconds()`, `getUTCMilliseconds()`	Month between 0 and 11, date between 1 and 31, hour between 0 and 23
`getUTCDay()`	The weekday, between 0 (Sunday) and 6 (Saturday)
`getTime()`	Milliseconds from the epoch
`toISOString()`	The ISO 8601 string such as `'1969-07-20T20:17:40.000Z'`
`toLocaleString(locale, options)`, `toLocaleDateString(locale, options)`, `toLocaleTimeString(locale, options)`	Humanly readable date and time, date only, time only. See Chapter 8 for locales and a description of all options.

See Table 5-3 for the most useful features of the `Date` class.

You can construct a date from its ISO 8601 string, or by giving the number of milliseconds from the epoch:

```
const epoch = new Date('1970-01-01T00:00:00.000Z')
const oneYearLater = new Date(365 * 86400 * 1000) // 1971-01-01T00:00:00.000Z
```

Constructing a `Date` without arguments yields the current time.

```
const now = new Date()
```

CAUTION: Don't call the `Date` function without `new`. That call ignores any arguments and does not yield a `Date` object but a string describing the current time—and not even in ISO 8601 format:

```
Date(365 * 86400 * 1000)
   // Ignores its argument and yields a string
   // 'Mon Jun 24 2020 07:23:10 GMT+0200 (Central European Summer Time)'
```

 CAUTION: If you use `Date` objects with arithmetic expressions, they are automatically converted, either into the string format from the preceding note, or the number of milliseconds from the epoch:

```
oneYearLater + 1
   // 'Fri Jan 01 1971 01:00:00 GMT+0100 (Central European Summer Time)1'
oneYearLater * 1 // 31536000000
```

This is only useful to compute the distance between two dates:

```
const before = new Date()
// Do some work
const after = new Date()
const millisecondsElapsed = after - before
```

You can construct a `Date` object *in your local time zone* as

```
new Date(year, zeroBasedMonth, day, hours, minutes, seconds, milliseconds)
```

All arguments starting from `day` are optional. (At least two arguments are needed to distinguish this form from the call `new Date(millisecondsFromEpoch)`.)

For historical reasons, the month is zero-based but the day is not.

For example, as I am writing these words, I am an hour east of the Greenwich observatory. When I evaluate

```
new Date(1970, 0 /* January */, 1, 0, 0, 0, 0) // Caution—local time zone
```

I get

```
1969-12-30T23:00:00.000Z
```

When you try it, you may get a different result, depending on your time zone.

 CAUTION: If you supply out-of-range values for `zeroBasedMonth`, `day`, `hours`, and so on, the date is silently adjusted. For example, `new Date(2019, 13, -2)` is January 29, 2020.

5.8 Date Functions and Methods

The `Date` class has three static functions:

- `Date.UTC(year, zeroBasedMonth, day, hours, minutes, seconds, milliseconds)`
- `Date.parse(dateString)`
- `Date.now()`

The `UTC` function is similar to the constructor with multiple arguments, but it produces the date in UTC.

The `parse` function parses ISO 8601 strings and may, depending on the implementation, also accept other formats (see Exercise 17).

`Date.now()` produces the current date and time.

 CAUTION: Tragically, all three functions yield milliseconds since the epoch and *not* `Date` objects.

To actually construct a date from UTC components, call:

```
const deadline = new Date(Date.UTC(2020, 0 /* January */, 31))
```

The `Date` class has Java-style getter and setter methods, such as `getHours/setHours`, not JavaScript `get/set` methods.

To get the components of a `Date` object, call the methods `getUTCFullYear`, `getUTCMonth` (between `0` and `11`), `getUTCDate` (between `1` and `31`), `getUTCHours` (between `0` and `23`), `getUTCMinutes`, `getUTCSeconds`, `getUTCMilliseconds`.

The methods without `UTC` (that is, `getFullYear`, `getMonth`, `getDate`, and so on) yield the same information in local time. Unless you need to show local time to a user, you probably don't want those. And if you do display a local time, you should use one of the date-formatting methods described in Section 5.9, "Date Formatting" (page 110).

The `getUTCDay` method yields the weekday between `0` (Sunday) and `6` (Saturday):

```
const epoch = new Date('1970-01-01T00:00:00.000Z')
epoch.getUTCDay() // 4 (Thursday)
epoch.getDay() // 3, 4, or 5, depending on when and where the call is made
```

 NOTE: The obsolete `getYear` method yields a two-digit year. Apparently, when JavaScript was created in 1995, nobody could have predicted that two-digit years might be problematic.

JavaScript copies the Java mistake of having mutable Date objects, and makes it worse by having setters for each time unit—see Exercise 16. The setters silently adjust to the next valid date:

```
const appointment = new Date('2020-05-31T00:00:00.000Z')
appointment.setUTCMonth(5 /* June */) // appointment is now July 1
```

5.9 Date Formatting

The methods toString, toDateString, toTimeString, and toUTCString yield "humanly readable" strings in a format that is not particularly human-friendly:

```
'Sun Jul 20 1969 21:17:40 GMT+0100 (Mitteleuropäische Sommerzeit)'
'Sun Jul 20 1969'
'21:17:40 GMT+0100  (Mitteleuropäische Sommerzeit)'
'Sun, 20 Jul 1969 20:17:40 GMT'
```

Note that the time zone (but not the weekday or month name) appears in the user's locale.

To actually present date and time to a human user, use the methods toLocaleString, toLocaleDateString, or toLocaleTimeString that format a date and time, only the date portion, or only the time portion. The format uses the rules of the user's current locale or a locale that you specify:

```
moonlanding.toLocaleDateString() // '20.7.1969' if the locale is German
moonlanding.toLocaleDateString('en-US') // '7/20/1969'
```

The default format is rather short, but you can change it by supplying formatting options:

```
moonlanding.toLocaleDateString(
  'en-US', { year: 'numeric', month: 'long', day: 'numeric' })
  // 'July 20, 1969'
```

Chapter 8 explains the locale concept and presents these options in detail.

For machine-readable dates, simply call the toISOString method which yields an ISO 8601 string:

```
moonlanding.toISOString() // '1969-07-20T20:17:40.000Z'
```

Exercises

1. The values 0 and −0 are distinct in the IEEE 754 standard. Provide at least two distinct implementations of a function plusMinusZero(x) that returns +1 if x is 0, -1 if x is -0, and 0 otherwise. Hints: Object.is, 1/-0.

2. There are three kinds of IEEE 754 "double precision" floating-point values:

   - "Normalized" values of the form $\pm 1.m \times 2^e$, where m has 52 bits and e ranges from -1022 to 1023

   - ± 0 and "denormalized" values close to zero, of the form $\pm 0.m \times 2^{-1022}$, where m has 52 bits

   - Special values $\pm\infty$, NaN

   Write a function that produces a string `'normalized'`, `'denormalized'`, or `'special'` for a given floating-point number.

3. Suppose the number `x`, when shown in exponential format, has an exponent of `e`. Give a condition depending on `e` and `p` under which the call `x.toPrecision(p)` shows the result in fixed format.

4. Write a function that formats a numeric value according to a `printf`-style specification. For example, `format(42, "%04x")` should print `002A`.

5. Write a function that yields the exponent of a floating-point number—that is, the value that would be printed after `e` in exponential notation. Use binary search, and don't call any `Math` or `Number` methods.

6. Explain the values for `Number.MAX_VALUE`, `Number.MIN_VALUE`, and `Number.EPSILON` given in Section 5.4, "Number Functions and Constants" (page 102).

7. Write a function that computes the smallest representable floating-point number after a given integer `n`. Hint: What is the smallest representable number after 1? After 2? After 3? After 4? You may want to consult an article describing the IEEE floating-point representation. Extra credit if you can obtain the result for an arbitrary number.

8. Produce a big integer with the digit 3 repeated a thousand times, using no loops or recursion, in a single line of code that is no more than 80 characters long.

9. Write a function that converts a `Date` object into an object with properties `year, month, day, weekday, hours, minutes, seconds, millis`.

10. Write a function that determines how many hours a user is away from UTC.

11. Write a function that determines whether a year is a leap year. Provide two different implementations.

12. Write a function that yields the weekday of a given day without calling the `Date.getUTCDay`/`getDay` methods. Hint: The epoch fell on a Thursday.

13. Write a function that, given a month and year (which should default to the current month and year), prints a calendar such as

```
      1  2  3  4  5
 6  7  8  9 10 11 12
13 14 15 16 17 18 19
20 21 22 23 24 25 26
27 28 29 30 31
```

14. Write a function with two Date parameters that yields the number of days between the dates, with the fractional part indicating the fraction of the day.

15. Write a function with two Date parameters that yields the number of years between the dates. This is more complex than the preceding problem because years have varying lengths.

16. Suppose you are given this deadline and you need to move it to February 1:

```
const deadline = new Date(Date.UTC(2020, 0 /* January */, 31))
```

    What is the result of

```
deadline.setUTCMonth(1 /* February */)
deadline.setUTCDate(1)
```

    Perhaps one should always call setUTCDate before setUTCMonth? Give an example where that doesn't work.

17. Experiment which strings are accepted by Date.parse(dateString) or new Date(dateString) in your favorite JavaScript runtime. Examples to try:

    The string returned by Date()
    '3/14/2020'
    'March 14, 2020'
    '14 March 2020'
    '2020-03-14'
    '2020-03-14 '

    Scarily, the last two strings yield *different* dates in Node.js version 13.11.0.

Strings and Regular Expressions

Chapter 6

In this chapter, you will learn about the methods that the standard library provides for string processing. We will then turn to regular expressions, which let you find strings that match patterns. After an introduction into the syntax of regular expressions and the JavaScript-specific idiosyncrasies, you will see how to use the API for finding and replacing matches.

6.1 Converting between Strings and Code Point Sequences

A string is a sequence of Unicode code points. Each code point is an integer between zero and `0x10FFFF`. The `fromCodePoint` function of the `String` class assembles a string from code point arguments:

```
let str = String.fromCodePoint(0x48, 0x69, 0x20, 0x1F310, 0x21) // 'Hi 🌐!'
```

If the code points are in an array, use the spread operator:

```
let codePoints = [0x48, 0x69, 0x20, 0x1F310, 0x21]
str = String.fromCodePoint(...codePoints)
```

Conversely, you can turn a string into an array of code points:

```
let characters = [...str] // [ 'H', 'i', ' ', '🌐', '!' ]
```

The result is an array of strings, each containing a single code point. You can obtain the code points as integers:

```
codePoints = [...str].map(c => c.codePointAt(0))
```

> **CAUTION:** JavaScript stores strings as sequences of UTF-16 code units. The offset in a call such as `'Hi ☺'.codePointAt(i)` refers to the UTF-16 encoding. In this example, valid offsets are `0`, `1`, `2`, `3`, and `5`. If the offset falls in the middle of a pair of code units that make up a single code point, then an invalid code point is returned.

If you want to traverse the code points of a string without putting them in an array, use this loop:

```
for (let i = 0; i < str.length; i++) {
  let cp = str.codePointAt(i)
  if (cp > 0xFFFF) i++
  . . . // Process the code point cp
}
```

6.2 Substrings

The `indexOf` method yields the index of the first occurrence of a substring:

```
let index = 'Hello yellow'.indexOf('el') // 1
```

The `lastIndexOf` method yields the index of the last occurrence:

```
index = 'Hello yellow'.lastIndexOf('el') // 7
```

As with all offsets into JavaScript strings, these values are offsets into the UTF-16 encoding:

```
index = 'I♡yellow'.indexOf('el') // 4
```

The offset is 4 because the "yellow heart" emoji ♡ is encoded with two UTF-16 code units.

If the substring is not present, these methods return `-1`.

The methods `startsWith`, `endsWith`, and `includes` return a Boolean result:

```
let isHttps = url.startsWith('https://')
let isGif = url.endsWith('.gif')
let isQuery = url.includes('?')
```

The `substring` method extracts a substring, given two offsets in UTF-16 code units. The substring contains all characters from the first offset up to, but not including, the second offset.

```
let substring = 'I♡yellow'.substring(3, 7) // 'yell'
```

If you omit the second offset, all characters until the end of the string are included:

```
substring = 'I♡yellow'.substring(3) // 'yellow'
```

The slice method is similar to substring, except that negative offsets are counted from the end of the string. -1 is the offset of the last code unit, -2 the offset of its predecessor, and so on. This is achieved by adding the string length to a negative offset.

```
'I♡yellow'.slice(-6, -2) // 'yell', same as slice(3, 7)
```

The length of 'I♡yellow' is 9—recall that the ♡ takes two code units. The offsets -6 and -2 are adjusted to 3 and 7.

With both the substring and slice methods, offsets larger than the string length are truncated to the length. Negative and NaN offsets are truncated to 0. (In the slice method, this happens after adding the string length to negative offsets.)

 CAUTION: If the first argument to substring is larger than the second, the arguments are switched!

```
substring = 'I♡yellow'.substring(7, 3) // 'yell', same as substring(3, 7)
```

In contrast, str.slice(start, end) yields the empty string if start ≥ end.

I prefer the slice method over substring. It is more versatile, has a saner behavior, and the method name is shorter.

Another way of taking a string apart is the split method. That method splits a string into an array of substrings, removing the provided separator.

```
let parts = 'Mary had a little lamb'.split(' ')
  // ['Mary', 'had', 'a', 'little', 'lamb']
```

You can supply a limit for the number of parts:

```
parts = 'Mary had a little lamb'.split(' ', 4)
  // ['Mary', 'had', 'a', 'little']
```

The separator can be a regular expression—see Section 6.12, "String Methods with Regular Expressions" (page 133).

 CAUTION: Calling str.split('') with an empty separator splits the string into strings that each hold a 16-bit code unit, which is not useful if str contains characters above \u{FFFF}. Use [...str] instead.

6.3 Other String Methods

In this section, you will find miscellaneous methods of the String class. Since strings are immutable in JavaScript, none of the string methods change the contents of a given string. They all return a new string with the result.

The repeat method yields a string repeated a given number of times:

```
const repeated = 'ho '.repeat(3) // 'ho ho ho '
```

The trim, trimStart, and trimEnd methods yield strings that remove leading and trailing white space, or just leading or trailing white space. White space characters include the space character, the nonbreaking space \u{00A0}, newline, tab, and 21 other characters with the Unicode character property White_Space.

The padStart and padEnd methods do the opposite—they add space characters until the string has a minimum length:

```
let padded = 'Hello'.padStart(10) // '     Hello', five spaces are added
```

You can also supply your own padding string:

```
padded = 'Hello'.padStart(10, '=-') // =-=-=Hello
```

> **CAUTION:** The first parameter is the length of the padded string in bytes. If your padding string contains characters that require two bytes, you may get a malformed string:
>
> ```
> padded = 'Hello'.padStart(10, '♡')
> // Padded with two hearts and an unmatched code unit
> ```

The toUpperCase and toLowerCase methods yield a string with all characters converted to upper- or lowercase.

```
let uppercased = 'Straße'.toUpperCase() // 'STRASSE'
```

As you can see, the toUpperCase method is aware of the fact that the uppercase of the German character 'ß' is the string 'SS'.

Note that toLowerCase does not recover the original string:

```
let lowercased = uppercased.toLowerCase() // 'strasse'
```

> **NOTE:** String operations such as conversion to upper- and lowercase can depend on the user's language preferences. See Chapter 8 for methods toLocaleUpperCase, toLocaleLowerCase, localeCompare, and normalize that are useful when you localize your applications.

NOTE: See Section 6.12, "String Methods with Regular Expressions" (page 133), for string methods `match`, `matchAll`, `search`, and `replace` that work with regular expressions.

The `concat` method concatenates a string with any number of arguments that are converted to strings.

```
const n = 7
let concatenated = 'agent'.concat(' ', n) // 'agent 7'
```

You can achieve the same effect with template strings or the `join` method of the `Array` class:

```
concatenated = `agent ${n}`
concatenated = ['agent', ' ', n].join('')
```

Table 6-1 shows the most useful features of the `String` class.

Table 6-1 Useful Functions and Methods of the `String` class

Name	Description
Functions	
`fromCodePoint(codePoints...)`	Yields a string consisting of the given code points
Methods	
`startsWith(s)`, `endsWith(s)`, `includes(s)`	`true` if a string starts or ends with `s`, or has `s` as a substring
`indexOf(s, start)`, `lastIndexOf(s, start)`	The index of the first or last occurrence of `s` beginning with index start (which defaults to 0)
`slice(start, end)`	The substring of code units with index between start inclusive and end exclusive. Negative index values are counted from the end of the string. end defaults to the length of the string. Prefer this method over `substring`.
`repeat(n)`	This string, repeated `n` times
`trimStart()`, `trimEnd()`, `trim()`	This string with leading, trailing, or leading and trailing white space removed
`padStart(minLength, padString)`, `padEnd(minLength, padString)`	This string, padded at the start or end until its length reaches `minLength`. The default `padString` is `' '`.

(Continues)

Table 6-1 Useful Functions and Methods of the `String` class *(Continued)*

Name	Description
`toLowerCase()`, `toUpperCase()`	This string with all letters converted to lower or upper case
`split(separator, maxParts)`	An array of parts obtained by removing all copies of the separator (which can be a regular expression). If `maxParts` is omitted, all parts are returned.
`search(target)`	The index of the first match of target (which can be a regular expression)
`replace(target, replacement)`	This string, with the first match of target replaced. If target is a global regular expression, all matches are replaced. See Section 6.13 about replacement patterns and functions.
`match(regex)`	An array of matches if regex is global, `null` if there is no match, and the match result otherwise. The match result is an array of all group matches, with properties `index` (the index of the match) and `groups` (an object mapping group names to matches).
`matchAll(regex)`	An iterable of the match results

Finally, there are global functions for encoding URL components and entire URLs—or, more generally, URIs using schemes such as `mailto` or `tel`—into their "URL encoded" form. That form uses only characters that were considered "safe" when the Internet was first created. Suppose you need to produce a query for translating a phrase from one language into another. You might construct a URL like this:

```
const phrase = 'à coté de'
const prefix = 'https://www.linguee.fr/anglais-francais/traduction'
const suffix = '.html'
const url = prefix + encodeURIComponent(phrase) + suffix
```

The phrase is encoded into `'%C3%A0%20cot%C3%A9%20de'`, the result of encoding characters into UTF-8 and encoding each byte into a code *%hh* with two hexadecimal digits. The only characters that are left alone are the "safe" characters

```
A-Z a-z 0-9 ! ' ( ) * . _ ~ -
```

In the less common case, if you need to encode an entire URI, use the `encodeURI` function. It also leaves the characters

```
# $ & + , / : ; = ? @
```
unchanged since they can have special meanings in URIs.

6.4 Tagged Template Literals

In Chapter 1, you saw template literals—strings with embedded expressions:

```
const person = { name: 'Harry', age: 42 }
message = `Next year, ${person.name} will be ${person.age + 1}.`
```

Template literals insert the values of the embedded expressions into the template string. In this example, the embedded expressions `person.name` and `person.age + 1` are evaluated, converted to strings, and spliced with the surrounding string fragments. The result is the string

```
'Next year, Harry will be 43.'
```

You can customize the behavior of template literals with a tag function. As an example, we will be writing a tag function `strong` that produces an HTML string, highlighting the embedded values. The call

```
strong`Next year, ${person.name} will be ${person.age + 1}.`
```

will yield an HTML string

```
'Next year, <strong>Harry</strong> will be <strong>43</strong>.'
```

The tag function is called with the fragments of the literal string around the embedded expressions, followed by the expression values. In our example, the fragments are `'Next year, '`, `' will be '`, and `'.'`, and the values are `'Harry'` and `43`. The tag function combines these pieces. The returned value is turned into a string if it is not already one.

Here is an implementation of the `strong` tag function:

```
const strong = (fragments, ...values) => {
  let result = fragments[0]
    for (let i = 0; i < values.length; i++)
     result += `<strong>${values[i]}</strong>${fragments[i + 1]}`
    return result
}
```

When processing the template string

```
strong`Next year, ${person.name} will be ${person.age + 1}.`
```

the `strong` function is called like this:

```
strong(['Next year, ', ' will be ', '.'], 'Harry', 43)
```

Note that all string fragments are put into an array, whereas the expression values are passed as separate arguments. The strong function uses the spread operator to gather them all in a second array.

Also note that there is always one more fragment than there are expression values.

This mechanism is infinitely flexible. You can use it for HTML templating, number formatting, internationalization, and so on.

6.5 Raw Template Literals

If you prefix a template literal with String.raw, then backslashes are not escape characters:

```
path = String.raw`c:\users\nate`
```

Here, \u does not denote a Unicode escape, and \n is not turned into a newline character.

CAUTION: Even in raw mode, you cannot enclose arbitrary strings in backticks. You still need to escape all ` characters, $ before {, and \ before ` and {.

That doesn't quite explain how String.raw works, though. Tag functions have access to a "raw" form of the template string fragments, in which backslash combinations such as \u and \n lose their special meanings.

Suppose we want to handle strings with Greek letters. We follow the convention of the LaTeX markup language for mathematical formulas. In that language, symbols start with backslashes. Therefore, raw strings are attractive—users want to write \nu and \upsilon, not \\nu and \\upsilon. Here is an example of a string that we want to be able to process:

```
greek`\nu=${factor}\upsilon`
```

As with any tagged template string, we need to define a function:

```
const greek = (fragments, ...values) => {
  const substitutions = { alpha: 'α', . . ., nu: 'v', . . . }
  const substitute = str => str.replace(/\\[a-z]+/g,
    match => substitutions[match.slice(1)])

  let result = substitute(fragments.raw[0])
  for (let i = 0; i < values.length; i++)
    result += values[i] + substitute(fragments.raw[i + 1])
  return result
}
```

You access the raw string fragments with the `raw` property of the first parameter of the tag function. The value of `fragments.raw` is an array of string fragments with unprocessed backslashes.

In the preceding tagged template literal, `fragments.raw` is an array of two strings. The first string is `\nu=`, and the second string is `\upsilon`.

```
\${\nu\upsilon{
```

including three backslashes. The second string has two characters:

```
}}
```

Note the following:

- The `\n` in `\nu` is not turned into a newline.

- The `\u` in `\upsilon` is not interpreted as a Unicode escape. In fact, it would not be syntactically correct. For that reason, `fragments[1]` cannot be parsed and is set to `undefined`.

- `${factor}` is an embedded expression. Its value is passed to the tag function.

The `greek` function uses regular expression replacement, which is explained in detail in Section 6.13, "More about Regex Replace" (page 135). Identifiers starting with a backslash are replaced with their substitutions, such as v for `\nu`.

6.6 Regular Expressions

Regular expressions specify string patterns. Use them whenever you need to locate strings that match a particular pattern. For example, suppose you want to find hyperlinks in an HTML file. You need to look for strings of the form `<a href=". . .">`. But wait—there may be extra spaces, or the URL may be enclosed in single quotes. Regular expressions give you a precise syntax for specifying what sequences of characters are legal matches.

In a regular expression, a character denotes itself unless it is one of the reserved characters

```
. * + ? { | ( ) [ \ ^ $
```

For example, the regular expression `href` only matches the string `href`.

The symbol `.` matches any single character. For example, `.r.f` matches `href` and `prof`.

The `*` symbol indicates that the preceding construct may be repeated 0 or more times; with the `+` symbol, the repetition is 1 or more times. A suffix of

? indicates that a construct is optional (0 or 1 times). For example, be+s? matches be, bee, and bees. You can specify other multiplicities with { }—see Table 6-2.

A | denotes an alternative: .(oo+|ee+)f matches beef or woof. Note the parentheses—without them, .oo+|ee+f would be the alternative between .oo+ and ee+f. Parentheses are also used for grouping—see Section 6.11, "Groups" (page 131).

A *character class* is a set of character alternatives enclosed in brackets, such as [Jj], [0-9], [A-Za-z], or [^0-9]. Inside a character class, the - denotes a range (all characters whose Unicode values fall within the two bounds). However, a - that is the first or last character in a character class denotes itself. A ^ as the first character in a character class denotes the complement—all characters except those specified. For example, [^0-9] denotes any character that is not a decimal digit.

There are six *predefined character classes*: \d (digits), \s (white space), \w (word characters), and their complements \D (non-digits), \S (nonwhite space), and \W (nonword characters).

The characters ^ and $ match the beginning and end of input. For example, ^[0-9]+$ matches a string entirely consisting of digits.

Be careful about the position of the ^ character. If it is the first character inside brackets, it denotes the complement: [^0-9]+$ matches a string of non-digits at the end of input.

 NOTE: I have a hard time remembering that ^ matches the start and $ the end. I keep thinking that $ should denote start, and on the US keyboard, $ is to the left of ^. But it's exactly the other way around, probably since the archaic text editor QED used $ to denote the last line.

Table 6-2 summarizes the JavaScript regular expression syntax.

If you need to have a literal . * + ? { | ( ) [\ ^ $, precede it by a backslash. Inside a character class, you only need to escape [and \, provided you are careful about the positions of] - ^. For example, []^-] is a class containing all three of them.

Table 6-2 Regular Expression Syntax

Expression	Description	Example
Characters		
A character other than .*+?{	( ) [\ ^ $	Matches only the given character	J
.	Matches any character except \n, or any character if the dotAll flag is set	
\u{hhhh}, \u{hhhhh}	The Unicode code point with the given hex value (requires unicode flag)	\u{1F310}
\uhhhh, \xhh	The UTF-16 code unit with the given hex value	\xA0
\f, \n, \r, \t, \v	Form feed (\x0C), newline (\x0A), carriage return (\x0D), tab (\x09), vertical tab (\x0B)	\n
\cL, where L is in [A-Za-z]	The control character corresponding to the character L	\cH is Ctrl-H or backspace (\x08)
\c, where c is not in [0-9BDPSWbcdfknprstv]	The character c	\\
Character Classes		
$[C_1C_2...]$, where C_i are characters, ranges c-d, or character classes	Any of the characters represented by $C_1, C_2, \ldots$	[0-9+-]
[^...]	Complement of a character class	[^\d\s]
\p{BooleanProperty} \p{Property=Value} \P{...}	A Unicode property (see Section 6.9); its complement (requires the unicode flag)	\p{L} are Unicode letters
\d, \D	A digit [0-9]; the complement	\d+ is a sequence of digits

(Continues)

Table 6-2 Regular Expression Syntax *(Continued)*

Expression	Description	Example
\w, \W	A word character [a-zA-Z0-9_]; the complement	
\s, \S	A space from [\t\n\v\f\r \xA0] or 18 additional Unicode space characters; same as \p{White_Space}	\s*,\s* is a comma surrounded by optional white space
Sequences and Alternatives		
XY	Any string from X, followed by any string from Y	[1-9][0-9]* is a positive number without leading zero
X|Y	Any string from X or Y	http|ftp
Grouping		
(*X*)	Captures the match of *X* into a group—see Section 6.11	'([^']*)' captures the quoted text
n	Matches the *n*th group	(['"]).*\1 matches 'Fred' or "Fred" but not "Fred'
(?<*name*>*X*)	Captures the match of *X* with the given name	'(?<qty>[0-9]+)' captures the match with name qty
\k<*name*>	The group with the given name	\k<qty> matches the group with name qty
(?:*X*)	Use parentheses without capturing *X*	In (?:http|ftp)://(.*) , the match after :// is \1
Other (?. . .)	See Section 6.14	
Quantifiers		
X?	Optional *X*	\+? is an optional + sign
X*, *X*+	0 or more *X*, 1 or more *X*	[1-9][0-9]+ is an integer ≥ 10
X{*n*}, *X*{*n*,}, *X*{*m*,*n*}	*n* times *X*, at least *n* times X, between *m* and *n* times *X*	[0-9]{4,6} are four to six digits

(Continues)

Table 6-2 Regular Expression Syntax *(Continued)*

Expression	Description	Example
X*? or X+?	Reluctant quantifier, attempting the shortest match before trying longer matches	.*(<.+?>).* captures the shortest sequence enclosed in angle brackets
Boundary Matches		
^ $	Beginning, end of input (or beginning, end of line if the `multiline` flag is set)	`^JavaScript$` matches the input or line `JavaScript`
\b, \B	Word boundary, nonword boundary	`\bJava\B` matches `JavaScript` but not `Java code`

6.7 Regular Expression Literals

A regular expression literal is delimited by slashes:

```
const timeRegex = /^([1-9]|1[0-2]):[0-9]{2} [ap]m$/
```

Regular expression literals are instances of the `RegExp` class.

The `typeof` operator, when applied to a regular expression, yields `'object'`.

Inside the regular expression literal, use backslashes to escape characters that have special meanings in regular expressions, such as the . and + characters:

```
const fractionalNumberRegex = /[0-9]+\.[0-9]*/
```

Here, the escaped . means a literal period.

In a regular expression literal, you also need to escape a forward slash so that it is not interpreted as the end of the literal.

To convert a string holding a regular expression into a `RegExp` object, use the `RegExp` function, with or without `new`:

```
const fractionalNumberRegex = new RegExp('[0-9]+\\.[0-9]*')
```

Note that the backslash in the string must be escaped.

6.8 Flags

A *flag* modifies a regular expression's behavior. One example is the `i` or `ignoreCase` flag. The regular expression

/[A-Z]+\.com/**i**

matches `Horstmann.COM`.

You can also set the flag in the constructor:

```
const regex = new RegExp(/[A-Z]+\.com/, 'i')
```

To find the flag values of a given `RegExp` object, you can use the `flags` property which yields a string of all flags. There is also a Boolean property for each flag:

```
regex.flags // 'i'
regex.ignoreCase // true
```

JavaScript supports six flags, shown in Table 6-3.

Table 6-3 Regular Expression Flags

Single Letter	Property Name	Description
i	ignoreCase	Case-insensitive match
m	multiline	^, $ match start, end of line
s	dotAll	. matches newline
u	unicode	Match Unicode characters, not code units—see Section 6.9
g	global	Find all matches—see Section 6.10
y	sticky	Match must start at *regex*.lastIndex—see Section 6.10

The `m` or `multiline` flag changes the behavior of the start and end anchors ^ and $. By default, they match the beginning and end of the entire string. In multiline mode, they match the beginning and end of a line. For example,

/^[0-9]+/m

matches digits at the beginning of a line.

With the `s` or `dotAll` flag, the . pattern matches newlines. Without it, . matches any non-newline character.

The other three flags are explained in later sections.

You can use more than one flag. The following regular expression matches upper- or lowercase letters at the start of each line:

/^[A-Z]/im

6.9 Regular Expressions and Unicode

For historical reasons, regular expressions work with UTF-16 code units, not Unicode characters. For example, the . pattern matches a single UTF-16 code unit. For example, the string

```
'Hello 🌐'
```

does not match the regular expression

```
/Hello .$/
```

The 🌐 character is encoded with two code units. The remedy is to use the u or unicode flag:

```
/Hello .$/u
```

With the u flag, the . pattern matches a single Unicode character, no matter how it is encoded in UTF-16.

If you need to keep your source files in ASCII, you can embed Unicode code points into regular expressions, using the \u{ } syntax:

```
/[A-Za-z]+ \u{1F310}/u
```

 CAUTION: Without the u flag, /\u{1F310}/ matches the string 'u{1F310}'.

When working with international text, you should avoid patterns such as [A-Za-z] for denoting letters. These patterns won't match letters in other languages. Instead, use \p{*Property*}, where *Property* is the name of a Boolean Unicode property. For example, \p{L} denotes a Unicode letter. The regular expression

```
/Hello, \p{L}+!/u
```

matches

```
'Hello, värld!'
```

and

```
'Hello, 世界!'
```

Table 6-4 shows the names of other common Boolean properties.

For Unicode properties whose values are not Boolean, use the syntax \p{*Property=Value*}. For example, the regular expression

```
/p{Script=Han}+/u
```

matches any sequence of Chinese characters.

Using an uppercase \P yields the complement: \P{L} matches any character that is not a letter.

Table 6-4 Common Boolean Unicode Properties

Name	Description
L	Letter
Lu	Uppercase letter
Ll	Lowercase letter
Nd	Decimal number
P	Punctuation
S	Symbol
White_Space	White space, same as \s
Emoji	Emoji characters, modifiers, or components

6.10 The Methods of the RegExp Class

The test method yields true if a string *contains* a match for the given regular expression:

```
/[0-9]+/.test('agent 007') // true
```

To test whether the entire string matches, your regular expression must use start and end anchors:

```
/^[0-9]+$/.test('agent 007') // false
```

The exec method yields an array holding the first matched subexpression, or null if there was no match.

For example,

```
/[0-9]+/.exec('agents 007 and 008')
```

returns an array containing the string '007'. (As you will see in the following section, the array can also contain group matches.)

In addition, the array that exec returns has two properties:

• index is the index of the subexpression

• input is the argument that was passed to exec

In other words, the array returned by the preceding call to exec is actually

```
['007', index: 7, input: 'agents 007 and 008']
```

To match multiple subexpressions, use the g or global flag:

```
let digits = /[0-9]+/g
```

Now each call to exec returns a new match:

```
result = digits.exec('agents 007 and 008') // ['007', index: 7, . . .]
result = digits.exec('agents 007 and 008') // ['008', index: 15, . . .]
result = digits.exec('agents 007 and 008') // null
```

To make this work, the RegExp object has a property lastIndex that is set to the first index after the match in each successful call to exec. The next call to exec starts the match at lastIndex. The lastIndex property is set to zero when a regular expression is constructed or a match failed.

You can also set the lastIndex property to skip a part of the string.

With the y or sticky flag, the match must start *exactly* at lastIndex:

```
digits = /[0-9]+/y
digits.lastIndex = 5
result = digits.exec('agents 007 and 008') // null
digits.lastIndex = 8
result = digits.exec('agents 007 and 008') // ['07', index: 8, . . .]
```

 NOTE: If you simply want an array of all matched substrings, use the match method of the String class instead of repeated calls to exec—see Section 6.12, "String Methods with Regular Expressions" (page 133).

```
let results = 'agents 007 and 008'.match(/[0-9]+/g) // ['007', '008']
```

6.11 Groups

Groups are used for extracting components of a match. For example, here is a regular expression for parsing times with groups for each component:

```
let time = /([1-9]|1[0-2]):([0-5][0-9])([ap]m)/
```

The group matches are placed in the array returned by exec:

```
let result = time.exec('Lunch at 12:15pm')
 // ['12:15pm', '12', '15', 'pm', index: 9, . . .]
```

As in the preceding section, result[0] is the entire matched string. For i > 0, result[i] is the match for the ith group.

Groups are numbered by their *opening* parentheses. This matters if you have nested parentheses. Consider this example. We want to analyze line items of invoices that have the form

```
Blackwell Toaster    USD29.95
```

Here is a regular expression with groups for each component:

```
/(\p{L}+(\s+\p{L}+)*)\s+([A-Z]{3})([0-9.]*)/u
```

In this situation, group 1 is `Blackwell Toaster`, the substring matched by the expression `(\p{L}+(\s+\p{L}+)*)`, from the first opening parenthesis to its matching closing parenthesis.

Group 2 is `' Toaster'`, the substring matched by `(\s+\p{L}+)`.

Groups 3 and 4 are `USD` and `29.95`.

We aren't interested in group 2; it only arose from the parentheses that were required for the repetition. For greater clarity, you can use a noncapturing group, by adding `?:` after the opening parenthesis:

```
/(\p{L}+(?:\s+\p{L}+)*)\s+([A-Z]{3})([0-9.]*)/u
```

Now `USD` and `29.95` are captured as groups 2 and 3.

 NOTE: When you have a group inside a repetition, such as `(\s+\p{L}+)*` in the example above, the corresponding group only holds the *last* match, not all matches.

If the repetition happened zero times, then the group match is set to `undefined`.

You can match against the contents of a captured group. For example, consider the regular expression:

```
/(['"]).*\1/
```

The group `(['"])` captures either a single or double quote. The pattern `\1` matches the captured string, so that `"Fred"` and `'Fred'` match the regular expression but `"Fred'` does not.

 CAUTION: Even though they are supposed be outlawed in strict mode, several JavaScript engines still support octal character escapes in regular expressions. For example, `\11` denotes `\t`, the character at code point 9.

However, if the regular expression has 11 or more capturing groups, then `\11` denotes a match of the 11th group.

Numbered groups are rather fragile. It is much better to capture by name:

```
let lineItem = /(?<item>\p{L}+(\s+\p{L}+)*)\s+(?<currency>[A-Z]{3})(?<price>[0-9.]*)/u
```

When a regular expression has one or more named groups, the array returned by exec has a property groups whose value is an object holding group names and matches:

```
let result = lineItem.exec('Blackwell Toaster    USD29.95')
let groupMatches = result.groups
  // { item: 'Blackwell Toaster', currency: 'USD', price: '29.95' }
```

The expression \k<*name*> matches against a group that was captured by name:

```
/(?<quote>['"]).*\k<quote>/
```

Here, the group with the name "quote" matches a single or double quote at the beginning of the string. The string must end with the same character. For example, "Fred" and 'Fred' are matches but "Fred' is not.

The features of the RegExp are summarized in Table 6-5.

Table 6-5 Features of the RegExp Class

Name	Description
Constructors	
new RegExp(regex, flags)	Constructs a regular expression from the given regex (a string, regular expression literal, or RegExp object) and the given flags
Properties	
flags	A string of all flags
ignoreCase, multiline, dotAll, unicode, global, sticky	Boolean properties for all flag types
Methods	
test(str)	true if str contains a match for this regular expression
exec(str)	Match results for the current match of this regular expression inside str. See Section 6.10 for details. The match and matchAll methods of the String class are simpler to use than this method.

6.12 String Methods with Regular Expressions

As you saw in Section 6.10, "The Methods of the RegExp Class" (page 130), the workhorse method for getting match information is the exec method of the RegExp class. But its API is far from elegant. The String class has several methods that work with regular expressions and produce commonly used results more easily.

For a regular expression without the global flag set, the call `str.match(regex)` returns the same match results as `regex.exec(str)`:

```
'agents 007 and 008'.match(/[0-9]+/) // ['007', index: 7, . . .]
```

With the global flag set, `match` simply returns an array of matches, which is often just what you want:

```
'agents 007 and 008'.match(/[0-9]+/g) // ['007', '008']
```

If there is no match, the `String.match` method returns `null`.

 NOTE: `RegExp.exec` and `String.match` are the only methods in the ECMAScript standard library that yield `null` to indicate the absence of a result.

If you have a global search and want all match results without calling `exec` repeatedly, you will like the `matchAll` method of the `String` class that is currently a stage 3 proposal. It returns an iterable of the match results. Let's say you want to look for all matches of the regular expression

```
let time = /([1-9]|1[0-2]):([0-5][0-9])([ap]m)/g
```

The loop

```
for (const [, hours, minutes, period] of input.matchAll(time)) {
   . . .
}
```

iterates over all match results, using destructuring to set `hours`, `minutes`, and `period` to the group matches. The initial comma ignores the entire matched expression.

The `matchAll` method yields the matches lazily. It is efficient if there are many matches but only a few are examined.

The `search` method returns the index of the first match or -1 if no match is found:

```
let index = 'agents 007 and 008'.search(/[0-9]+/) // Yields index 7
```

The `replace` method replaces the first match of a regular expression with a replacement string. To replace all matches, set the global flag:

```
let replacement = 'agents 007 and 008'.replace(/[0-9]/g, '?')
   // 'agents ??? and ???'
```

NOTE: The split method can have a regular expression as argument. For example,

```
str.split(/\s*,\s*/)
```

splits str along commas that are optionally surrounded by white space.

6.13 More about Regex Replace

In this section, we have a closer look at the replace method of the String class.

The replacement string parameter can contain patterns starting with a $ that are processed as shown in Table 6-6.

Table 6-6 Replacement String Patterns

Pattern	Description
$\`, $'	The portion before or after the matched string
$&	Matched string
$n	The nth group
$<name>	The group with the given name
$$	Dollar sign

For example, the following replacement repeats each vowel three times:

```
'hello'.replace(/[aeiou]/g, '$&$&$&') // 'heeellooo'
```

The most useful pattern is the group pattern. Here, we use groups to match the first and last name of a person in each line and flip them:

```
let names = 'Harry Smith\nSally Lin'
let flipped = names.replace(
  /^([A-Z][a-z]+) ([A-Z][a-z]+)/gm, "$2, $1")
  // 'Smith, Harry\nLin, Sally'
```

If the number after the $ sign is larger than the number of groups in the regular expression, the pattern is inserted verbatim:

```
let replacement = 'Blackwell Toaster $29.95'.replace('\$29', '$19')
  // 'Blackwell Toaster $19.95'—there is no group 19
```

You can also use named groups:

```
flipped = names.replace(/^(?<first>[A-Z][a-z]+) (?<last>[A-Z][a-z]+)$/gm,
  "$<last>, $<first>")
```

For more complex replacements, you can provide a function instead of a replacement string. The function receives the following arguments:

- The string that was matched by the regular expression
- The matches of all groups
- The offset of the match
- The entire string

In this example, we just process the group matches:

```
flipped = names.replace(/^([A-Z][a-z]+) ([A-Z][a-z]+)/gm,
  (match, first, last) => `${last}, ${first[0]}.`)
  // 'Smith, H.\nLin, S.'
```

 NOTE: The `replace` method also works with strings, replacing the first match of the string itself:

```
let replacement = 'Blackwell Toaster $29.95'.replace('$', 'USD')
  // Replaces $ with USD
```

Note that the $ is not interpreted as an end anchor.

 CAUTION: If you call the `search` method with a string, it is converted to a regular expression:

```
let index = 'Blackwell Toaster $29.95'.search('$')
  // Yields 24, the end of the string, not the index of $
```

Use `indexOf` to search for a plain string.

6.14 Exotic Features

In the final section of this chapter, you will see several complex and uncommon regular expression features.

The + and * repetition operators are "greedy"—they match the longest possible strings. That's generally desirable. You want /[0-9]+/ to match the longest possible string of digits, and not a single digit.

However, consider this example:

```
'"Hi" and "Bye"'.match(/".*"/g)
```

The result is

```
'"Hi" and "Bye"'
```

because .* greedily matches everything until the final ". That does not help us if we want to match quoted substrings.

One remedy is to require non-quotes in the repetition:

```
'"Hi" and "Bye"'.match(/"[^"]*"/g)
```

Alternatively, you can specify that the match should be *reluctant*, by using the *? operator:

```
'"Hi" and "Bye"'.match(/".*?"/g)
```

Either way, now each quoted string is matched separately, and the result is

```
['"Hi"', '"Bye"']
```

There is also a reluctant version +? that requires at least one repetition.

The *lookahead* operator $p(?=q)$ matches p provided it is followed by q, but does not include q in the match. For example, here we find the hours that precede a colon.

```
let hours = '10:30 - 12:00'.match(/[0-9]+(?=:)/g) // ['10, 12']
```

The inverted lookahead operator $p(?!q)$ matches p provided it is *not followed* by q.

```
let minutes = '10:30 - 12:00'.match(/[0-9][0-9](?!:)/g) // ['10, 12']
```

There is also a *lookbehind* $(?<=p)q$ that matches q as long as it is preceded by p.

```
minutes = '10:30 - 12:00'.match(/(?<=[0-9]+:)[0-9]+/g) // ['30', '00']
```

Note that the argument inside $(?<=[0-9]+:)$ is itself a regular expression.

Finally, there is an inverted lookbehind $(?<!p)q$, matching q as long as it is not preceded by p.

```
hours = '10:30 - 12:00'.match(/(?<![0-9:])[0-9]+/g)
```

Regular expressions such as this one may have motivated Jamie Zawinski's timeless quote, "Some people, when confronted with a problem, think: 'I know, I'll use regular expressions.' Now they have two problems."

Exercises

1. Write a function that, given a string, produces an escaped string delimited by ' characters. Turn all non-ASCII Unicode into \u{. . .}. Produce escapes \b, \f, \n, \r, \t, \v, \', \\.

2. Write a function that fits a string into a given number of Unicode characters. If it is too long, trim it and append an ellipsis ... (\u{2026}). Be sure

to correctly handle characters that are encoded with two UTF-16 code units.

3. The substring and slice methods are very tolerant of bad arguments. Can you get them to yield an error with any arguments? Try strings, objects, array, no arguments.

4. Write a function that accepts a string and returns an array of all substrings. Be careful about characters that are encoded with two UTF-16 code units.

5. In a more perfect world, all string methods would take offsets that count Unicode characters, not UTF-16 code units. Which String methods would be affected? Provide replacement functions for them, such as indexOf(str, sub) and slice(str, start, end).

6. Implement a printf tagged template function that formats integers, floating-point numbers, and strings with the classic printf formatting instructions, placed after embedded expressions:

   ```
   const formatted = printf`${item}%-40s | ${quantity}%6d | ${price}%10.2f`
   ```

7. Write a tagged template function spy that displays both the raw and "cooked" string fragments and the embedded expression values. In the raw string fragments, remove the backslashes that were needed for escaping backticks, dollar signs, and backslashes.

8. List as many different ways as you can to produce a regular expression that matches only the empty string.

9. Is the m/multiline flag actually useful? Couldn't you just match \n? Produce a regular expression that can find all lines containing just digits without the multiline flag. What about the last line?

10. Produce regular expressions for email addresses and URLs.

11. Produce regular expressions for US and international telephone numbers.

12. Use regular expression replacement to clean up phone numbers and credit card numbers.

13. Produce a regular expression for quoted text, where the delimiters could be matching single or double quotes, or curly quotes "".

14. Produce a regular expression for image URLs in an HTML document.

15. Using a regular expression, extract all decimal integers (including negative ones) from a string into an array.

16. Suppose you have a regular expression and you want to use it for a complete match, not just a match of a substring. You just want to surround it with ^ and $. But that's not so easy. The regular expression needs to

be properly escaped before adding those anchors. Write a function that accepts a regular expression and yields a regular expression with the anchors added.

17. Use the `replace` method of the `String` class with a function argument to replace all °F measurements in a string with their °C equivalents.

18. Enhance the `greek` function of Section 6.5, "Raw Template Literals" (page 122), so that it handles escaped backslashes and $ symbols. Also check whether a symbol starting with a backslash has a substitution. If not, include it verbatim.

19. Generalize the `greek` function of the preceding exercise to a general purpose substitution function that can be called as subst(*dictionary*)`templateString`.

Arrays and Collections

Topics in This Chapter

Chapter 7

Whenever you learn a new programming language, you want to know how to store your data. The traditional data structure of choice for sequential data is the humble array. In this chapter, you will learn the various array methods that the JavaScript API provides. We then turn to typed arrays and array buffers—advanced constructs for efficient handling of binary data blocks. Unlike Java or C++, JavaScript does not provide a rich set of data structures, but there are simple map and set classes that we discuss at the end of the chapter.

7.1 Constructing Arrays

You already know how to construct an array with a given sequence of elements—simply write a literal:

```
const names = ['Peter', 'Paul', 'Mary']
```

Here is how to construct an empty array with ten thousand elements, all initially `undefined`:

```
const bigEmptyArray = []
bigEmptyArray.length = 10000
```

In an array literal, you can place spreads of any *iterable*. Arrays and strings, the sets and maps that you will see later in this chapter, as well as `NodeList` and `HTMLCollection` from the DOM API, are iterable. For example, here is how to form an array containing the elements of two iterables `a` and `b`:

```
const elements = [...a, ...b]
```

As you will see in Chapter 9, an iterable object has a somewhat complex structure. The `Array.from` method collects elements from a simpler *array-like* object. An array-like object is an object with an integer-valued property with name `'length'` and properties with names `'0'`, `'1'`, `'2'`, and so on. Of course, arrays are array-like, but some methods of the DOM API yield array-like objects that aren't arrays or iterables. Then you can call `Array.from(arrayLike)` to place the elements into an array.

```
const arrayLike = { length: 3 , '0': 'Peter', '1': 'Paul', '2': 'Mary'}
const elements = Array.from(arrayLike)
  // elements is the array ['Peter', 'Paul', 'Mary']
  // Array.isArray(arrayLike) is false, Array.isArray(elements) is true
```

The `Array.from` method accepts an optional second argument, a function that is called for all index values from 0 up to `length` − 1, passing the element (or `undefined` for missing elements) and the index. The results of the function are collected into an array. For example,

```
const squares = Array.from({ length: 5 }, (element, index) => index * index)
  // [0, 1, 4, 9, 16]
```

 CAUTION: There is a constructor for constructing an array with given elements that you can invoke with or without `new`:

```
names = new Array('Peter', 'Paul', 'Mary')
names = Array('Peter', 'Paul', 'Mary')
```

But it has a pitfall. Calling `new Array` or `Array` with a single numeric argument has an entirely different effect. The single argument denotes the length of the array:

```
numbers = new Array(10000)
```

The result is an array of length 10000 and no elements!

I suggest to stay away from the `Array` constructor and use array literals:

```
names = ['Peter', 'Paul', 'Mary']
numbers = [10000]
```

 NOTE: The factory function `Array.of` doesn't suffer from the problem of the `Array` constructor:

```
names = Array.of('Peter', 'Paul', 'Mary')
littleArray = Array.of(10000) // An array of length 1, same as [10000]
```

But it offers no advantage over array literals either. (Exercise 2 shows a subtle and uncommon use case for the `of` method.)

7.2 The length Property and Index Properties

Every array has a `'length'` property whose value is an integer between 0 and $2^{32} - 1$. The properties whose numeric values are non-negative integers are called *index properties*. For example, the array

```
const names = ['Peter', 'Paul', 'Mary']
```

is an object with a `'length'` property (whose value is 3) and index properties `'0'`, `'1'`, `'2'`. Recall that property keys are always strings.

The length is always one more than the highest index:

```
const someNames = [ , 'Smith', , 'Jones'] // someNumbers.length is 4
```

The length is adjusted when a value is assigned to an index property:

```
someNames[5] = 'Miller' // Now someNames has length 6
```

You can adjust the length manually:

```
someNames.length = 100
```

If you decrease the length, any element whose index is at least the new length gets deleted.

```
someNames.length = 4 // someNames[4] and beyond are deleted
```

There is no requirement that an array has an index property for every index between 0 and length − 1. The ECMAScript standard uses the term *missing elements* for gaps in the index sequence.

To find out whether an element is missing, you can use the `in` operator:

```
'2' in someNames // false—no property '2'
3 in someNames // true; there is a property '3'
  // Note that the left operand is converted to a string
```

 NOTE: An array can have properties that are not index properties. This is occasionally used to attach other information to an array. For example, the `exec` method of the `RegExp` class yields an array of matches, with additional properties `index` and `input`.

```
/([1-9]|1[0-2]):([0-5][0-9])([ap]m)/.exec('12:15pm')
 // ['12:15pm', '12', '15', 'pm', index: 0, input: '12:15pm']
```

 CAUTION: A string containing a negative number, such as `'-1'`, is a valid property, but it is not an index property.

```
const squares = [0, 1, 4, 9]
squares[-1] = 1 // [ 0, 1, 4, 9, '-1': 1 ]
```

7.3 Deleting and Adding Elements

The calls

```
let arr = [0, 1, 4, 9, 16, 25]
const deletedElement = arr.pop() // arr is now [0, 1, 4, 9, 16]
const newLength = arr.push(x) // arr is now [0, 1, 4, 9, 16, x]
```

delete or add an element at the end of an array, adjusting the length.

 NOTE: Instead of calling pop and push, you could write

```
arr.length--
arr[arr.length] = x
```

I prefer pop and push since they indicate the intent better.

To delete or add the initial element, call

```
arr = [0, 1, 4, 9, 16, 25]
const deletedElement = arr.shift() // arr is now [1, 4, 9, 16, 25]
const newLength = arr.unshift(x) // arr is now [x, 1, 4, 9, 16, 25]
```

The push and unshift methods can add any number of elements at once:

```
arr = [9]
arr.push(16, 25) // 16, 25 are appended; arr is now [9, 16, 25]
arr.unshift(0, 1, 4) // 0, 1, 4 are prepended; arr is now [0, 1, 4, 9, 16, 25]
```

Use the splice method to delete or add elements in the middle:

```
const deletedElements = arr.splice(start, deleteCount, x1, x2, . . .)
```

First, deleteCount elements are removed, starting at offset start. Then the provided elements are inserted at start.

```
arr = [0, 1, 12, 24, 36]
const start = 2
// Replace arr[start] and arr[start + 1]
arr.splice(start, 2, 16, 25) // arr is now [0, 1, 16, 25, 36]
// Add elements at index start
arr.splice(start, 0, 4, 9) // arr is now [0, 1, 4, 9, 16, 25, 36]
// Delete the elements at index start and start + 1
arr.splice(start, 2) // arr is now [0, 1, 16, 25, 36]
// Delete all elements at index start and beyond
arr.splice(start) // arr is now [0, 1]
```

If start is negative, it is counted from the *end* of the array (that is, it is adjusted by adding arr.length).

```
arr = [0, 1, 4, 16]
arr.splice(-1, 1, 9) // arr is now [0, 1, 4, 9]
```

The `splice` method returns an array of the removed elements.

```
arr = [1, 4, 9, 16]
const spliced = arr.splice(1, 2) // spliced is [4, 9], arr is [1, 16]
```

7.4 Other Array Mutators

In this section, you will see the mutator methods of the `Array` class other than those for deleting and adding elements.

The `fill` method overwrites existing elements with a new value:

```
arr.fill(value, start, end)
```

The `copyWithin` method overwrites existing elements with other elements from the same array:

```
arr.copyWithin(targetIndex, start, end)
```

With both methods, `start` defaults to `0` and `end` to `arr.length`.

If `start`, `end`, or `targetIndex` are negative, they count from the end of the array.

Here are some examples:

```
let arr = [0, 1, 4, 9, 16, 25]
arr.copyWithin(0, 1) // arr is now [1, 4, 9, 16, 25, 25]
arr.copyWithin(1) // arr is now [1, 1, 4, 9, 16, 25]
arr.fill(7, 3, -1)  // arr is now [1, 1, 4, 7, 7, 25]
```

`arr.reverse()` reverses `arr` in place:

```
arr = [0, 1, 4, 9, 16, 25]
arr.reverse() // arr is now [25, 16, 9, 4, 1, 0]
```

The call

```
arr.sort(comparisonFunction)
```

sorts `arr` in place. The comparison function compares two elements `x, y` and returns

- A negative number if `x` should come before `y`
- A positive number if `x` should come after `y`
- `0` if they are indistinguishable

For example, here is how you can sort an array of numbers:

```
arr = [0, 1, 16, 25, 4, 9]
arr.sort((x, y) => x - y) // arr is now [0, 1, 4, 9, 16, 25]
```

CAUTION: If the comparison function is not provided, the `sort` method turns elements to strings and compares them—see Exercise 5. For numbers, this might be the world's worst comparison function:

```
arr = [0, 1, 4, 9, 16, 25]
arr.sort() // arr is now [0, 1, 16, 25, 4, 9]
```

The most useful methods of the `Array` class are summarized in Table 7-1.

Table 7-1 Useful Functions and Methods of the `Array` Class

Name	Description
Functions	
`from(arraylike, f)`	Produces an array from any object with properties named `'length'`, `'0'`, `'1'`, and so on. If present, the function `f` is applied to each element.
Mutating Methods	
`pop(), shift()`	Removes and returns the last element
`push(value), unshift(value)`	Appends or prepends `value` to this array and returns the new length
`fill(value, start, end)`	Overwrites the given range with `value`. For this and the following methods, the following apply unless otherwise mentioned: If `start` or `end` are negative, they are counted from the end of the array. The range includes `start` and excludes `end`. The default for `start` and `end` are `0` and the array length. The method returns this array.
`copyWithin(targetIndex, start, end)`	Copies the given range to the target index
`reverse()`	Reverses the elements of this array
`sort(comparisonFunction)`	Sorts this array
`splice(start, deleteCount, values...)`	Removes and returns `deleteCount` elements at index `start`, then inserts the given values at `start`

(Continues)

Table 7-1 Useful Functions and Methods of the `Array` Class *(Continued)*

Name	Description
Nonmutating Methods	
`slice(start, end)`	Returns the elements in the given range
`includes(target, start)`, `firstIndex(target, start)`, `lastIndex(target, start)`	If the array includes `target` at or after index `start`, these methods return `true` or the index; otherwise, `false` or -1
`flat(k)`	Returns the elements of this array, replacing any arrays of dimension ≤k with their elements. The default for `k` is 1.
`map(f)`, `flatMap(f)`, `forEach(f)`	Calls the given function on each element and returns an array of the results, or the flattened results, or `undefined`
`filter(f)`	Returns all elements for which `f` returns a truish result
`findIndex(f)`, `find(f)`	Return the index or value of the first element for which `f` returns a truish value. The function `f` is called with three arguments: the element, index, and array.
`every(f)`, `some(f)`	Return `true` if `f` returns a truish value for every, or at least one, element
`join(separator)`	Returns a string consisting of all elements turned to strings and separated by the given separator (which defaults to `','`)

For sorting strings in a human language, the `localeCompare` method can be a good choice:

```
const titles = . . .
titles.sort((s, t) => s.localeCompare(t))
```

Chapter 8 has more information about locale-based comparisons.

 NOTE: Since 2019, the `sort` method is guaranteed to be *stable*. That is, the order of indistinguishable elements is not disturbed. For example, suppose you have a sequence of messages that was previously sorted by date. If you now sort it by the sender, then messages with the same sender will continue to be sorted by date.

7.5 Producing Elements

All methods that are introduced from this point on do not mutate the array on which they operate.

The following methods produce arrays containing elements from an existing array.

The call

```
arr.slice(start, end)
```

yields an array containing the elements in the given range. The start index defaults to 0, end to arr.length.

arr.slice() is the same as [...arr].

The flat method flattens multidimensional arrays. The default is to flatten one level.

```
[[1, 2], [3, 4]].flat()
```

is the array

```
[1, 2, 3, 4]
```

In the unlikely case that you have an array of more than two dimensions, you can specify how many levels you want to flatten. Here is a flattening from three dimensions to one:

```
[[[1, 2], [3, 4]], [[5, 6], [7, 8]]].flat(2) // [1, 2, 3, 4, 5, 6, 7, 8]
```

The call

```
arr.concat(arg1, arg2, . . .)
```

yields an array starting with arr, to which the arguments are appended. However, there is a twist: Array arguments are flattened.

```
const arr = [1, 2]
const arr2 = [5, 6]
const result = arr.concat(3, 4, arr2) // result is [1, 2, 3, 4, 5, 6]
```

Since you can nowadays use spreads in array literals, the concat method is no longer very useful. A simpler way of achieving the same result is:

```
const result = [...arr, 3, 4, ...arr2]
```

There is one remaining use case for the concat method: to concatenate a sequence of items of unknown type and flatten just those that are arrays.

NOTE: You can control the flattening with the `isConcatSpreadable` symbol. (Symbols are covered in Chapter 8.)

If the symbol is `false`, arrays are not flattened:

```
arr = [17, 29]
arr[Symbol.isConcatSpreadable] = false
[].concat(arr) // An array with a single element [17, 29]
```

If the symbol is `true`, then array-like objects are flattened:

```
[].concat({ length: 2, [Symbol.isConcatSpreadable]: true,
  '0': 17, '1': 29 }) // An array with two elements 17, 29
```

7.6 Finding Elements

The following calls check whether a specific value is contained in an array.

```
const found = arr.includes(target, start) // true or false
const firstIndex = arr.indexOf(target, start) // first index or -1
const lastIndex = arr.lastIndexOf(target, start) // last index or -1
```

The target must match the element strictly, using the `===` comparison.

The search starts at `start`. If `start` is less than `0`, it counts from the end of the array. If `start` is omitted, it defaults to `0`.

If you want to find a value that fulfills a condition, then call one of the following:

```
const firstIndex = arr.findIndex(conditionFunction)
const firstElement = arr.find(conditionFunction)
```

For example, here is how you can find the first negative number in an array:

```
const firstNegative = arr.find(x => x < 0)
```

For this and the subsequent methods of this section, the condition function receives three arguments:

- The array element
- The index
- The entire array

The calls

```
arr.every(conditionFunction)
arr.some(conditionFunction)
```

yield `true` if `conditionFunction(element, index, arr)` is `true` for every element or at least one element.

For example,

```
const atLeastOneNegative = arr.some(x => x < 0)
```

The `filter` method yields all values that fulfill a condition:

```
const negatives = [-1, 7, 2, -9].filter(x => x < 0) // [-1, -9]
```

7.7 Visiting All Elements

To visit all elements of an array, you can use a `for of` loop to visit all elements in order, or the `for in` loop to visit all index values.

```
for (const e of arr) {
  // Do something with the element e
}
for (const i in arr) {
  // Do something with the index i and the element arr[i]
}
```

 NOTE: The `for of` loop looks up elements for all index values between 0 and `length − 1`, yielding `undefined` for missing elements. In contrast, the `for in` loop only visits keys that are present.

In other words, the `for in` loop views an array as an object, whereas the `for of` loop views an array as an iterable. (As you will see in Chapter 12, iterables are sequences of values without gaps.)

If you want to visit both the index values and elements, use the iterator that the `entries` method returns. It produces arrays of length 2 holding each index and element. This loop uses the `entries` method, a `for of` loop, and destructuring:

```
for (const [index, element] of arr.entries())
  console.log(index, element)
```

 NOTE: The `entries` method is defined for all JavaScript data structures, including arrays. There are corresponding methods `keys` and `values` that yield iterators over the keys and values of the collection. These are useful for working with generic collections. If you know that you are working with an array, you won't need them.

The call `arr.forEach(f)` invokes `f(element, index, arr)` for each element, skipping missing elements. The call

```
arr.forEach((element, index) => console.log(index, element))
```

is equivalent to

```
for (const index in arr) console.log(index, arr[index])
```

Instead of specifying an action for each element, it is often better to transform the elements and collect the results. The call `arr.map(f)` yields an array of all values returned from `f(arr[index], index, arr)`:

```
[1, 7, 2, 9].map(x => x * x) // [1, 49, 4, 81]
[1, 7, 2, 9].map((x, i) => x * 10 ** i) // [1, 70, 200, 9000]
```

Consider a function that returns an array of values:

```
function roots(x) {
  if (x < 0) {
    return [] // No roots
  } else if (x === 0) {
    return [0] // Single root
  } else {
    return [Math.sqrt(x), -Math.sqrt(x)] // Two roots
  }
}
```

When you map this function to an array of inputs, you get an array of the array-valued answers:

```
[-1, 0, 1, 4].map(roots) // [[], [0], [1, -1], [2, -2]]
```

If you want to flatten out the results, you can call `map` followed by `flat`, or you can call `flatMap` which is slightly more efficient:

```
[-1, 0, 1, 4].flatMap(roots) // [0, 1, -1, 2, -2]
```

Finally, the call `arr.join(separator)` converts all elements to strings and joins them with the given separator. The default separator is `','`.

```
[1,2,3,[4,5]].join(' and ') // '1 and 2 and 3 and 4,5'
```

NOTE: The `forEach`, `map`, `filter`, `find`, `findIndex`, `some`, and `every` methods (but not `sort` or `reduce`), as well as the `from` function, take an optional argument after the function argument:

```
arr.forEach(f, thisArg)
```

The `thisArg` argument becomes the `this` parameter of f. That is,

```
thisArg.f(arr[index], index, arr)
```

is called for each index.

You only need the `thisArg` argument if you pass a method instead of a function. Exercise 4 shows how you can avoid this situation.

7.8 Sparse Arrays

An array with one or more missing elements is called *sparse*. Sparse arrays can arise in four situations:

1. Missing elements in an array literal:

   ```
   const someNumbers = [ , 2, , 9] // No index properties 0, 2
   ```

2. Adding an element beyond the length:

   ```
   someNumbers[100] = 0 // No index properties 4 to 99
   ```

3. Increasing the length:

   ```
   const bigEmptyArray = []
   bigEmptyArray.length = 10000 // No index properties
   ```

4. Deleting an element:

   ```
   delete someNumbers[1] // No longer an index property 1
   ```

Most methods in the array API skip over the missing elements in sparse arrays. For example, [, 2, , 9].forEach(f) only invokes f twice. No call is made for the missing elements at indices 0 and 2.

As you have seen in Section 7.1, "Constructing Arrays" (page 141), Array.from(arrayLike, f) is an exception, invoking f for every index.

You can use Array.from to replace missing elements with undefined:

```
Array.from([ , 2, , 9]) // [undefined, 2, undefined, 9]
```

The join method turns missing and undefined elements into empty strings:

```
[ , 2, undefined, 9].join(' and ') // ' and 2 and  and 9'
```

Most methods that produce arrays from given arrays keep the missing elements in place. For example, [, 2, , 9].map(x => x * x) yields [, 4, , 81].

However, the sort method places missing elements at the end:

```
let someNumbers = [ , 2, , 9]
someNumbers.sort((x, y) => y - x) // someNumbers is now [9, 2, , , ]
```

(Eagle-eyed readers may have noted that there are four commas. The last comma is a trailing comma. If it had not been present, then the preceding comma would have been a trailing comma and the array would only have had one undefined element.)

The filter, flat, and flatMap skip missing elements entirely.

A simple way of eliminating missing elements from an array is to filter with a function that accepts all elements:

```
[ , 2, , 9].filter(x => true) // [2, 9]
```

7.9 Reduction

This section discusses a general mechanism for computing a value from the elements of an array. The mechanism is elegant, but frankly, it is never necessary—you can achieve the same effect with a simple loop. Feel free to skip this section if you don't find it interesting.

The `map` method applies a unary function to all elements of a collection. The `reduce` and `reduceRight` methods that we discuss in this section combine elements with a *binary* operation. The call `arr.reduce(op)` applies `op` to successive elements like this:

```
              .
            .
          .
         op
        / \
      op    arr[3]
     / \
   op    arr[2]
  / \
arr[0]  arr[1]
```

For example, here is how to compute the sum of array elements:

```
const arr = [1, 7, 2, 9]
const result = arr.reduce((x, y) => x + y) // ((1 + 7) + 2) + 9
```

Here is a more interesting reduction that computes the value of a decimal number from an array of digits:

```
[1, 7, 2, 9].reduce((x, y) => 10 * x + y) // 1729
```

This tree diagram shows the intermediate results:

```
        1729
        / \
      172    9
      / \
    17    2
    / \
   1    7
```

In most cases, it is useful to start the computation with an initial value other than the initial array element. The call `arr.reduce(op, init)` computes

```
         op
        /  \
      op    arr[2]
     /  \
   op    arr[1]
  /  \
init   arr[0]
```

Compared with the tree diagram of `reduce` without an initial value, this diagram is more regular. All array elements are on the right of the tree. Each operation combines an accumulated value (starting with the initial value) and an array element.

For example,

```
[1, 7, 2, 9].reduce((accum, current) => accum - current, 0)
```

is

$$0 - 1 - 7 - 2 - 9 = -19$$

Without the initial value, the result would have been $1 - 7 - 2 - 9$, which is not the difference of all elements.

The initial value is returned when the array is empty. For example, if you define

```
const sum = arr => arr.reduce((accum, current) => accum + current, 0)
```

then the sum of the empty array is `0`. Reducing an empty array without an initial value throws an exception.

The callback function actually takes four arguments:

- The accumulated value
- The current array element
- The index of the current element
- The entire array

In this example, we collect the positions of all elements fulfilling a condition:

```
function findAll(arr, condition) {
  return arr.reduce((accum, current, currentIndex) =>
    condition(current) ? [...accum, currentIndex] : accum, [])
}

const odds = findAll([1, 7, 2, 9], x => x % 2 !== 0)
  // [0, 1, 3], the positions of all odd elements
```

The reduceRight method starts at the end of the array, visiting the elements in reverse order.

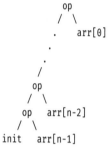

For example,

```
[1, 2, 3, 4].reduceRight((x, y) => [x, y], [])
```

is

```
[[[[[], 4], 3], 2], 1]
```

 NOTE: Right reduction in JavaScript is similar to a right fold in Lisp-like languages, but the order of the operands is reversed.

Reducing can be used instead of a loop. Suppose, for example, that we want to count the frequencies of the letters in a string. One way is to visit each letter and update an object.

```
const freq = {}
for (const c of 'Mississippi') {
  if (c in freq) {
    freq[c]++
  } else {
    freq[c] = 1
  }
}
```

Here is another way of thinking about this. At each step, combine the frequency map and the newly encountered letter, yielding a new frequency map. That's a reduction:

```
              .
            .
          .
        op
       / \
      op  's'
     / \
    op  'i'
   / \
empty map 'M'
```

What is op? The left operand is the partially filled frequency map, and the right operand is the new letter. The result is the augmented map. It becomes the input to the next call to op, and at the end, the result is a map with all counts. The code is

```
[...'Mississippi'].reduce(
  (freq, c) => ({ ...freq, [c]: (c in freq ? freq[c] + 1 : 1) }),
  {})
```

In the reduction function, a new object is created, starting with a copy of the freq object. Then the value associated with the c key is set either to an increment of the preceding value if there was one, or to 1.

Note that in this approach, no state is mutated. In each step, a new object is computed.

It is possible to replace any loop with a call to reduce. Put all variables updated in the loop into an object, and define an operation that implements one step through the loop, producing a new object with the updated variables. I am not saying this is always a good idea, but you may find it interesting that loops can be eliminated in this way.

7.10 Maps

The JavaScript API provides a Map class that implements the classic map data structure: a collection of key/value pairs.

Of course, every JavaScript object is a map, but there are advantages of using the Map class instead:

- Object keys must be strings or symbols, but Map keys can be of any type.

- A Map instance remembers the order in which elements were inserted.

- Unlike objects, maps do not have a prototype chain.

- You can find out the number of entries with the `size` property.

To construct a map, you can provide an iterable with [*key*, *value*] pairs:

```
const weekdays = new Map(
  [["Mon", 0], ["Tue", 1], ["Wed", 2], ["Thu", 3], ["Fri", 4], ["Sat", 5], ["Sun", 6], ])
```

Or you can construct an empty map and add entries later:

```
const emptyMap = new Map()
```

You must use `new` with the constructor.

The API is very straightforward. The call

```
map.set(key, value)
```

adds an entry and returns the map for chaining:

```
map.set(key1, value1).set(key2, value2)
```

To remove an entry, call:

```
map.delete(key) // Returns true if the key was present, false otherwise
```

The `clear` method removes all entries.

To test whether a key is present, call

```
if (map.has(key)) . . .
```

Retrieve a key's value with

```
const value = map.get(key) // Returns undefined if the key is not present
```

A map is an iterable yielding [`key`, `value`] pairs. Therefore, you can easily visit all entries with a `for of` loop:

```
for (const [key, value] of map) {
  console.log(key, value)
}
```

Alternatively, use the `forEach` method:

```
map.forEach((key, value) => {
  console.log(key, value)
})
```

Maps are traversed in insertion order. Consider this map:

```
const weekdays = new Map([['Mon', 0], ['Tue', 1], . . ., ['Sun', 6]])
```

Both the `for of` loop and the `forEach` method will respect the order in which you inserted the elements.

 NOTE: In Java, you would use a `LinkedHashMap` to visit elements in insertion order. In JavaScript, tracking insertion order is automatic.

NOTE: Maps, like all JavaScript collections, have methods `keys`, `values`, and `entries` that yield iterators over the keys, values, and key/value pairs. If you just want to iterate over the keys, you can use a loop:

```
for (const key of map.keys()) . . .
```

In programming languages such as Java and C++, you get the choice between hash maps and tree maps, and you have to come up with a hash or comparison function. In JavaScript, you always get a hash map, and you have no choice of the hash function.

The hash function for a JavaScript `Map` is compatible with *key equality*: `===` except that all `NaN` are equal. Hash values are derived from primitive type values or object references.

This is fine if your keys are strings or numbers, or if you are happy to compare keys by identity. For example, you can use a map to associate values with DOM nodes. That is better than adding properties directly into the node objects.

But you have to be careful when you use other objects as keys. Distinct objects are separate keys, even if their values are the same:

```
const map = new Map()
const key1 = new Date('1970-01-01T00:00:00.000Z')
const key2 = new Date('1970-01-01T00:00:00.000Z')
map.set(key1, 'Hello')
map.set(key2, 'Epoch') // Now map has two entries
```

If that's not what you want, consider choosing different keys, such as the date strings in this example.

7.11 Sets

A `Set` is a data structure that collects elements without duplicates.

Construct a set as

```
const emptySet = new Set()
const setWithElements = new Set(iterable)
```

where `iterable` produces the elements.

As with maps, the `size` property yields the number of elements.

The API for sets is even simpler than that for maps:

```
set.add(x)
  // Adds x if not present and returns set for chaining
set.delete(x)
  // If x is present, deletes x and returns true, otherwise returns false
set.has(x) // Returns true if x is present
set.clear() // Deletes all elements
```

To visit all elements of a set, you can use a `for of` loop:

```
for (const value of set) {
  console.log(value)
}
```

Alternatively, you can use the `forEach` method:

```
set.forEach(value => {
  console.log(value)
})
```

Just like maps, sets remember their insertion order. For example, suppose you add weekday names in order:

```
const weekdays = new Set(['Mon', 'Tue', 'Wed', 'Thu', 'Fri', 'Sat', 'Sun'])
```

Then the `for of` loop and `forEach` method iterate over the elements in this order.

 NOTE: A set is considered as a map of [value, value] pairs. Both the keys and values methods yield an iterator over the values, and the entries method yield an iterator over [value, value] pairs. None of these methods are useful when you work with a known set. They are intended for code that deals with generic collections.

As with maps, sets are implemented as hash tables with a predefined hash function. Set elements are considered to be the same if they are the same primitive type values or the same object references. In addition, `NaN` values equal each other.

7.12 Weak Maps and Sets

An important use case for JavaScript maps and sets is to attach properties to DOM nodes. Suppose we want to categorize certain nodes to indicate success, work in progress, or an error. We could attach the properties directly to the nodes:

```
node.outcome = 'success'
```

That generally works fine, but it is a bit fragile. DOM nodes have lots of properties, and trouble lies ahead if someone else, or a future version of the DOM API, uses the same property.

It is more robust to use a map:

```
const outcome = new Map()
. . .
outcome.set(node, 'success')
```

DOM nodes come and go. If a particular node is no longer needed, it should be garbage-collected. However, if a node reference resides in the outcome map, that reference will keep the node object alive.

That is where *weak maps* come in. If a key in a weak map is the only reference to an object, that object is not kept alive by the garbage collector.

Simply use a weak map to collect properties:

```
const outcome = new WeakMap()
```

Weak maps have no traversal methods, and the map objects are not iterable. The only methods are set, delete, has, and get. That is enough to set properties and to check the properties of a given object.

If the property that you want to monitor is binary, you can use a WeakSet instead of a WeakMap. Then the only methods are set, delete, and has.

The keys of weak maps and the elements of weak sets can only be objects, not primitive type values.

7.13 Typed Arrays

JavaScript arrays store sequences of elements of any kind, possibly with missing elements. If all you want to store is a sequence of numbers, or the raw bytes of an image, a generic array is quite inefficient.

If you need to store sequences of numbers of the same type efficiently, you can use a *typed array*. The following array types are available:

```
Int8Array
Uint8Array
Uint8ClampedArray
Int16Array
Uint16Array
Int32Array
Uint32Array
Float32Array
Float64Array
```

All elements are of the given type. For example, an `Int16Array` stores 16-bit integers between –32768 and 32767. The `Uint` prefix denotes unsigned integers. An `UInt16Array` holds integers from 0 to 65535.

When constructing an array, specify the length. You cannot change it later.

```
const iarr = new Int32Array(1024)
```

Upon construction, all array elements are zero.

There are no typed array literals, but each typed array class has a function named `of` for constructing an instance with given values:

```
const farr = Float32Array.of(1, 0.5, 0.25, 0.125, 0.0625, 0.03215, 0.015625)
```

As with arrays, there is a `from` function that takes elements from any iterable, with an optional mapping function:

```
const uarr = Uint32Array.from(farr, x => 1 / x)
  // An Uint32Array with elements [1, 2, 4, 8, 16, 32, 64]
```

Assigning to a numerical array index that is not an integer between 0 and `length` – 1 has no effect. However, as with regular arrays, you can set other properties:

```
farr[-1] = 2 // No effect
farr[0.5] = 1.414214 // No effect
farr.lucky = true // Sets the lucky property
```

When you assign a number to an integer array element, any fractional part is discarded. Then the number is truncated to fit into the integer range. Consider this example:

```
iarr[0] = 40000.25 // Sets iarr[0] to -25536
```

Only the integer part is used. Since `40000` is too large to fit in the range of 32-bit integers, the last 32 bits are taken, which happen to represent –25536.

An exception to this truncation process is the `Uint8ClampedArray` which sets an out-of-range value to 0 or 255 and rounds non-integer values to the nearest integer.

The `Uint8ClampedArray` type is intended for use with HTML canvas images. The `getImageData` method of a canvas context yields an object whose `data` property is an `Uint8ClampedArray` containing the RGBA values of a rectangle on a canvas:

```
const canvas = document.getElementById('canvas')
const ctx = canvas.getContext('2d')
ctx.drawImage(img, 0, 0)
let imgdata = ctx.getImageData(0, 0, canvas.width, canvas.height)
let rgba = imgdata.data // an Uint8ClampedArray
```

Figure 7-1 The canvas content turns into negative when clicked

The companion code for this book has a sample program that turns the canvas contents into negative when you click on it—see Figure 7-1.

```
canvas.addEventListener('click', event => {
  for (let i = 0; i < rgba.length; i++) {
    if (i % 4 != 3) rgba[i] = 255 - rgba[i]
  }
  ctx.putImageData(imgdata, 0, 0)
})
```

Typed arrays have all methods of regular arrays, except for:

- push, pop, shift, unshift—you can't change the size of a typed array

- flat, flatMap—a typed array can't hold arrays

- concat—use set instead

There are two methods that regular arrays don't have. The set method copies values from an array or typed array at an offset:

```
targetTypedArray.set(source, offset)
```

By default, the offset is zero. The source must fit entirely into the target. If the offset and source length exceed the target length, a RangeError is thrown. (This means you cannot use this method to shift elements of a typed array.)

The subarray method yields a view into a subrange of the elements:

```
const sub = iarr.subarray(16, 32)
```

If omitted, the end index is the length of the array, and the start index is zero.

This seems to be just the same as the slice method, but there is an important difference. The array and subarray share the same elements. Modifying either is visible in the other.

```
sub[0] = 1024 // Now iarr[16] is also 1024
```

7.14 Array Buffers

An *array buffer* is a contiguous byte sequence that can hold data from a file, a data stream, an image, and so on. The data from typed arrays are also stored in array buffers.

A number of web APIs (including the File API, XMLHttpRequest, and WebSockets) yield array buffers. You can also construct an array buffer with a given number of bytes:

```
const buf = new ArrayBuffer(1024 * 2)
```

Usually, the binary data in an array buffer has a complex structure, such as an image or sound file. Then use a DataView to look at the data inside:

```
const view = new DataView(buf)
```

Read values at a given offset with the DataView methods getInt8, getInt16, getInt32, getUInt8, getUInt16, getUInt32, getFloat32, getFloat64:

```
const littleEndian = true // false or omitted for big-endian byte order
const value = view.getUint32(offset, littleEndian)
```

Write data with the set method:

```
view.setUint32(offset, newValue, littleEndian)
```

 NOTE: There are two ways of storing binary data as a sequence of bytes, called "big-endian" and "little-endian." Consider the 16-bit value 0x2122. In the big-endian way, the more significant byte comes first: 0x21 followed by 0x22. Little-endian is the other way around: 0x22 0x21.

Most modern processors are little-endian, but a number of common file formats (such as PNG and JPEG) use big-endian numbers.

The "big-endian" and "little-endian" terms, while eminently sensible on their own, are actually borrowed from a satirical passage in *Gulliver's Travels*.

The buffer of a typed array always uses the endianness of the host platform. If the entire buffer data is an array, and you know that the endianness matches that of the host platform, you can construct a typed array from the buffer contents:

```
const arr = new Uint16Array(buf) // An array of 1024 Uint16, backed by buf
```

Exercises

1. Implement a function that works exactly like the `from` function of the `Array` class. Pay careful attention to missing elements. What happens with objects that have keys whose numeric values are ≥ the `length` property? With properties that are not index properties?

2. The `Array.of` method was designed for a very specific use case: to be passed as a "collector" to a function that produces a sequence of values and sends them to some destination—perhaps printing them, summing them, or collecting them in an array. Implement such a function:

    ```
    mapCollect(values, f, collector)
    ```

    The function should apply `f` to all values and then send the result to the collector, a function with a variable number of arguments. Return the result of the collector.

    Explain the advantage of using `Array.of` over `Array` (i.e., `(...elements) => new Array(...elements)`) in this context.

3. An array can have properties whose numeric values are negative integers, such as `'-1'`. Do they affect the length? How can you iterate over them in order?

4. Google for "JavaScript forEach thisArg" to find blog articles explaining the `thisArg` parameter of the `forEach` method. Rewrite the examples without using the `thisArg` parameter. If you find a call such as

    ```
    arr.forEach(function() { . . . this.something() . . . }, thisArg)
    ```

    where `thisArg` is `this`, replace the function with an arrow function. Otherwise, replace the inner `this` with whatever `thisArg` is. If the call has the form

    ```
    arr.forEach(method, thisArg)
    ```

    use an arrow function invoking `thisArg.method(. . .)`. Can you come up with any situation where `thisArg` is required?

5. If you do not supply a comparison function in the `sort` method of the `Array` class, then elements are converted to strings and lexicographically compared by UTF-16 code units. Why is this a terrible idea? Come up with arrays of integers or objects where the sort results are useless. What about characters above \u{FFFF}?

6. Suppose an object representing a message has properties for dates and for senders. Sort an array of messages first by date, then by sender. Verify that the `sort` method is stable: Messages with the same sender continue to be sorted by date after the second sort.

7. Suppose an object representing a person has properties for first and last names. Provide a comparison function that compares last names and then breaks the ties using first names.

8. Implement a comparison function that compares two strings by their Unicode code points, not their UTF-16 code units.

9. Write a function that yields all positions of a target value in an array. For example, `indexOf(arr, 0)` yields all array index values i where `arr[i]` is zero. Use `map` and `filter`.

10. Write a function that yields all positions at which a given function is `true`. For example, `indexOf(arr, x => x > 0)` yields all array index values i where `arr[i]` is positive.

11. Compute the spread (that is, the difference between maximum and minimum) of an array using `reduce`.

12. Given an array of functions $[f_1, f_2, \ldots, f_n]$, obtain the composition function $x => f_1(f_2(\ldots (f_n(x)) \ldots))$ using `reduceRight`.

13. Implement functions `map`, `filter`, `forEach`, `some`, `every` for sets.

14. Implement functions `union(set1, set2)`, `intersection(set1, set2)`, `difference(set1, set2)` that yield the union, intersection, or difference of the sets, without mutating the arguments.

15. Write a function that constructs a `Map` from an object, so that you can easily construct a map as `toMap({ Monday: 1, Tuesday: 2, ... })`.

16. Suppose you use a `Map` whose keys are point objects of the form `{ x:. . ., y:. . . }`. What can go wrong when you make queries such as `map.get({ x: 0, y: 0 })`? What can you do to overcome that?

17. Show that weak sets really work as promised. Start Node.js with the flag `--expose-gc`. Call `process.memoryUsage()` to find out how much of the heap is used. Allocate an object:

    ```
    let fred = { name: 'Fred', image: new Int8Array(1024*1024) }
    ```

    Verify that the heap usage has gone up by about a megabyte. Set `fred` to `null`, run the garbage collector by calling `global.gc()`, and check that the object was collected. Now repeat, inserting the object into a weak set. Verify that the weak set allows the object to be collected. Repeat with a regular set and show that the object won't be collected.

18. Write a function to find the endianness of host platform. Use an array buffer and view it both as a data view and a typed array.

Internationalization

Topics in This Chapter

Chapter 8

There's a big world out there, and hopefully many of its inhabitants will be interested in your software. Some programmers believe that all they need to do to internationalize their application is to support Unicode and translate the messages in the user interface. However, as you will see, there is a lot more to internationalizing programs. Dates, times, currencies, even numbers are formatted differently in different parts of the world. In this chapter, you will learn how to use the internationalization features of JavaScript so that your programs present and accept information in a way that makes sense to your users, wherever they may be.

8.1 The Locale Concept

When you look at an application that is adapted to an international audience, the most obvious difference is the language. But there are many more subtle differences; for example, numbers are formatted differently in different countries. The number

    123,456.78

should be displayed as

    123.456,78

for a German user—that is, the roles of the decimal point and the decimal comma separator are reversed. In other locales, users prefer different digits. Here is the same number in Thai digits:

๑๒๓,๔๕๖.๗๘

There are similar variations in the display of dates. In the United States, dates are displayed as month/day/year; Germany uses the less idiosyncratic order of day/month/year, whereas in China, the usage is the even more sensible year/month/day. Thus, the American date

3/22/61

should be presented as

22.03.1961

to a German user. If the month names are written out explicitly, then the difference in languages becomes even more apparent. The English

March 22, 1961

should be presented as

22. März 1961

in German, or

1961年月22日

in Chinese.

A *locale* specifies the language and location of a user, which allows formatters to take user preferences into account. The following sections show you how to specify a locale and how to control the locale settings of a JavaScript program.

8.2 Specifying a Locale

A locale consists of up to five components:

1. A language, specified by two or three lowercase letters, such as en (English), de (German), or zh (Chinese). Table 8-1 shows common codes.

2. Optionally, a script, specified by four letters with an initial uppercase, such as Latn (Latin), Cyrl (Cyrillic), or Hans (simplified Chinese characters). This can be useful because some languages, such as Serbian, are written in Latin or Cyrillic, and some Chinese readers prefer the traditional over the simplified characters.

3. Optionally, a country or region, specified by two uppercase letters or three digits, such as US (United States) or CH (Switzerland). Table 8-2 shows common codes.

Table 8-1 Common Language Codes

Language	Code	Language	Code
Chinese	zh	Japanese	ja
Danish	da	Korean	ko
Dutch	du	Norwegian	no
English	en	Portugese	pt
French	fr	Spanish	es
Finnish	fi	Swedish	sv
Italian	it	Turkish	tr

Table 8-2 Common Country Codes

Country	Code	Country	Code
Austria	AT	Japan	JP
Belgium	BE	Korea	KR
Canada	CA	The Netherlands	NL
China	CN	Norway	NO
Denmark	DK	Portugal	PT
Finland	FI	Spain	ES
Germany	DE	Sweden	SE
Great Britain	GB	Switzerland	CH
Greece	GR	Taiwan	TW
Ireland	IE	Turkey	TR
Italy	IT	United States	US

4. Optionally, a variant. Variants are rarely used nowadays. There used to be a "Nynorsk" variant of Norwegian, but it is now expressed with a different language code, nn. What used to be variants for the Japanese imperial calendar and Thai numerals are now expressed as extensions (see below).

5. Optionally, an extension. Extensions describe local preferences for calendars (such as the Japanese calendar), numbers (Thai instead of Western

digits), and so on. The Unicode standard specifies some of these extensions. These extensions start with u- and a two-letter code specifying whether the extension deals with the calendar (ca), numbers (nu), and so on. For example, the extension u-nu-thai denotes the use of Thai numerals. Other extensions are entirely arbitrary and start with x-, such as x-java.

Rules for locales are formulated in the "Best Current Practices" memo BCP 47 of the Internet Engineering Task Force (http://tools.ietf.org/html/bcp47). You can find a more accessible summary at www.w3.org/International/articles/language-tags.

 NOTE: The codes for languages and countries seem a bit random because some of them are derived from local languages. German in German is Deutsch, Chinese in Chinese is zhongwen—hence de and zh. And Switzerland is CH, derived from the Latin term *Confoederatio Helvetica* for the Swiss confederation.

Locales are described by tags—hyphenated strings of locale elements such as 'en-US'.

In Germany, you would use a locale 'de-DE'. Switzerland has four official languages (German, French, Italian, and Rhaeto-Romance). A German speaker in Switzerland would want to use a locale 'de-CH'. This locale uses the rules for the German language, but currency values are expressed in Swiss francs, not euros.

Pass the locale tags to locale-sensitive functions. For example:

```
const newYearsEve = new Date(1999, 11, 31, 23, 59)
newYearsEve.toLocaleString('de') // Yields the string '31.12.1999 23:59:00'
```

Instead of a single locale tag, you can provide an array in decreasing priority: ['de-CH', 'de', 'en']. With such a locale tag array, a locale-sensitive method can use a fallback locale if it cannot support the preferred one.

Additional options can be specified in an object that follows the locale tag:

```
newYearsEve.toLocaleString('de', { timeZone: 'Asia/Tokyo' })
    // The date as viewed in the given time zone, such as '1.1.2000, 07:59:00'
```

If you omit the locale and options, the default locale is used with no options. For the default locale with options, you can provide an empty locale tag array:

```
newYearsEve.toLocaleString([], { timeZone: 'Asia/Tokyo' })
```

 NOTE: The toLocaleString method is defined in the Object class. You can override it in any class—see Exercise 1.

8.3 Formatting Numbers

To format numbers, invoke the `toLocaleString` method of the `Number` method and pass the locale tag as an argument:

```
let number = 123456.78
let result = number.toLocaleString('de') // '123,456.78'
```

Alternatively, you can construct an instance of the `Intl.NumberFormat` class and invoke its `format` method:

```
let formatter = new Intl.NumberFormat('de')
result = formatter.format(number) // '123,456.78'
```

In the perhaps unlikely case that you need to analyze such a result further, the `formatToParts` method yields an array of the parts. For example, `formatter.formatToParts(number)` is the following array:

```
[ { type: 'integer', value: '123' },
  { type: 'group', value: ',' },
  { type: 'integer', value: '456' },
  { type: 'decimal', value: '.' },
  { type: 'fraction', value: '78' } ]
```

For any locale-specific methods, you want to know which locale tag extensions and options are supported. Table 8-3 shows this information for the `toLocaleString` method of the `Number` class and the `format` method of the `Intl.NumberFormat` class.

Recall that locale tag extensions are prefixed with `u`. The `format` method recognizes the `u-nu` extension, such as:

```
number.toLocaleString('th-u-nu-thai')
new Intl.NumberFormat('th-u-nu-thai').format(number)
    // Both yield '๑๒๓,๔๕๖.๗๘'
```

The options are provided as a second argument following the locale tag:

```
number.toLocaleString('de', { style: 'currency', currency: 'EUR' })
formatter = new Intl.NumberFormat('de', { style: 'currency', currency: 'EUR' })
formatter.format(number)
    // Both yield '123.456,78 €'
```

As you can see, if you need to repeatedly carry out complex formatting, it makes sense to construct a formatter object.

Exercise 2 asks you to explore various options.

 NOTE: A stage 3 proposal adds more formatting options for measurement units (`'299,792,458 m/s'`), scientific notation (`'6.022E23'`), and compact decimals (`'8.1 billion'`).

CAUTION: Unfortunately, there is currently no standard way for parsing localized numbers with grouping separators or digits other than 0–9.

Table 8-3 Configuring `toLocaleString` for Numbers and the `Intl.NumberFormat` Constructor

Name	Value
Locale Tag Extensions	
`nu` (numbering)	`latn, arab, thai, . . .`
Options	
`style`	`decimal` (default), `currency`, `percent`
`currency`	ISO 4217 currency code such as `USD` or `EUR`. Required for currency style.
`currencyDisplay`	`symbol` (€, default), `code` (EUR), `name` (Euro)
`useGrouping`	`true` (default) to use grouping separators

`minimumIntegerDigits,`
`minimumFractionDigits,`
`maximumFractionDigits,`
`minimumSignificantDigits,`
`maximumSignificantDigits`
	Bounds on the digits before and after the decimal separator, or the total number of digits

8.4 Localizing Dates and Times

When formatting date and time, there are many locale-dependent issues:

1. The names of months and weekdays should be presented in the local language.

2. There will be local preferences for the order of year, month, and day.

3. The Gregorian calendar might not be the local preference for expressing dates.

4. The time zone of the location must be taken into account.

In the following sections, you will see how to localize `Date` objects, date ranges, and relative dates (such as "in 3 days").

8.4.1 Formatting Date Objects

Given a Date object, you can format its date part, time part, or both:

```
const newYearsEve = new Date(1999, 11, 31, 23, 59)
newYearsEve.toLocaleDateString('de') // '31.12.1999'
newYearsEve.toLocaleTimeString('de') // '23:59:00'
newYearsEve.toLocaleString('de') // '31.12.1999, 23:59:00'
```

As with number formatting, you can also construct a formatter for a given locale and invoke its format method:

```
const germanDateTimeFormatter = new Intl.DateTimeFormat('de')
germanDateTimeFormatter.format(newYearsEve) // '31.12.1999'
```

You can provide options to control how each of the parts is formatted:

```
newYearsEve.toLocaleDateString('en', {
  year: 'numeric',
  month: 'short',
  day: 'numeric',
}) // 'Dec 31, 1999'

new Intl.DateTimeFormat('de', {
  hour: 'numeric',
  minute: '2-digit'
}).format(newYearsEve) // '23:59'
```

However, this approach is cumbersome and illogical. After all, the format of each part, and even which parts to include, is a locale-specific preference. The ECMAScript specification prescribes a tedious algorithm for matching the requested format with one that makes sense for a given locale, and a formatMatcher option to choose between the specification algorithm and a potentially better one. That complexity should have tipped them off that they were on the wrong track. There is a stage 3 proposal to fix this mess. You specify which style you want for the date and time part (full, long, medium, or short). Then the formatter picks appropriate fields and formats for the locale:

```
newYearsEve.toLocaleDateString('en', { dateStyle: 'medium' })
  // 'Dec 31, 1999'
newYearsEve.toLocaleDateString('de', { dateStyle: 'medium' })
  // '31.12.1999'
```

Table 8-4 shows all locale tag extensions and options.

Table 8-4 Formatting Options for Dates

Name	Value
Locale Tag Extensions	
nu (numbering)	latn, arab, thai
ca (calendar)	gregory, hebrew, buddhist, . . .
hc (hour cycle)	h11, h12, h23, h24
Options	
timeZone	UTC, Europe/Berlin, . . . (default: local time)
dateStyle, timeStyle (stage 3)	full, long, medium, short. If you can use these, avoid the options below.
hour12	true, false (whether to use 12 hour time; default is locale-dependent)
hourCycle	h11, h12, h23, h24
month	2-digit (09), numeric (9), narrow (S), short (Sep), long (September)
year, day, hour, minute, second	2-digit, numeric
weekday, era	long, short, narrow
timeZoneName	short (GMT+9), long (Japan Standard Time)
formatMatcher	basic (a standard algorithm for matching the requested format with those provided by the locale), best fit (default, a potentially better implementation by the JavaScript runtime)

8.4.2 Ranges

The formatRange method of the Intl.DateTimeFormat class formats a range between two dates as concisely as possible:

```
const christmas = new Date(1999, 11, 24)
const newYearsDay = new Date(2000, 0, 1)
const formatter = new Intl.DateTimeFormat('en', { dateStyle: 'long' })
formatter.formatRange(christmas, newYearsEve) // 'December 24 – 31, 1999'
formatter.formatRange(newYearsEve, newYearsDay) // 'December 31, 1999 – January 1, 2000'
```

8.4.3 Relative Time

The `Intl.RelativeTimeFormat` class produces expressions such as "yesterday" or "in 3 hours":

```
new Intl.RelativeTimeFormat('en', { numeric: 'auto'}).format(-1, 'day') // 'yesterday'
new Intl.RelativeTimeFormat('fr').format(3, 'hours') // 'dans 3 heures'
```

The `format` method has two arguments: a quantity and a unit. The unit is one of `year`, `quarter`, `month`, `week`, `day`, `hour`, `minute`, or `second`. The plural form is also accepted, such as `years`.

You can specify the following options:

* `numeric`: `always` (1 day ago, default), `auto` (yesterday)

* `style`: `long`, `short`, `narrow`

8.4.4 Formatting to Parts

As with number formatters, the `Intl.DateTimeFormat` and `Intl.RelativeTimeFormat` classes have `formatToParts` methods that produce arrays of objects describing each part of the formatted result. Here are a couple of examples:

The call

```
new Intl.RelativeTimeFormat('fr').formatToParts(3, 'hours')
```

returns the array

```
[
  { type: 'literal', value: 'dans '},
  { type: 'integer', value: '3', unit: 'hour' },
  { type: 'literal', value: ' heures'}
]
```

The call

```
Intl.DateTimeFormat('en',
  {
    dateStyle: 'long',
    timeStyle: 'short'
  }).formatToParts(newYearsEve)
```

yields an array with eleven entries, describing the parts of the string `'December 31, 1999 at 11:59 PM'`, namely

```
{ type: 'month', value: 'December' },
{ type: 'literal', value: ' ' },
{ type: 'day', value: '31' },
```

and so on.

8.5 Collation

In JavaScript, you can compare strings with the <, <=, >, and >= operators. Unfortunately, when interacting with human users, these operators are not very useful. They lead to absurd results, even in English. For example, the following five strings are ordered according to the < operator:

```
Athens
Zulu
able
zebra
Ångström
```

For dictionary ordering, you would want to consider upper case and lower case equivalent, and accents should not be significant. To an English speaker, the sample list of words should be ordered as

```
able
Ångström
Athens
zebra
Zulu
```

However, that order would not be acceptable to a Swedish user. In Swedish, the letter Å is different from the letter A, and it is collated *after* the letter Z! That is, a Swedish user would want the words to be sorted as

```
able
Athens
zebra
Zulu
Ångström
```

Whenever you need to sort strings that are provided by a human user, you should use a locale-aware comparison.

The simplest way is to use the localeCompare method of the String class. Pass the locale as a second argument:

```
const words = ['Alpha', 'Ångström', 'Zulu', 'able', 'zebra']
words.sort((x, y) => x.localeCompare(y, 'en'))
   // words is now ['able', 'Alpha', 'Ångström', 'zebra', 'Zulu']
```

Alternatively, you can construct a collator object:

```
const swedishCollator = new Intl.Collator('sv')
```

Then pass the collator's compare function to the Array.sort method:

```
words.sort(swedishCollator.compare)
   // words is now ['able', 'Alpha', 'zebra', 'Zulu', 'Ångström']
```

Table 8-5 shows the extensions and options supported by the `localeCompare` method and the `Intl.Collator` constructor.

A useful extension is numeric sort, where numeric substrings are sorted in increasing order:

```
const parts = ['part1', 'part10', 'part2', 'part9']
parts.sort((x, y) => x.localeCompare(y, 'en-u-kn-true'))
  // Now parts is ['part1', 'part2', 'part9', 'part10']
```

Many of the other constructs are of limited use. For example, in German phonebooks (but not dictionaries), Ö is considered the same as Oe. The following call does not modify the given array:

```
['Österreich', 'Offenbach'].sort((x, y) => x.localeCompare(y, 'de-u-co-phonebk'))
```

Table 8-5 String Collation with `localeCompare` and the `Intl.Collator` Constructor

Name	Value
Locale Tag Extensions	
co (collation)	phonebook, phonetic, reformed, pinyin, . . .
kn (numeric collation)	true ('1' < '2' < '10'), false (default)
kf (case first)	upper, lower, false (default)
Options	
sensitivity	base (a = A = Å), accent (a = A ≠ Å), case (a ≠ A = Å), variant (a, A, Å all different; default)
ignorePunctuation	true, false (default)
numeric, caseFirst	true, false (default)—see kn, kf above
usage	sort (use for sorting, default), search (use for searching, where only equality matters)

8.6 Other Locale-Sensitive String Methods

The `String` class has several methods that work with locales. You have already seen the `localeCompare` method in the preceding section. The `toLocaleUpperCase` and `toLocaleLowerCase` methods take language rules into account. For example, in German, the uppercase of the "double s" character ß is a sequence of two S:

```
'Großhändler'.toLocaleUpperCase('de') // 'GROSSHÄNDLER'
```

The `localeCompare` method accepts options just like the `Intl.Collator` constructor of the preceding section. For example, the comparison

```
'part10'.localeCompare('part2', 'en', { numeric: true })
```

yields a positive number because with numeric comparison, 'part10' comes after 'part2'.

A character or sequence of characters can sometimes be described in more than one way in Unicode. For example, an Å (\u{00C5}) can also be expressed as a plain A (\u{0041}) followed by a combining ring above Å (\u{030A}).

You might want to convert strings into a normalized form when you store them or communicate with another program. The Unicode standard defines four normalization forms (C, D, KC, and KD)—see www.unicode.org/unicode/reports /tr15/tr15-23.html. In the normalization form C, accented characters are always composed. For example, a sequence of A and Å is combined into a single character Å. In form D, accented characters are always decomposed into their base letters and combining accents: Å is turned into A followed by Å. In forms KC and KD, characters such the trademark symbol ™ (\u{2122}) are decomposed. The W3C recommends that you use the normalization form C for transferring data over the Internet.

The normalize method of the String class carries out this process. Let's try it with all four modes. For each mode, we spread out the result of the call to normalize, so that you can clearly see the individual characters.

```
const str = 'Å™'
['NFC', 'NFD', 'NFKC', 'NFKD'].map(mode => [...str.normalize(mode)])
  // Yields ['Å', '™'], ['A', '°', '™'], ['Å', 'T', 'M'], ['A', '°', 'T', 'M']
```

8.7 Plural Rules and Lists

Many languages have special forms for small quantities. In English, we count 0 dollars, 1 dollar, 2 dollars, 3 dollars and so on. The form for a quantity of 1 is special.

With Russian rubles, it is more complex. There are special forms for one and for "a few": 0 рублей, 1 рубль, 2, 3, or 4 рубля. With 5 or more, it is again рублей.

You need to know about these rules when you format messages such as "Found *n* matches".

The Intl.PluralRules class helps with this problem. The select method yields a key that describes which word form is required for a given quantity. Here are the results in English and Russian:

```
[0, 1, 2, 3, 4, 5].map(i => (new Intl.PluralRules('en').select(i)))
  // ['other', 'one', 'other', 'other', 'other', 'other']
```

```
[0, 1, 2, 3, 4, 5].map(i => (new Intl.PluralRules('ru').select(i)))
  // ['many', 'one', 'few', 'few', 'few', 'many']
```

The `PluralRules` class just produces the English form names. They still need to be mapped to the localized word forms. Provide a map for each language:

```
dollars = { one: 'dollar', other: 'dollars' }
rubles = { one: 'рубль', few: 'рубля', many: 'рублей' }
```

Then you can call

```
dollars[new Intl.PluralRules('en').select(i)]
rubles[new Intl.PluralRules('ru').select(i)]
```

The `select` method has one option:

• type: `cardinal` (default), `ordinal`

Let's try out English ordinals:

```
const rules = new Intl.PluralRules('en', { type: 'ordinal' })
[0, 1, 2, 3, 4, 5].map(i => rules.select(i))
  // ['other', 'one', 'two', 'few', 'other', 'other']
```

What is going on? It turns out that the English language is no simpler than Russian: English ordinals are 0th, 1st, 2nd, 3rd, 4th, 5th, and so on.

The `Intl.ListFormat` class helps with formatting lists of values. It is easiest to understand with an example:

```
let list = ['Goethe', 'Schiller', 'Lessing']
new Intl.ListFormat('en', { type: 'conjunction' }).format(list)
  // Yields the string 'Goethe, Schiller, and Lessing'
```

As you can see, the `format` method knows about the conjunction word "and" and the Oxford comma.

When the type is `'disjunction'`, the elements are joined with "or". Let's try it in German:

```
new Intl.ListFormat('de', { type: 'disjunction' }).format(list)
  // 'Goethe, Schiller oder Lessing'
```

The `format` method has the following options:

• type: `conjunction` (default), `disjunction`, `unit`

• style: `long` (default), `short`, `narrow` (with `unit` type only)

The `unit` type is for unit lists like "7 pounds 11 ounces." Unfortunately, with the `'long'` and `'short'` styles, the formatter produces commas in English:

```
list = ['7 pounds', '11 ounces']
new Intl.ListFormat('en', { type: 'unit', style: 'long' }).format(list)
  // '7 pounds, 11 ounces'
```

The Chicago and AP style guides would not approve.

8.8 Miscellaneous Locale Features

In modern browsers, the `navigator.languages` property is an array of the user's preferred locale tags, in decreasing preference. The value `navigator.language` is the most preferred locale tag, the same as `navigator.languages[0]`. Browsers typically use the locale of the host operating system unless users personalize the browser's language settings.

You can use `navigator.languages` as the locale argument of the various locale-sensitive methods and constructors that you saw in the preceding sections.

The `Intl.getCanonicalLocales` accepts a locale tag or an array of locale tags and returns an array with cleaned-up tags, removing duplicates.

Each of the formatter classes described in the preceding sections has a `supportedLocalesOf` method. Pass a locale tag or array of locale tags. Unsupported tags are dropped, and supported tags are normalized. For example, assuming your browser's `Intl.NumberFormat` class does not support Welsh, the call

```
Intl.NumberFormat.supportedLocalesOf(['cy', 'en-uk'])
```

returns `['en-UK']`.

When you pass an array of locale choices to a locale-sensitive method, it is up to the browser to find the best available locale that matches the preferences. All locale-specific functions support the `localeMatcher` option for setting the matching algorithm. The option has two values:

- `'lookup'` uses a standard algorithm that is specified in ECMA-402.

- `'best fit'` (default) allows the JavaScript runtime to find a better match.

At this point, the common JavaScript runtimes use the standard algorithm, so this option is not something to worry about.

 NOTE: If you want to present your users with a locale choice, you need to be able to display that choice in a language that your users understand. A stage 3 proposal defines a class `Intl.DisplayNames` for this purpose. Here are a few usage samples:

```
const regionNames = new Intl.DisplayNames(['fr'], { type: 'region' })
const languageNames = new Intl.DisplayNames(['fr'], { type: 'language' })
const currencyNames = new Intl.DisplayNames(['zh-Hans'],
  { type: 'currency' })
regionNames.of('US') // 'États-Unis'
languageNames.of('fr') // 'Français'
currencyNames.of('USD') // '世界'
```

To obtain more information about the properties of an internationalization object, call the `resolvedOptions` method. For example, given the following collator object:

```
const collator = new Intl.Collator('en-US-u-kn-true', { sensitivity: 'base' })
```

the call

```
collator.resolvedOptions()
```

returns the object

```
{
  locale: 'en-US',
  usage: 'sort',
  sensitivity: 'base',
  ignorePunctuation: false,
  numeric: true,
  caseFirst: 'false',
  collation: 'default'
}
```

 NOTE: A stage 3 proposal is the `Intl.Locale` class that provides a convenient way for denoting a locale with options:

```
const germanCurrency = new Intl.Locale('de-DE',
  { style: 'currency', currency: 'EUR' })
```

Exercises

1. Implement a class `Person` with instance fields for the first name, last name, sex, and marital status. Provide a `toLocaleString` method that formats names, for example `'Ms. Smith'`, `'Frau Smith'`, `'Mme Smith'`. Look up the honorific forms for a few languages and design options for variations such as Ms. vs. Mrs./Miss.

2. Write a program that formats a value as a number, percentage, and dollar amount. Explore all currency display options. Turn grouping on and off, and show the meanings of the various bounds on the number of digits.

3. Show how numbers look different when using English, Arabic, and Thai numerals. What other numerals can you produce?

4. Write a program that demonstrates the date and time formatting styles in France, China, Egypt, and Thailand (with Thai digits).

5. Make an array with all two-letter (ISO 639-1) language codes. For each of them, format a date and time. How many different formats do you find?

6. Write a program that lists all Unicode characters that are expanded to two or more ASCII characters in normalization form KC or KD.

7. Provide examples to demonstrate the different sensitivity options for collation.

8. What happens with the Turkish locale when you form the uppercase of 'i' or the lowercase of 'I'? Suppose you write a program that checks for a particular HTTP header, If-Modified-Since. HTTP headers are case-insensitive. How do you find the header so that your program works everywhere, including Turkey?

9. The Java library has a useful concept of a "message bundle" where you can look up localized messages by locale, with fallbacks. Provide a similar mechanism for JavaScript. For each locale, there is a map of keys to translated messages.

```
{ de: { greeting: 'Hallo', farewell: 'Auf Wiedersehen' },
  'de-CH' : { greeting: 'Grüezi' },
  fr: { greeting: 'Bonjour', farewell: 'Au revoir' },
  . . .
}
```

When looking for a message, first look at the most specific locale, then move to more general ones. Support overrides for more specialized locales. For example, when looking up a message with key 'greeting' in the locale 'de-CH', locate 'Grüezi', but for 'farewell', fall back to 'de'.

10. The Java library has a useful class for formatting locale-dependent messages. Consider the template '{0} has {1} messages'. The French version would be 'Il y a {1} messages pour {0}'. When formatting the message, you provide the items in a fixed order, irrespective of the order required by the language. Implement a function messageFormat that accepts a template string and a variable number of items. Come up with a mechanism for including literal braces.

11. Provide a class for locale-dependent display of paper sizes, using the preferred dimensional unit and default paper size in the given locale. Everyone on the planet, with the exception of the United States and Canada, uses ISO 216 paper sizes. Only three countries in the world have not yet officially adopted the metric system: Liberia, Myanmar (Burma), and the United States.

Asynchronous Programming

Topics in This Chapter

Chapter 9

In this chapter, you will learn how to coordinate tasks that must be executed at some point in the future. We start with an in-depth look at the notion of *promises*. A promise is just what it sounds: an action that will produce a result at some point in the future, unless it dies with an exception. As you will see, promises can be executed in sequence or in parallel.

One drawback of promises is that you need to use method calls to combine them. The `async`/`await` constructs give you a much more pleasant syntax. You write code that uses regular control flow, and the compiler translates your code to a chain of promises.

Ideally, you could skip promises and move straight to the `async`/`await` syntax. However, I think it would be quite a challenge to understand the complexities and limitations of the syntax without knowing what it does behind your back.

We end the chapter with a discussion of asynchronous generators and iterators. All but the last section of this chapter should be required reading for intermediate JavaScript developers because asynchronous processing is ubiquitous in web applications.

9.1 Concurrent Tasks in JavaScript

A program is "concurrent" when it manages multiple activities with overlapping timelines. Concurrent programs in Java or C++ use multiple threads of execution. When a processor has more than one core, these threads truly run in parallel. But there is a problem—programmers must be careful to protect data, so that there is no corruption when a value is updated by different threads at the same time.

In contrast, a JavaScript program runs in a single thread. In particular, once a function starts, it will run to completion before any other part of your program starts running. That is good. You know that no other code will corrupt the data that your function uses. No other code will try to read any of the data until after the function returns. Inside your function, you can modify the program's variables to your heart's content, as long as you clean up before the function returns. You never have to worry about mut or deadlocks.

The problem with having a single thread is obvious: If a program needs to wait for something to happen—most commonly, for data across the Internet—it cannot do anything else. Therefore, time-consuming operations in JavaScript are always *asynchronous*. You specify what you want, and provide callback functions that are invoked when data is available or when an error has occurred. The current function continues execution so that other work can be done.

Let us look at a simple example: loading an image. The following function loads an image with a given URL and appends it to a given DOM element:

```
const addImage = (url, element) => {
  const request = new XMLHttpRequest()
  request.open('GET', url)
  request.responseType = 'blob'

  request.addEventListener('load', () => {
    if (request.status == 200) {
      const blob = new Blob([request.response], { type: 'image/png' })
      const img = document.createElement('img')
      img.src = URL.createObjectURL(blob)
      element.appendChild(img)
    } else {
      console.log(`${request.status}: ${request.statusText}`)
    }
  })
  request.addEventListener('error', event => console.log('Network error'));
  request.send()
}
```

The details of the XMLHttpRequest API are not important, except for one crucial fact. The image data are processed in a callback—the listener to the load event.

If you call addImage, the call returns immediately. The image is added to the DOM element much later, once the data is loaded.

Consider this example, where we load four images (taken from the Japanese Hanafuda card deck—see https://en.wikipedia.org/wiki/Hanafuda):

```
const imgdiv = document.getElementById('images')
addImage('hanafuda/1-1.png', imgdiv)
addImage('hanafuda/1-2.png', imgdiv)
addImage('hanafuda/1-3.png', imgdiv)
addImage('hanafuda/1-4.png', imgdiv)
```

All four calls to addImage return immediately. Whenever the data for an image arrive, a callback is invoked and the image is added. Note that you do *not* need to worry about corruption by concurrent callbacks. The callbacks are never intermingled. They run one after another in the single JavaScript thread. However, they can come in any order. If you load the web page with this program multiple times, the image order can change—see Figure 9-1.

 NOTE: All sample programs in this chapter are designed to be run in a web browser. The companion code has web pages that you can load into your browser and code snippets that you can paste into the development tools console.

To experiment with these files on your local system, you need to run a local web server. You can install light-server with the command

```
npm install -g light-server
```

Change to the directory containing the files to serve and run the command

```
light-server -s .
```

Then point your browser to URLs such as http://localhost:4000/images.html.

Figure 9-1 Images may load out of order

When loading images, it is fairly easy to cope with out-of-order arrival—see Exercise 1. But consider a more complex situation. Suppose you need to read remote data, and then, depending on the received data, read more data. For example, a web page might contain the URL of an image that you want to load.

In that case, you need to asynchronously read the web page, with a callback that scans the contents for the image URL. Then that image must be retrieved asynchronously, with another callback that adds the image to the desired location. Each retrieval requires error handling, which leads to more callbacks. With a few levels of processing, this programming style turns into "callback hell"—deeply nested callbacks with hard-to-understand success and failure paths.

In the following sections, you will learn how *promises* allow you to compose asynchronous tasks without nested callbacks.

A promise is an object that promises to produce a result eventually, hopefully. The result may not be available right away, and it might never be available if an error occurs.

That does not sound very promising, but as you will soon see, it is much easier to chain completion and error actions with promises than with callbacks.

9.2 Making Promises

In this section and the next, you will see how to make promises. This is a bit technical, and you rarely need to do it yourself. It is much more common to call library functions that return a promise. Feel free to gloss over these sections until you actually need to construct promises yourself.

 NOTE: A typical example for an API that produces promises is the *Fetch API* that all modern browsers support. The call

```
fetch('https://horstmann.com/javascript-impatient/hanafuda/index.html')
```

returns a promise that will yield the response from the HTTP request when it is available.

The Promise constructor has a single argument, a function that has two arguments: handlers for success and failure outcomes. This function is called the "executor function."

```
const myPromise = new Promise((resolve, reject) => {
  // Body of the executor function
})
```

In the body of the executor function, you start the task that yields the desired result. Once the result is available, you pass it to the `resolve` handler. Or, if you know that there won't be a result, you invoke the `reject` handler with the reason for failure. When work is completed asynchronously, these handlers will be invoked in some callback.

Here is an outline of the process:

```
const myPromise = new Promise((resolve, reject) => {
  const callback = (args) => {
    . . .
    if (success) resolve(result) else reject(reason)
  }
  invokeTask(callback)
})
```

Let us put this to work in the simplest case: delivering a result after a delay. This function yields a promise to do that:

```
const produceAfterDelay = (result, delay) => {
  return new Promise((resolve, reject) => {
    const callback = () => resolve(result)
    setTimeout(callback, delay)
  })
}
```

In the executor function that is passed to the constructor, we call `setTimeout` with a callback and the given delay. The callback will be invoked when the delay has passed. In the callback, we pass the result on to the `resolve` handler. We don't need to worry about errors, and the `reject` handler is unused.

Here is a more complex function that yields a promise whose result is an image:

```
const loadImage = url => {
  return new Promise((resolve, reject) => {
    const request = new XMLHttpRequest()
    const callback = () => {
      if (request.status == 200) {
        const blob = new Blob([request.response], { type: 'image/png' })
        const img = document.createElement('img')
        img.src = URL.createObjectURL(blob)
        resolve(img)
      } else {
        reject(Error(`${request.status}: ${request.statusText}`))
      }
    }
```

```
    request.open('GET', url)
    request.responseType = 'blob'
    request.addEventListener('load', callback)
    request.addEventListener('error', event => reject(Error('Network error')));
    request.send()
  })
}
```

The executor function configures an XMLHttpRequest object and sends it. Upon receipt of the response, a callback produces an image and invokes the resolve handler to pass it on. If an error occurs, it is passed to the reject handler.

Let us look at the control flow of a promise in slow motion.

1. The Promise constructor is called.

2. The executor function is called.

3. The executor function initiates an asynchronous task with one or more callbacks.

4. The executor function returns.

5. The constructor returns. The promise is now in the *pending* state.

6. The code invoking the constructor runs to completion.

7. The asynchronous task finishes.

8. A task callback is invoked.

9. That callback calls the resolve or reject handler, and the promise transitions to the *fulfilled* or *rejected* state. In either case, the promise is now *settled*.

 NOTE: There is one variation of the last step in the control flow. You can call resolve with another promise. Then the current promise is resolved but not fulfilled. It stays pending until the subsequent promise is settled. For this reason, the handler function is called resolve and not fulfill.

Be sure to always call resolve or reject in your task callbacks, or the promise never exits the pending state.

That means that you have to pay attention to exceptions in task callbacks. If a task callback terminates with an exception instead of calling resolve or reject, then the promise cannot settle. In the loadImage example, I carefully vetted the code to ensure that no exception was going to be thrown. In general, it is a good idea to use a try/catch statement in the callback and pass any exceptions to the reject handler.

However, if an exception is thrown in the executor function, you don't need to catch it. The constructor simply yields a rejected promise.

9.3 Immediately Settled Promises

The call `Promise.resolve(value)` makes a promise that is fulfilled immediately with the given value. This is useful in methods that returns promises, and where the answer is available right away in some cases:

```
const loadImage = url => {
  if (url === undefined) return Promise.resolve(brokenImage)
  . . .
}
```

If you have a value that might be a promise or a plain value, the result of `Promise.resolve(value)` definitely turns it into a promise. If the value is already a promise, it is simply returned.

 NOTE: For compatibility with libraries that predate standard ECMAScript promises, the `Promise.resolve` method provides special treatment for "thenable" objects—that is, objects with a `then` method. The `then` method is invoked with a resolve handler and a reject handler, and returns a promise that is settled when either of the two handlers is called—see Exercise 6.

The call `Promise.reject(error)` yields a promise that is immediately rejected with the given error.

Use it when a promise-producing function fails:

```
const loadImage = url => {
  if (url === undefined) {
    return Promise.reject(Error('No URL'))
  } else {
    return new Promise(. . .)
  }
}
```

9.4 Obtaining Promise Results

Now that you know how to construct a promise, you will want to obtain its result. You do not wait for the promise to settle. Instead, you provide actions that process the result or error once the promise has settled. Those actions will execute at some point *after* the end of the function that has scheduled them.

Use the `then` method to specify an action that should be carried out once the promise is resolved. The action is a function that consumes the result.

```
const promise1 = produceAfterDelay(42, 1000)
promise1.then(console.log) // Log the value when ready

const promise2 = loadImage('hanafuda/1-1.png')
promise2.then(img => imgdiv.appendChild(img)) // Append the image when ready
```

 NOTE: The `then` method is the only way to get a result out of a promise.

You will see in Section 9.6, "Rejection Handling" (page 194), how to deal with rejected promises.

 CAUTION: When you experiment with the `loadImage` or `fetch` function with different URLs, you will likely run into "cross-origin" errors. The JavaScript engine inside a browser will not allow JavaScript code to see results of web requests from third-party hosts unless those hosts agree that the access is safe and set a response header. Unfortunately, few sites have gone through the trouble. You can fetch the URLs at `https://horstmann` `.com/javascript-impatient` or (as I write this) `https://developer.mozilla.org` and `https://aws.random.cat/meow`. If you want to experiment with other sites, you can use a CORS proxy or a browser plugin to overcome the browser check.

9.5 Promise Chaining

In the preceding section, you saw how to obtain the result of a promise. Now we tackle a more interesting case, where the promise result is passed to another asynchronous task.

If the action that you pass to `then` yields another promise, the result is that other promise. To process its result, call the `then` method once again.

Here is an example. We load an image, and then another:

```
const promise1 = loadImage('hanafuda/1-1.png')
const promise2 = promise1.then(img => {
  imgdiv.appendChild(img)
  return loadImage('hanafuda/1-2.png') // Another promise
})
promise2.then(img => {
  imgdiv.appendChild(img)
})
```

There is no need to save each promise in a separate variable. Normally, one processes a chain of promises as a "pipeline."

```
loadImage('hanafuda/1-1.png')
  .then(img => {
    imgdiv.appendChild(img)
    return loadImage('hanafuda/1-2.png')
  })
  .then(img => imgdiv.appendChild(img))
```

NOTE: With the Fetch API, you need to chain promises to read the contents of a web page:

```
fetch('https://developer.mozilla.org')
  .then(response => response.text())
  .then(console.log)
```

The `fetch` function returns a promise yielding the response, and the `text` method yields another promise for the text content of the page.

You can intermingle synchronous and asynchronous tasks:

```
loadImage('hanafuda/1-1.png')
  .then(img => imgdiv.appendChild(img)) // Synchronous
  .then(() => loadImage('hanafuda/1-2.png')) // Asynchronous
  .then(img => imgdiv.appendChild(img)) // Synchronous
```

Technically, if a `then` action yields a value that isn't a promise, the `then` method returns an immediately fulfilled promise. This allows further chaining with another `then` method.

TIP: You can make promise pipelines more symmetric by starting out with an immediately fulfilled promise:

```
Promise.resolve()
  .then(() => loadImage('hanafuda/1-1.png'))
  .then(img => imgdiv.appendChild(img))
  .then(() => loadImage('hanafuda/1-2.png'))
  .then(img => imgdiv.appendChild(img))
```

The preceding examples showed how to compose a fixed number of tasks. You can build an arbitrarily long pipeline of tasks with a loop:

```
let p = Promise.resolve()
for (let i = 1; i <= n; i++) {
  p = p.then(() => loadImage(`hanafuda/1-${i}.png`))
    .then(img => imgdiv.appendChild(img))
}
```

 CAUTION: If the argument of the then method is not a function, the argument is discarded! The following is wrong:

```
loadImage('hanafuda/1-1.png')
  .then(img => imgdiv.appendChild(img))
  .then(loadImage('hanafuda/1-2.png'))
    // Error—argument of then isn't a function
  .then(img => imgdiv.appendChild(img))
```

Here, then is called with the return value of loadImage—that is, a Promise. If you call p.then(arg) with an argument that is not a function, there is no error message. The argument is discarded, and the then method returns a promise with the same result as p. Also, note that the second call to loadImage happens right after the first, without waiting for the first promise to settle.

9.6 Rejection Handling

In the preceding section, you saw how to carry out multiple asynchronous tasks in sequence. We focused on the "happy day" scenario when all of the tasks succeeded. Handling error paths can greatly complicate the program logic. Promises make it fairly easy to propagate errors through a pipeline of tasks.

You can supply a rejection handler when calling the then method:

```
loadImage(url)
  .then(
    img => { // Promise has settled
      imgdiv.appendChild(img)
    },
    reason => { // Promise was rejected
      console.log({reason})
      imgdiv.appendChild(brokenImage)
    })
```

However, it is usually better to use the catch method:

```
loadImage(url)
  .then(
    img => { // Promise has settled
      imgdiv.appendChild(img)
    })
  .catch(
    reason => { // A prior promise was rejected
      console.log({reason})
      imgdiv.appendChild(brokenImage)
    })
```

That way, errors in the resolve handler are also caught.

The catch method yields a new promise based on the returned value, returned promise, or thrown exception of its handler argument.

If the handler returns without throwing an exception, then the resulting promise is resolved, and you can keep the pipeline going.

Often, a pipeline has a single rejection handler that is invoked when any of the tasks fails:

```
Promise.resolve()
  .then(() => loadImage('hanafuda/1-1.png'))
  .then(img => imgdiv.appendChild(img))
  .then(() => loadImage('hanafuda/1-2.png'))
  .then(img => imgdiv.appendChild(img))
  .catch(reason => console.log({reason}))
```

If a then action throws an exception, the then method yields a rejected promise. Chaining a rejected promise with another then simply propagates that rejected promise. Therefore, the catch handler at the end will handle a rejection at any stage of the pipeline.

The finally method invokes a handler whether or not a promise has settled. The handler has no arguments since it is intended for cleanup, not for analyzing the promise result. The finally method returns a promise with the same outcome as the one on which it was invoked, so that it can be included in a pipeline:

```
Promise.resolve()
  .then(() => loadImage('hanafuda/1-1.png'))
  .then(img => imgdiv.appendChild(img))
  .finally(() => { doCleanup(. . .) })
  .catch(reason => console.log({reason}))
```

9.7 Executing Multiple Promises

When you have multiple promises and you want them all resolved, you can place them into an array or any iterable, and call Promise.all(iterable). You then obtain a promise that is resolved when all promises in the iterable are resolved. The value of the combined promise is an iterable of all promise results, in the same order as the promises themselves.

This gives us an easy way to load a sequence of images and append them in order:

```
const promises = [
  loadImage('hanafuda/1-1.png'),
  loadImage('hanafuda/1-2.png'),
  loadImage('hanafuda/1-3.png'),
  loadImage('hanafuda/1-4.png')]
Promise.all(promises)
  .then(images => { for (const img of images) imgdiv.appendChild(img) })
```

The Promise.all does not actually run tasks in parallel. All tasks are executed sequentially in a single thread. However, the order in which they are scheduled is not predictable. For example, in the image loading example, you don't know which image data arrives first.

As already mentioned, Promise.all returns a promise for an iterable. That iterable contains the results of the individual promises in the correct order, regardless of the order in which they were obtained.

In the preceding sample code, the then method is invoked when all images have been loaded, and they are appended from the images iterable in the correct order.

If the iterable that you pass to Promise.all contains non-promises, they are simply included in the result iterable.

If any of the promises is rejected, then Promise.all yields a rejected promise whose error is that of the first rejected promise.

If you need more fine-grained control over rejections, use the Promise.allSettled method instead. It yields a promise for an iterable whose elements are objects of the form

```
{ status: 'fulfilled', value: result }
```

or

```
{ status: 'rejected', reason: exception }
```

Exercise 8 shows how to process the results.

9.8 Racing Multiple Promises

Sometimes, you want to carry out tasks in parallel, but you want to stop as soon as the first one has completed. A typical example is a search where you are satisfied with the first result. The `Promise.race(iterable)` runs the promises in the iterable until one of them settles. That promise determines the outcome of the race.

 CAUTION: If the iterable has non-promises, then one of them will be the result of the race. If the iterable is empty, then `Promise.race(iterable)` never settles.

It is possible that a rejected promise wins the race. In that case, all other promises are abandoned, even though one of them might produce a result. A more useful method, `Promise.any`, is currently a stage 3 candidate.

The `Promise.any` method continues until one of the tasks has *resolved*. In the unhappy case that all promises are rejected, the resulting promise is rejected with an `AggregateError` that collects all reasons for rejection.

```
Promise.any(promises)
  .then(result => . . .) // Process the result of the first settled promise
  .catch(error => . . .) // None of the promises settled
```

9.9 Async Functions

You have just seen how to build pipelines of promises with the `then` and `catch` methods, and how to execute a sequence of promises concurrently with `Promise.all` and `Promise.any`. However, this programming style is not very convenient. Instead of using familiar statement sequences and control flow, you need to set up a pipeline with method calls.

The `await`/`async` syntax makes working with promises much more natural.

The expression

```
let value = await promise
```

waits for the promise to settle and yields its value.

But wait. . .didn't we learn at the beginning of this chapter that it is a terrible idea to keep waiting in a JavaScript function? Indeed it is, and you cannot use `await` in a normal function. The `await` operator can only occur in a function that is tagged with the `async` keyword:

```
const putImage = async (url, element) => {
  const img = await loadImage(url)
  element.appendChild(img)
}
```

The compiler transforms the code of an `async` function so that any steps that occur after an `await` operator are executed when the promise resolves. For example, the `putImage` function is equivalent to:

```
const putImage = (url, element) => {
  loadImage(url)
    .then(img => element.appendChild(img))
}
```

Multiple `await` are OK:

```
const putTwoImages = async (url1, url2, element) => {
  const img1 = await loadImage(url1)
  element.appendChild(img1)
  const img2 = await loadImage(url2)
  element.appendChild(img2)
}
```

Loops are OK too:

```
const putImages = async (urls, element) => {
  for (url of urls) {
    const img = await loadImage(url)
    element.appendChild(img)
  }
}
```

As you can see from these examples, the rewriting that the compiler does behind the scenes is not trivial.

 CAUTION: If you forget the `await` keyword when calling an `async` function, the function is called and returns a promise, but the promise just sits there and does nothing. Consider this scenario, adapted from one of many confused blogs:

```
const putImages = async (urls, element) => {
  for (url of urls)
    putImage(url, element) // Error—no await for async putImage
}
```

This function produces and forgets a number of `Promise` objects, then returns a `Promise.resolve(undefined)`. If all goes well, the images will be appended in some order. But if an exception occurs, nobody will catch it.

You can apply the `async` keyword to the following:

- Arrow functions:

```
async url => { . . . }
async (url, params) => { . . . }
```

- Methods:

```
class ImageLoader {
  async load(url) { . . . }
}
```

- Named and anonymous functions:

```
async function loadImage(url) { . . . }
async function(url) { . . . }
```

- Object literal methods:

```
obj = {
  async loadImage(url) { . . . },
  . . .
}
```

 NOTE: In all cases, the resulting function is an `AsyncFunction` instance, not a `Function`, even though `typeof` still reports `'function'`.

9.10 Async Return Values

An `async` function looks as if it returned a value, but it always returns a promise. Here is an example. The URL `https://aws.random.cat/meow` serves up locations of random cat pictures, returning a JSON object such as { `file:` `'https://purr.objects-us-east-1.dream.io/i/mDh7a.jpg' }`.

Using the Fetch API, we can get a promise for the content like this:

```
const result = await fetch('https://aws.random.cat/meow')
const imageJSON = await result.json()
```

The second `await` is necessary because in the Fetch API, JSON processing is asynchronous—the call `result.json()` yields another promise.

Now we are ready to write a function that returns the URL of the cat image:

```
const getCatImageURL = async () => {
  const result = await fetch('https://aws.random.cat/meow')
  const imageJSON = await result.json()
  return imageJSON.file
}
```

Of course, the function must be tagged as async because it uses the await operator.

The function appears to return a string. The point of the await operator is to let you work with values, not promises. But that illusion ends when you leave an async function. The value that appears in a return statement always becomes a promise.

What can you do with an async function? Since it returns a promise, you can harvest the result by calling then:

```
getCatImageURL()
  .then(url => loadImage(url))
  .then(img => imgdiv.appendChild(img))
```

Or you can get the result with the await operator:

```
const url = await getCatImageURL()
const img = await loadImage(url)
imgdiv.appendChild(img)
```

The latter looks nicer, but it has to happen in another async function. As you can see, once you are in the async world, it is hard to leave.

Consider the last line in this async function:

```
const loadCatImage = async () => {
  const result = await fetch('https://aws.random.cat/meow')
  const imageJSON = await result.json()
  return await loadImage(imageJSON.file)
}
```

You can omit the last await operator:

```
const loadCatImage = async () => {
  const result = await fetch('https://aws.random.cat/meow')
  const imageJSON = await result.json()
  return loadImage(imageJSON.file)
}
```

Either way, this method returns a promise for the image that is asynchronously produced by the call to loadImage.

I find the first version easier to understand since the async/await syntax consistently hides all promises.

 CAUTION: Inside a try/catch statement, there is a subtle difference between return await promise and return promise—see Exercise 11. Here, you do not want to drop the await operator.

If an `async` function returns a value before ever having called `await`, the value is wrapped into a resolved promise:

```
const getJSONProperty = async (url, key) => {
  if (url === undefined) return null
    // Actually returns Promise.resolve(null)
  const result = await fetch(url)
  const json = await result.json()
  return json[key]
}
```

NOTE: The `async` functions of this section return a single value in the future. In Chapter 12, you will see how an `async` iterator produces a sequence of values in the future. Here is an example that yields a range of integers, with a given delay between them.

```
async function* range(start, end, delay) {
  for (let current = start; current < end; current++) {
    yield await produceAfterDelay(current, delay)
  }
}
```

Don't worry about the syntax of this "async generator function." You are unlikely to implement one, but you might use one that is provided by a library. You can harvest the results with a `for await of` loop:

```
for await (const value of range(0, 10, 1000)) {
  console.log(value)
}
```

This loop must be inside an `async` function since it awaits all values.

9.11 Concurrent Await

Successive calls to `await` are done one after another:

```
const img1 = await loadImage(url)
const img2 = await loadCatImage() // Only starts after the first image was loaded
```

It would be more efficient to load the images concurrently. Then you need to use `Promise.all`:

```
const [img1, img2] = await Promise.all([loadImage(url), loadCatImage()])
```

To make sense of this expression, it is not sufficient to understand the async/await syntax. You really need to know about promises.

The argument of `Promise.all` is an iterable of promises. Here, the `loadImage` function is a regular function that returns a promise, and `loadCatImage` is an `async` function that implicitly returns a promise.

The `Promise.all` method returns a promise, so we can call `await` on it. The result of the promise is an array that we destructure.

If you don't understand what goes on under the hood, it is easy to make mistakes. Consider this statement:

```
const [img1, img2] = Promise.all([await loadImage(url), await loadCatImage()])
   // Error—still sequential
```

The statement compiles and runs. But it does not load the images concurrently. The call `await loadImage(url)` must complete before the call `await loadCatImage()` is initiated.

9.12 Exceptions in Async Functions

Throwing an exception in an `async` function yields a rejected promise.

```
const getAnimalImageURL = async type => {
  if (type === 'cat') {
    return getJSONProperty('https://aws.random.cat/meow', 'file')
  } else if (type === 'dog') {
    return getJSONProperty('https://dog.ceo/api/breeds/image/random', 'message')
  } else {
    throw Error('bad type') // Async function returns rejected promise
  }
}
```

Conversely, when the `await` operator receives a rejected promise, it throws an exception. The following function catches the exception from the `await` operator:

```
const getAnimalImage = async type => {
  try {
    const url = await getAnimalImageURL(type)
    return loadImage(url)
  } catch {
    return brokenImage
  }
}
```

You do not have to surround every `await` with a `try`/`catch` statement, but you need some strategy for error handling with `async` functions. Perhaps your top-level `async` function catches all asynchronous exceptions, or you document the fact that its callers must call `catch` on the returned promise.

When a promise is rejected at the top level in Node.js, a stern warning occurs, stating that future versions of Node.js may instead terminate the process—see Exercise 12.

Exercises

1. The sample program in Section 9.1, "Concurrent Tasks in JavaScript" (page 185), may not load the images in the correct order. How can you modify it without using futures so that the images are always appended in the correct order, no matter when they arrive?

2. Implement a function `invokeAfterDelay` that yields a promise, invoking a given function after a given delay. Demonstrate by yielding a promise for a random number between 0 and 1. Print the result on the console when it is available.

3. Invoke the `produceRandomAfterDelay` function from the preceding exercise twice and print the sum once the summands are available.

4. Write a loop that invokes the `produceRandomAfterDelay` function from the preceding exercises `n` times and prints the sum once the summands are available.

5. Provide a function `addImage(url, element)` that is similar to that in Section 9.1, "Concurrent Tasks in JavaScript" (page 185). Return a promise so that one can chain the calls:

   ```
   addImage('hanafuda/1-1.png')
     .then(() => addImage('hanafuda/1-2.png', imgdiv))
     .then(() => addImage('hanafuda/1-3.png', imgdiv))
     .then(() => addImage('hanafuda/1-4.png', imgdiv))
   ```

   Then use the tip in Section 9.5, "Promise Chaining" (page 192), to make the chaining more symmetrical.

6. Demonstrate that the `Promise.resolve` method turns any object with a `then` method into a `Promise`. Supply an object whose `then` method randomly calls the resolve or reject handler.

7. Often, a client-side application needs to defer work until after the browser has finished loading the DOM. You can place such work into a listener for the `DOMContentLoaded` event. But if `document.readyState != 'loading'`, the loading has already happened, and the event won't fire again. Capture both cases with a function yielding a promise, so that one can call

   ```
   whenDOMContentLoaded().then(. . .)
   ```

8. Make an array of image URLs, some good, and some failing because of CORS (see the note at the end of Section 9.2, "Making Promises," page 188). Turn each into a promise:

   ```
   const urls = [. . .]
   const promises = urls.map(loadImage)
   ```

Call `allSettled` on the array of promises. When that promise resolves, traverse the array, append the loaded images into a DOM element, and log those that failed:

```
Promise.allSettled(promises)
  .then(results => {
    for (result of results)
      if (result.status === 'fulfilled') . . . else . . .
  })
```

9. Repeat the preceding exercise, but use `await` instead of `then`.

10. Implement a function `sleep` that yields a promise so that one can call

    ```
    await sleep(1000)
    ```

11. Describe the difference between

    ```
    const loadCatImage = async () => {
      try {
        const result = await fetch('https://aws.random.cat/meow')
        const imageJSON = await result.json()
        return loadImage(imageJSON.file)
      } catch {
        return brokenImage
      }
    }
    ```

    and

    ```
    const loadCatImage = async () => {
      try {
        const result = await fetch('https://aws.random.cat/meow')
        const imageJSON = await result.json()
        return await loadImage(imageJSON.file)
      } catch {
        return brokenImage
      }
    }
    ```

    Hint: What happens if the future returned by `loadImage` is rejected?

12. Experiment with calling an `async` function that throws an exception in Node.js. Given

    ```
    const rejectAfterDelay = (result, delay) => {
      return new Promise((resolve, reject) => {
        const callback = () => reject(result)
        setTimeout(callback, delay)
      })
    }
    ```

    try

```
const errorAfterDelay = async (message, delay) =>
    await rejectAfterDelay(new Error(message), delay)
```

Now invoke the `errorAfterDelay` function. What happens? How can you avoid this situation?

13. Explain how the error message from the preceding exercise can be useful for locating a forgotten `await` operator, such as

```
const errorAfterDelay = async (message, delay) => {
    try {
        return rejectAfterDelay(new Error(message), 1000)
    } catch(e) { console.error(e) }
}
```

14. Write complete programs that demonstrate the `Promise.all` and `Promise.race` functions of Section 9.7, "Executing Multiple Promises" (page 196).

15. Write a function `produceAfterRandomDelay` that produces a value after a random delay between 0 and a given maximum milliseconds. Then produce an array of futures where the function is applied to 1, 2, . . . , 10, and pass it to `Promise.all`. In which order will the results be collected?

16. Use the Fetch API to load a (CORS-friendly) image. Fetch the URL, then call `blob()` on the response to get a promise for the BLOB. Turn it into an image as in the `loadImage` function. Provide two implementations, one using `then` and one using `await`.

17. Use the Fetch API to obtain the HTML of a (CORS-friendly) web page. Search all image URLs and load each image.

18. When work is scheduled for the future, it may happen that due to changing circumstances the work is no longer needed and it should be canceled. Design a scheme for cancellation. Consider a multistep process, such as in the preceding exercise. At each stage, you will want to be able to abort the process. There is no standard way yet of doing this in JavaScript, but typically, APIs provide "cancellation tokens." A `fetchImages` function might receive an additional argument

```
const token = new CancellationToken()
const images = fetchImages(url, token)
```

The caller can later decide to call

```
token.cancel()
```

In the implementation of an cancelable `async` function, the call

```
token.throwIfCancellationRequested()
```

throws an exception if cancellation was indeed requested. Implement this mechanism and demonstrate it with an example.

19. Consider this code that carries out some asynchronous work such as fetching remote data, handles the data, and returns the promise for further processing:

```
const doAsyncWorkAndThen = handler => {
  const promise = asyncWork();
  promise.then(result => handler(result));
  return promise;
}
```

What happens if `handler` throws an exception? How should this code be reorganized?

20. What happens when you add `async` to a function that doesn't return promises?

21. What happens if you apply the `await` operator to an expression that isn't a promise? What happens if the expression throws an exception? Is there any reason why you would want to do this?

Modules

Chapter 10

When providing code to be reused by many programmers, it is important to separate the public interface from the private implementation. In an object-oriented programming language, this separation is achieved with classes. A class can evolve by changing the private implementation without affecting its users. (As you saw in Chapter 4, hiding private features is not yet fully supported in JavaScript, but this will surely come.)

A module system provides the same benefits for programming at larger scales. A module can make certain classes and functions available, while hiding others, so that the module's evolution can be controlled.

Several ad-hoc module systems were developed for the JavaScript. In 2015, ECMAScript 6 codified a simple module system that is the topic of this short chapter.

10.1 The Module Concept

A *module* provides features (classes, functions, or other values) for programmers, called the *exported* features. Any features that are not exported are private to the module.

A module also specifies on which other modules it depends. When a module is needed, the JavaScript runtime loads it together with its dependent modules.

Modules manage name conflicts. Since the private features of a module are hidden from the public, it does not matter what they are called. They will never clash with any names outside the module. When you use a public feature, you can rename it so that it has a unique name.

 NOTE: In this regard, JavaScript modules differ from Java packages or modules which rely on globally unique names.

It is important to understand that a module is different from a class. A class can have many instances, but a module doesn't have instances. It is just a container for classes, functions, or values.

10.2 ECMAScript Modules

Consider a JavaScript developer who wants to make features available to other programmers. The developer places those features into a file. The programmers who use the features include the file in their project.

Now suppose a programmer includes such files from multiple developers. There is a good chance that some of those feature names will conflict with each other. More ominously, each file contains quite a few helper functions and variables whose names give rise to further conflicts.

Clearly, there needs to be some way of hiding implementation details. For many years, JavaScript developers have simulated modules through closures, placing helper functions and classes inside a wrapper function. This is similar to the "hard objects" technique from Chapter 3. They also developed ad-hoc ways of publishing exported features and dependencies.

Node.js implements a module system (called Common.js) that manages module dependencies. When a module is needed, it and its dependencies are loaded. That loading happens *synchronously*, as soon as the demand for a module occurs.

The AMD (Asynchronous Module Definition) standard defines a system for loading modules asynchronously, which is better suited for browser-based applications.

ECMAScript modules improve on both of these systems. They are parsed to quickly establish their dependencies and exports, without having to execute their bodies first. This allows asynchronous loading and circular dependencies. Nowadays, the JavaScript world is transitioning to the ECMAScript module system.

NOTE: For Java programmers, an analog of a JavaScript module is a Maven artifact, or, since Java 9, a Java platform module. Artifacts provide dependency information but no encapsulation (beyond that of Java classes and packages). Java platform modules provide both, but they are quite a bit more complex than ECMAScript modules.

10.3 Default Imports

Only a few programmers write modules; many more programmers consume them. Let us therefore start with the most common activity: importing features from an existing module.

Most commonly, you import functions and classes. But you can also import objects, arrays, and primitive values.

A module implementor can tag one feature (presumably the most useful one) as the *default*. The import syntax makes it particularly easy to import the default feature. Consider this example where we import a class from a module that provides an encryption service:

```
import CaesarCipher from './modules/caesar.mjs'
```

This statement specifies the name that you choose to give to the default feature, followed by the file that contains the module implementation. For more details on specifying module locations, see Section 10.7, "Packaging Modules" (page 217).

The choice of the feature name in your program is entirely yours. If you prefer, you can give it a shorter name:

```
import CC from './modules/caesar.mjs'
```

If you work with modules that provide their services as a default feature, that is all you need to know about the ECMAScript module system.

 NOTE: In a browser, the module location must be a full URL or a relative URL that starts with ./, ../, or /. This restriction leaves open the possibility of special handling for well-known package names or paths in the future.

In Node.js, you can use a relative URL that starts with ./, ../, or a file:// URL. You can also specify a package name.

10.4 Named Imports

A module can export named features in addition to, or instead of, the default. The module implementor gives a name to each nondefault feature. You can import as many of these named features as you like.

Here we import two functions that the module calls encrypt and decrypt:

```
import { encrypt, decrypt } from './modules/caesar.mjs'
```

Of course, there is a potential pitfall. What if you want to import encryption functions from two modules, and they both call it encrypt? Fortunately, you can rename the imported features:

```
import { encrypt as caesarEncrypt, decrypt as caesarDecrypt }
  from './modules/caesar.mjs'
```

In this way, you can always avoid name clashes.

If you want to import both the default feature and one or more named features, combine the two syntax elements:

```
import CaesarCipher, { encrypt, decrypt } from './modules/caesar.mjs'
```

or

```
import CaesarCipher, { encrypt as caesarEncrypt, decrypt as caesarDecrypt} . . .
```

 NOTE: Be sure to use braces when importing a single nondefault feature:

```
import { encrypt } from './modules/caesar.mjs'
```

Without the braces, you would give a name to the default feature.

If a module exports many names, then it would be tedious to name each of them in the import statement. Instead, you can pour all exported features into an object:

```
import * as CaesarCipherTools from './modules/caesar.mjs'
```

You then use the imported functions as CaesarCipherTools.encrypt and CaesarCipherTools.decrypt. If there is a default feature, it is accessible as CaesarCipherTools.default. You can also name it:

```
import CaesarCipher, * as CaesarCipherTools . . .
```

You can use the import statement without importing anything:

```
import './app/init.mjs'
```

Then the statements in the file are executed but nothing is imported. This is not common.

10.5 Dynamic Imports

A stage 4 proposal allows you to import a module whose location is not fixed. Loading a module on demand can be useful to reduce the start-up cost and footprint of an application.

For dynamic import, use the `import` keyword as if it were a function with the module location as argument:

```
import(`./plugins/${action}.mjs`)
```

The dynamic `import` statement loads the module asynchronously. The statement yields a promise for an object containing all exported features. The promise is fulfilled when the module is loaded. You can then use its features:

```
import(`./plugins/${action}.mjs`)
  .then(module => {
    module.default()
    module.namedFeature(args)
    . . .
  })
```

Of course you can use the `async/await` notation:

```
async load(action) {
  const module = await import(`./plugins/${action}.mjs`)
  module.default()
  module.namedFeature(args)
  . . .
}
```

When you use a dynamic import, you do not import features by name, and there is no syntax for renaming features.

 NOTE: The `import` keyword is not a function, even though it looks like one. It is just given a function-like syntax. This is similar to the `super(. . .)` syntax of the `super` keyword.

10.6 Exports

Now that you have seen how to import features from modules, let us switch to the module implementor's perspective.

10.6.1 Named Exports

In a module, you can tag any number of functions, classes, or variable declarations with `export`:

```
export function encrypt(str, key) { . . . }
export class Cipher { . . . }
export const DEFAULT_KEY = 3
```

Alternatively, you can provide an `export` statement with the names of the exported features:

```
function encrypt(str, key) { . . . }
class Cipher { . . . }
const DEFAULT_KEY = 3

. . .
export { encrypt, Cipher, DEFAULT_KEY }
```

With this form of the `export` statement, you can provide different names for exported features:

```
export { encrypt as caesarEncrypt, Cipher, DEFAULT_KEY }
```

Keep in mind that the `export` statement defines the name under which the feature is exported. As you have seen, an importing module may use the provided name or choose a different name to access the feature.

 NOTE: The exported features must be defined at the top-level scope of the module. You cannot export local functions, classes, or variables.

10.6.2 The Default Export

At most one function or class can be tagged as `export default`:

```
export default class Cipher { . . . }
```

In this example, the `Cipher` class becomes the default feature of the module.

You cannot use `export default` with variable declarations. If you want the default export to be a value, do not declare a variable. Simply write `export default` followed by the value:

```
export default 3 // OK
export default const DEFAULT_KEY = 3
    // Error—export default not valid with const/let/var
```

It isn't likely that someone would make a simple constant the default value. A more realistic choice would be to export an object with multiple features:

```
export default { encrypt, Cipher, DEFAULT_KEY }
```

You can use this syntax with an anonymous function or class:

```
export default (s, key) => { . . . } // No need to name this function
```

or

```
export default class { // No need to name this class
  encrypt(key) { . . . }
  decrypt(key) { . . . }
}
```

Finally, you can use the renaming syntax to declare the default feature:

```
export { Cipher as default }
```

 NOTE: The default feature is simply a feature with the name `default`. However, since `default` is a keyword, you cannot use it as an identifier and must use one of the syntactical forms of this section.

10.6.3 Exports Are Variables

Each exported feature is a variable with a name and a value. The value may be a function, a class, or an arbitrary JavaScript value.

The value of an exported feature can change over time. Those changes are visible in importing modules. In other words, an exported feature captures a variable, not just a value.

For example, a logging module might export a variable with the current logging level and a function to change it:

```
export const Level = { FINE: 1, INFO: 2, WARN: 3, ERROR: 4 }
export let currentLevel = Level.INFO
export const setLevel = level => { currentLevel = level }
```

Now consider a module that imports the logging module with the statement:

```
import * as logging from './modules/logging.mjs'
```

Initially, in that module, `logging.currentLevel` has value `Level.INFO` or `2`. If the module calls

```
logging.setLevel(logging.Level.WARN)
```

the variable is updated, and `logging.currentLevel` has value `3`.

However, in the importing module, the variable is read-only. You cannot set

```
logging.currentLevel = logging.Level.WARN
  // Error—cannot assign to imported variable
```

The variables holding exported features are created as soon as the module is parsed, but they are only filled when the module body is executed. This enables circular dependencies between modules (see Exercise 6).

CAUTION: If you have a cycle of modules that depends on each other, then it can happen that an exported feature is still `undefined` when it is used in another module—see Exercise 11.

10.6.4 Reexporting

When you provide a module with a rich API and a complex implementation, you will likely depend on other modules. Of course, the module system takes care of dependency management, so the module user doesn't have to worry about that. However, it can happen that one of the modules contains useful features that you want to make available to your users. Instead of asking users to import those features themselves, you can *reexport* them.

Here, we reexport features from another module:

```
export { randInt, randDouble } from './modules/random.mjs'
```

Whoever imports this module will have the features `randInt` and `randDouble` from the `'./modules/random.mjs'` module available, as if they had been defined in this module.

If you like, you can rename features that you reexport:

```
export { randInt as randomInteger } from './modules/random.mjs'
```

To reexport the default feature of a module, refer to it as `default`:

```
export { default } from './modules/stringutil.mjs'
export { default as StringUtil } from './modules/stringutil.mjs'
```

Conversely, if you want to reexport another feature and make it the default of this module, use the following syntax:

```
export { Random as default } from './modules/random.mjs'
```

Finally, you can reexport all nondefault features of another module.

```
export * from './modules/random.mjs'
```

You might want to do this if you split up your project into many smaller modules and then provide a single module that is a façade for the smaller ones, reexporting all of them.

The `export *` statement skips the default feature because there would be a conflict if you were to reexport default features from multiple modules.

10.7 Packaging Modules

Modules are different from plain "scripts":

- The code inside a module always executes in strict mode.

- Each module has its own top-level scope that is distinct from the global scope of the JavaScript runtime.

- A module is only processed once even if it is loaded multiple times.

- A module is processed asynchronously.

- A module can contain import and export statements.

When the JavaScript runtime reads the module content, it must know that it is processing a module and not a plain script.

In a browser, you load a module with a script tag whose type attribute is module.

```
<script type="module" src="./modules/caesar.mjs"></script>
```

In Node.js, you can use the file extension .mjs to indicate that a file is a module. If you want to use a plain .js extension, you need to mark modules in the package.json configuration file. When invoking the node executable in interactive mode, use the command-line option --input-type=module.

It seems simplest to always use the .mjs extension for modules. All runtimes and build tools recognize that extension.

 NOTE: When you serve .mjs files from a web server, the server needs to be configured to provide the header Content-Type: text/javascript with the response.

 CAUTION: Unlike regular scripts, browsers fetch modules with CORS restrictions. If you load modules from a different domain, the server must return an Access-Control-Allow-Origin header.

 NOTE: The import.meta object is a stage 3 proposal to provide information about the current module. Some JavaScript runtimes provide the URL from which the module was loaded as import.meta.url.

Exercises

1. Find a JavaScript library for statistical computation (such as `https://github.com` `/simple-statistics/simple-statistics`). Write a program that imports the library as an ECMAScript module and computes the mean and standard deviation of a data set.

2. Find a JavaScript library for encryption (such as `https://github.com/brix` `/crypto-js`). Write a program that imports the library as an ECMAScript module and encrypts a message, then decrypts it.

3. Implement a simple logging module that supports logging messages whose log level exceeds a given threshold. Export a log function, constants for the log level, and a function to set the threshold.

4. Repeat the preceding exercise, but export a single class as a default feature.

5. Implement a simple encryption module that uses the Caesar cipher (adding a constant to each code point). Use the logging module from one of the preceding exercises to log all calls to `decrypt`.

6. As an example of a circular dependency between modules, repeat the preceding exercise, but provide an option to encrypt the logs in the logging module.

7. Implement a simple module that provides random integers, arrays of random integers, and random strings. Use as many different forms of the `export` syntax as you can.

8. What is the difference between

    ```
    import Cipher from './modules/caesar.mjs'
    ```

    and

    ```
    import { Cipher } from './modules/caesar.mjs'
    ```

9. Explain the difference between

    ```
    export { encrypt, Cipher, DEFAULT_KEY }
    ```

    and

    ```
    export default { encrypt, Cipher, DEFAULT_KEY }
    ```

10. Which of the following are valid JavaScript?

    ```
    export function default(s, key) { . . . }
    export default function (s, key) { . . . }
    export const default = (s, key) => { . . . }
    export default (s, key) => { . . . }
    ```

11. Trees have two kinds of nodes: those with children (parents) and those without (leaves). Let's model that with inheritance:

```
class Node {
  static from(value, ...children) {
    return children.length === 0 ? new Leaf(value)
      : new Parent(value, children)
  }
}

class Parent extends Node {
  constructor(value, children) {
    super()
    this.value = value
    this.children = children
  }
  depth() {
    return 1 + Math.max(...this.children.map(c => c.depth()))
  }
}

class Leaf extends Node {
  constructor(value) {
    super()
    this.value = value
  }
  depth() {
    return 1
  }
}
```

Now a module-happy developer wants to put each class into a separate module. Do that and try it out with a demo program:

```
import { Node } from './node.mjs'

const myTree = Node.from('Adam',
  Node.from('Cain', Node.from('Enoch')),
  Node.from('Abel'),
  Node.from('Seth', Node.from('Enos')))
console.log(myTree.depth())
```

What happens? Why?

12. Of course, the issue in the preceding exercise could have been easily avoided by not using inheritance, or by placing all classes into one module. In a larger system, those alternatives may not be feasible. In this exercise, keep each class in its own module and provide a façade module tree.mjs that reexports all three modules. In all modules, import from './tree.mjs', not the individual modules. Why does this solve the issue?

Metaprogramming

Topics in This Chapter

Chapter 11

This chapter is a deep dive into advanced APIs that you can use to create objects that have nonstandard behavior, and to write code that works with generic objects.

We start by looking at symbols, the only type other than strings that can be used for object property names. By defining properties with certain "well-known" symbols, you can customize the behavior of certain API methods.

Then we look at object properties in detail. Properties can have attributes, and you will learn how to analyze, create, and update properties with the appropriate attributes. As an application, we will walk through a robust clone function for making deep copies.

We then turn to function objects and methods for binding parameters and invoking functions with given parameters. Finally, you will see how proxies can intercept every aspect of working with objects. We will study two applications in detail: spying on object access and dynamically creating properties.

11.1 Symbols

As you have seen throughout this book, a JavaScript object has keys of type String. However, using strings as keys has some limitations. Modern JavaScript provides a second type that you can use for object keys—the Symbol type.

Symbols have string labels, but they are not strings. Create a symbol like this:

```
const sym = Symbol('label')
```

Symbols are unique. If you create a second symbol

```
const sym2 = Symbol('label')
```

then `sym !== sym2`.

This is the principal advantage of symbols. If you wanted to have a string key that is guaranteed to be unique, you might add a counter or a time stamp or a random number, and you'd still fret if that was good enough.

 NOTE: You cannot use `new` to make a symbol: `new Symbol('label')` throws an exception.

Since symbols are not strings, you cannot use the dot notation for symbol keys. Instead, use the bracket operator:

```
let obj = { [sym]: initialValue }
obj[sym] = newValue
```

If you want to attach some property to an existing object, such as a DOM node, it isn't a good idea to use a string key:

```
node.outcome = 'success'
```

Even if nodes don't currently have a key named `outcome`, they might in the future.

But a symbol is completely safe:

```
let outcomeSymbol = Symbol('outcome')
node[outcomeSymbol] = 'success'
```

Note that you need to save the symbol in a variable or object, so that it is available when you need it.

For example, the `Symbol` class has "well-known" symbols in the fields `Symbol.iterator` and `Symbol.species` that we will study in the next section.

If you need to share symbols across "realms" (such as different iframes or web workers), you can use the global symbol registry. To create or retrieve a previously created global symbol, call the `Symbol.for` method. Supply a key that should be globally unique:

```
let sym3 = Symbol.for('com.horstmann.outcome')
```

 NOTE: The `typeof` operator yields the string `'symbol'` when applied to a symbol.

11.2 Customization with Symbol Properties

Symbol properties are used in the JavaScript API for customizing the behavior of classes. The Symbol class defines a number of "well-known" symbol constants for this purpose, shown in Table 11-1. The following subsections examine three of them in detail.

Table 11-1 Well-Known Symbols

Symbol	Description
toStringTag	Customizes the toString method of the Object class—see Section 11.2.1
toPrimitive	Customizes conversion to a primitive type—see Section 11.2.2
species	A constructor function to create a result collection, used by methods such as map and filter—see Section 11.2.3
iterator, asyncIterator	Define iterators (Chapter 9) and asynchronous iterators (Chapter 10)

hasInstance	Customize the behavior of instanceof:
	
	```class Iterable {```
	``` static [Symbol.hasInstance](obj) {```
	``` return Symbol.iterator in obj```
	``` }```
	```}```
	```[1, 2, 3] instanceof Iterable```

match, matchAll, replace, search, split	Called from the String methods with the same name. Redefine for objects other than RegExp—see Exercise 2.

isConcatSpreadable	Used in the concat method of Array:
	
	```const a = [1, 2]```
	```const b = [3, 4]```
	```a[Symbol.isConcatSpreadable] = false```
	```[].concat(a, b) ⇒ [[1, 2], 3, 4]```

11.2.1 Customizing toString

You can change the behavior of the toString method in the Object class. By default, it yields '[object Object]'. But if an object has a property with the key Symbol.toStringTag, then that property value is used instead of Object. For example:

```
const harry = { name: 'Harry Smith', salary: 100000 }
harry[Symbol.toStringTag] = 'Employee'
console.log(harry.toString())
  // Now toString yields '[object Employee]
```

When you define a class, you can set the property in the constructor:

```
class Employee {
  constructor(name, salary) {
    this[Symbol.toStringTag] = 'Employee'
    . . .
  }
  . . .
}
```

Or you can provide a get method, using the following special syntax:

```
class Employee {
  . . .
  get [Symbol.toStringTag]() { return JSON.stringify(this) }
}
```

The point is that the well-known symbol provides a hook for customizing the behavior of an API method.

11.2.2 Controlling Type Conversion

The Symbol.toPrimitive symbol gives you additional control over the conversion to primitive types if overriding the valueOf method is not sufficient. Consider this class representing percentages:

```
class Percent {
  constructor(rate) { this.rate = rate }
  toString() { return `${this.rate}%` }
  valueOf() { return this.rate * 0.01 }
}
```

Now consider:

```
const result = new Percent(99.44)
console.log('Result: ' + result) // Prints Result: 0.9944
```

Why not '99.44%'? The + operator uses the valueOf method when it is available. The remedy is to add a method with key Symbol.toPrimitive:

```
[Symbol.toPrimitive](hint) {
  if (hint === 'number') return this.rate * 0.01
  else return `${this.rate}%`
}
```

The hint parameter is:

* 'number' with arithmetic other than + and comparisons

- 'string' with `` `${. . .}` `` or String(. . .)
- 'default' with + or ==

In practice, this mechanism is of limited utility because the hint doesn't give you enough information. What you really want is the type of the other operand—see Exercise 1.

11.2.3 Species

By default, the `Array` method `map` produces the same collection that it received:

```
class MyArray extends Array {}
let myValues = new MyArray(1, 2, 7, 9)
myValues.map(x => x * x) // Yields a MyArray
```

That's not always appropriate. Suppose we have a class `Range` extending `Array` that describes a range of integers.

```
class Range extends Array {
  constructor(start, end) {
    super()
    for (let i = 0; i < end - start; i++)
      this[i] = start + i
  }
}
```

Transforms of ranges aren't usually ranges:

```
const myRange = new Range(10, 99)
myRange.map(x => x * x) // Should not be a Range
```

Such a collection class can specify a different constructor as the value of the `Symbol.species` property:

```
class Range extends Array {
  . . .
  static get [Symbol.species]() { return Array }
}
```

This constructor function is used by the `Array` methods that create new arrays: `map`, `filter`, `flat`, `flatMap`, `subarray`, `slice`, `splice`, and `concat`.

11.3 Property Attributes

In this and the following sections, we will examine all functions and methods of the `Object` class that are summarized in Table 11-2.

Table 11-2 Object Functions and Methods

Name	Description
Functions	
defineProperty(obj, name, descriptor) defineProperties(obj, { name1: descriptor1, . . . })	Define one or multiple property descriptors
getOwnPropertyDescriptor(obj, name) getOwnPropertyDescriptors(obj) getOwnPropertyNames(obj) getOwnPropertySymbols(obj)	Gets one or all noninherited descriptors of an object, or just their string names/symbols
keys(obj) values(obj) entries(obj)	The names, values, and [name, value] pairs of own enumerable properties
preventExtensions(obj) seal(obj) freeze(obj)	Disallow prototype change and property addition; also, property deletion and configuration; also, property change
isExtensible(obj) isSealed(obj) isFrozen(obj)	Checks if obj has been protected by one of the functions from the preceding row
create(prototype, { name1: descriptor1, . . . }) fromEntries([[name1, value1], . . .])	Creates a new object with the given properties
assign(target, source1, source2, . . .)	Copies all enumerable own properties from the sources to the target. Use a spread instead.
getPrototypeOf(obj) setPrototypeOf(obj, proto)	Gets or sets the prototype
Methods	
hasOwnProperty(stringOrSymbol) propertyIsEnumerable(stringOrSymbol)	true if the object has the given property, or if it is enumerable
isPrototypeOf(other)	Checks if this object is a prototype of another

Let us start out with a close look at working with object properties. Every property of a JavaScript object has three *attributes*:

1. `enumerable`: When `true`, the property is visited in `for in` loops.

2. `writable`: When `true`, the property value can be updated.

3. `configurable`: When `true`, the property can be deleted and its attributes can be modified.

When you set a property in an object literal or by assignment, all three attributes are `true`, with one exception. Properties with symbol keys are not enumerable.

```
let james = { name: 'James Bond' }
// james.name is writable, enumerable, configurable
```

On the other hand, the `length` property of an array is writable but not enumerable or configurable.

 NOTE: The `writable` and `configurable` attributes are enforced in strict mode by throwing an exception. In non-strict mode, violations are silently ignored.

You can dynamically define properties with arbitrary names and attribute values by calling the `Object.defineProperty` function:

```
Object.defineProperty(james, 'id', {
  value: '007',
  enumerable: true,
  writable: false,
  configurable: true
})
```

The last argument is called the *property descriptor*.

When you define a new property and do not specify an attribute, it is set to `false`.

You can use the same function to change the attributes of an existing property, provided the property is configurable.

```
Object.defineProperty(james, 'id', {
  configurable: false
}) // Now james.id can't be deleted, and its attributes can't be changed
```

You can define getter and setter properties by providing functions with keys `get` and `set`:

```
Object.defineProperty(james, 'lastName', {
  get: function() { return this.name.split(' ')[1] },
  set: function(last) { this.name = this.name.split(' ')[0] + ' ' + last }
})
```

Note that you can't use arrow functions here since you need the `this` parameter.

The `get` function is invoked when using the property as a value:

```
console.log(james.lastName) // Prints Bond
```

The `set` function is invoked when a new value is assigned to the property:

```
james.lastName = 'Smith' // Now james.name is 'James Smith'
```

NOTE: You saw in Chapter 4 how to define getters and setters in a class: by prefixing a method with `get` or `set`. As you just saw, you don't need to define a class to have getters and setters.

Finally, the `Object.defineProperties` function can define or update multiple properties. Pass an object whose keys are property names and whose values are property descriptors.

```
Object.defineProperties(james, {
    id: { value: '007', writable: false, enumerable: true, configurable: false },
    age: { value: 42, writable: true, enumerable: true, configurable: true }
})
```

11.4 Enumerating Properties

In the preceding section, you saw how to define one or multiple properties. The `getOwnPropertyDescriptor/getOwnPropertyDescriptors` functions yield property descriptors in the same format as the arguments to the `defineProperty/defineProperties` functions. For example,

```
Object.getOwnPropertyDescriptor(james, 'name')
```

yields the descriptor

```
{ value: 'James Bond',
  writable: true,
  enumerable: true,
  configurable: true }
```

To get all descriptors, call

```
Object.getOwnPropertyDescriptors(james)
```

The result is an object whose keys are property names and whose values are descriptors:

```
{ name:
    { value: 'James Bond',
      writable: true,
      enumerable: true,
      configurable: true },
  lastName:
    { get: [Function: get],
      set: [Function: set],
      enumerable: false,
      configurable: false }
  . . .
}
```

The function is called get**Own**PropertyDescriptors since it only yields the properties that are defined with the object itself, not those inherited from the prototype chain.

 TIP: Object.getOwnPropertyDescriptors is very useful to "spy" on an object since it lists all properties, including those that are not enumerable—see Exercise 9.

If you don't want the firehose of information that Object.getOwnPropertyDescriptors yields, you can call Object.getOwnPropertyNames(obj) or Object.getOwnPropertySymbols(obj) to get all string or symbol-valued property keys, whether enumerable or not, and then look up those property descriptors that interest you.

Finally, there are Object.keys, Object.values, and Object.entries functions that yield the names, values, and [*name*, *value*] pairs of own enumerable properties. These are similar to the keys, values, and entries methods of the Map class that you saw in Chapter 7. However, they are not methods, and they yield arrays, not iterators.

```
const obj = { name: 'Fred', age: 42 }
Object.entries(obj) // [['name', 'Fred'], ['age', 42]]
```

You can iterate over the properties with this loop:

```
for (let [key, value] of Object.entries(obj))
  console.log(key, value)
```

11.5 Testing a Single Property

The condition

```
stringOrSymbol in obj
```

checks whether a property exists in an object or within its prototype chain.

Why not simply check whether `obj[stringOrSymbol] !== undefined`? The `in` operator yields `true` for properties whose value is `undefined`. Given the object

```
const harry = { name: 'Harry', partner: undefined }
```

the condition `'partner' in harry` is `true`.

Sometimes you may not want to look into the prototype chain. To find out whether an object itself has a property with a given name, call

```
obj.hasOwnProperty(stringOrSymbol)
```

To test for the presence of an enumerable property, call

```
obj.propertyIsEnumerable(stringOrSymbol)
```

Note that using these methods has a potential downside. An object can override the methods and lie about its properties. In this regard, it is safer to use the `in` operator and functions such as `Object.getOwnPropertyDescriptior`.

11.6 Protecting Objects

The `Object` class has three functions for protecting objects to increasing degrees:

1. `Object.preventExtensions(obj)`: Own properties cannot be added, and the prototype cannot be changed.

2. `Object.seal(obj)`: In addition, properties cannot be deleted or configured.

3. `Object.freeze(obj)`: In addition, properties cannot be set.

The three functions return the object that is being protected. For example, you can construct and freeze an object like this:

```
const frozen = Object.freeze({ . . . })
```

Note that these protections only apply in strict mode.

Even freezing doesn't make an object entirely immutable since property values might be mutable:

```
const fred = Object.freeze({ name: 'Fred', luckyNumbers: [17, 29] })
fred.luckyNumbers[0] = 13 // OK—luckyNumbers isn't frozen
```

If you want complete immutability, you need to recursively freeze all dependent objects—see Exercise 8.

To find out whether an object has been protected through one of these functions, call `Object.isExtensible(obj)`, `Object.isSealed(obj)`, or `Object.isFrozen(obj)`.

11.7 Creating or Updating Objects

The `Object.create` function gives you complete control over creating a new object. Specify the prototype and the names and descriptors of all properties:

```
const obj = Object.create(proto, propertiesWithDescriptors)
```

Here, `propertiesWithDescriptors` is an object whose keys are property names and whose values are descriptors, as in Section 11.4, "Enumerating Properties" (page 228).

If you have the property names and values in an iterable of key/value pair arrays, then call the `Object.fromEntries` function to make an object with these properties:

```
let james = Object.fromEntries([['name', 'James Bond'], ['id', '007']])
```

The call `Object.assign(target, source1, source2, . . .)` copies all enumerable own properties from the sources into the target and returns the updated target:

```
james = Object.assign(james, { salary: 300000 }, genericSpy)
```

These days, there is no good reason to use `Object.assign`. Just use a spread `{ ...james, salary: 300000, ...genericSpy }`.

11.8 Accessing and Updating the Prototype

As you know, the prototype chain is a key concept in JavaScript programming. If you use the `class` and `extends` keywords, the prototype chain is established for you. In this section, you will learn how to manage it manually.

To get the prototype of an object (that is, the value of the internal [[Prototype]] slot), call:

```
const proto = Object.getPrototypeOf(obj)
```

For example,

```
Object.getPrototypeOf('Fred') === String.prototype
```

When you have an instance of a class that was created with the `new` operator, such as

```
const obj = new ClassName(args)
```

then `Object.getPrototypeOf(obj)` is the same as `ClassName.prototype`. But you can set the prototype of any object by calling

```
Object.setPrototypeOf(obj, proto)
```

We have done this briefly in Chapter 4 before introducing the new operator.

However, changing the prototype of an existing object is a slow operation for JavaScript virtual machines because they speculatively assume that object prototypes do not change. If you need to make an object with a custom prototype, it is better to use the Object.create method from Section 11.7, "Creating or Updating Objects" (page 231).

The call proto.isPrototypeOf(obj) returns true if proto is in the prototype chain of obj. Unless you set a special prototype, you can just use the instanceof operator: obj instanceof ClassName is the same as ClassName.prototype.isPrototypeOf(obj).

 NOTE: Unlike all other prototype objects, Array.prototype is actually an array!

11.9 Cloning Objects

As an application of the material of the preceding sections, let us develop a function that can make a deep copy or "clone" of an object.

A naïve approach makes use of the spread operator:

```
const cloned = { ...original } // In general, not a true clone
```

However, this only copies the enumerable properties. And it does nothing about prototypes.

We can copy the prototype and all properties:

```
const cloned = Object.create(Object.getPrototypeOf(original),
    Object.getOwnPropertyDescriptors(original)) // Better, but still shallow
```

Now the clone has the same prototype and the same properties as the original, with all property attributes faithfully copied.

But the copy is still shallow. Mutable property values are not cloned. To see the problem with shallow copies, consider this object:

```
const original = { radius: 10, center: { x: 20, y: 30 } }
```

Then the original.center and clone.center are the same object, as you can see in Figure 11-1. Mutating original also mutates clone:

```
original.center.x = 40 // clone.center.x is also changed
```

The remedy is to recursively clone all values:

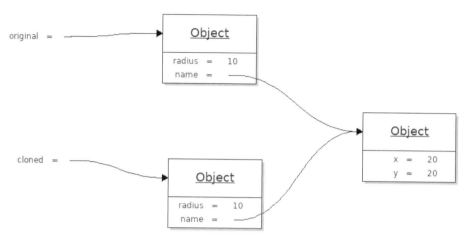

Figure 11-1 A shallow copy

```
const clone = obj => {
  if (typeof obj !== 'object' || Object.isFrozen(obj)) return obj
  const props = Object.getOwnPropertyDescriptors(obj)
  let result = Object.create(Object.getPrototypeOf(obj), props)
  for (const prop in props)
    result[prop] = clone(obj[prop])
  return result
}
```

However, this version fails when there are circular references.

Consider two people who are each other's best friend (see Figure 11-2):

```
const fred = { name: 'Fred' }
const barney = { name: 'Barney' }
fred.bestFriend = barney
barney.bestFriend = fred
```

Now suppose we recursively clone `fred`. The result is a new object

```
cloned = { name: 'Fred', bestFriend: clone(barney) }
```

What does `clone(barney)` do? It makes an object { name: 'Barney', bestFriend: clone(fred) }. But that is not right. We get an infinite recursion. And even if we didn't, we would get an object with the wrong structure. We expect an object so that

```
cloned.bestFriend.bestFriend === cloned
```

We need to refine the recursive cloning process. If an object has already been cloned, don't clone it again. Instead, use the reference to the existing clone. This can be implemented with a map from original to cloned objects. When

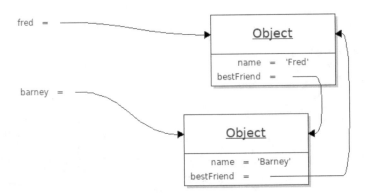

Figure 11-2 Circular references

a previously uncloned object is encountered, add the references to the original and the clone to the map. When the object has already been cloned, just look up the clone.

```
const clone = (obj, cloneRegistry = new Map()) => {
  if (typeof obj !== 'object' || Object.isFrozen(obj)) return obj
  if (cloneRegistry.has(obj)) return cloneRegistry.get(obj)
  const props = Object.getOwnPropertyDescriptors(obj)
  let result = Object.create(Object.getPrototypeOf(obj), props)
  cloneRegistry.set(obj, result)
  for (const prop in props)
    result[prop] = clone(obj[prop], cloneRegistry)
  return result
}
```

This is getting very close to the perfect clone function. However, it does not work for arrays. Calling clone([1, 2, 3]) yields an array-like object whose prototype is Array.prototype. However, it is not an array—Array.isArray returns false.

The remedy is to copy arrays with Arrays.from, not Object.create. Here is the final version:

```
const clone = (obj, cloneRegistry = new Map()) => {
  if (typeof obj !== 'object' || Object.isFrozen(obj)) return obj
  if (cloneRegistry.has(obj)) return cloneRegistry.get(obj)
  const props = Object.getOwnPropertyDescriptors(obj)
  let result = Array.isArray(obj) ? Array.from(obj)
    : Object.create(Object.getPrototypeOf(obj), props)
  cloneRegistry.set(obj, result)
  for (const prop in props)
    result[prop] = clone(obj[prop], cloneRegistry)
  return result
}
```

11.10 Function Properties

Now that we have discussed the methods of the `Object` class, let us move on to function objects. Every function that is an instance of the class `Function` has these three nonenumerable properties:

- `name`: the name with which the function was defined or, for anonymous functions, the name of the variable to which the function was assigned (see Exercise 14)

- `length`: the number of arguments, not counting a rest argument

- `prototype`: an object intended to be filled with prototype properties

Recall that in classic JavaScript, there is no difference between functions and constructors. Even in strict mode, every function can be called with `new`. Therefore, every function has a `prototype` object.

Let us look at the `prototype` object of a function more closely. It has no enumerable properties and one nonenumerable property `constructor` that points back to the constructor function—see Figure 11-3. For example, suppose we define a `class Employee`. The constructor function, `Employee`, like any function, has a `prototype` property, and

```
Employee.prototype.constructor === Employee
```

Any object inherits the `constructor` property from the prototype. Therefore, you can get the class name of an object as

```
obj.constructor.name
```

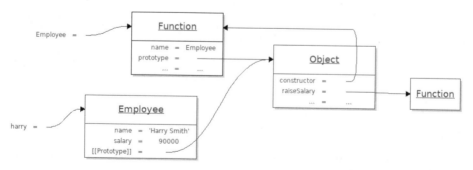

Figure 11-3 The `constructor` property

> **NOTE:** Inside a constructor, the odd-looking expression `new.target` evaluates to the function with which the object is constructed. You can use this expression to find out whether an object is constructed as an instance of a subclass, which may be of some utility—see Exercise 11. You can also tell if the function was called without `new`. In that case, `new.target === undefined`.

11.11 Binding Arguments and Invoking Methods

Given a function, the `bind` method yields a different function that has locked in the initial arguments:

```
const multiply = (x, y) => x * y
const triple = multiply.bind(null, 3)
triple(14) // Yields 42, or multiply(3, 14)
```

Because one argument of `multiply` is locked in by the `bind` method, the result is a function `triple` with a single argument.

The first argument of the `bind` method is the binding for the `this` parameter. Here is an example:

```
const isPet = Array.prototype.includes.bind(['cat', 'dog', 'fish'])
```

You can use `bind` for turning a method into a function:

```
button.onclick = this.handleClick.bind(this)
```

There is no need to use `bind` in any of these cases. You can define an explicit function:

```
const triple = y => multiply(3, y)
const isPet = x => ['cat', 'dog', 'fish'].includes(x)
button.onclick = (...args) => this.handleClick(...args)
```

The `call` method is similar to `bind`. However, all arguments are supplied, and the function or method is invoked. For example:

```
let answer = multiply.call(null, 6, 7)
let uppercased = String.prototype.toUpperCase.call('Hello')
```

Of course, it would be much simpler to call `multiply(6, 7)` or `'Hello'.toUpperCase()`.

However, there is one situation where a direct function call does not work. Consider this example:

```
const spacedOut = Array.prototype.join.call('Hello', ' ') // 'H e l l o'
```

We can't call

```
'Hello'.join(' ')
```

because `join` is not a method of the `String` class. It is a method of the `Array` class that happens to work with strings.

Finally, `apply` is like `call`, but the arguments other than `this` are in an array (or array-like object):

```
String.prototype.substring.apply('Hello', [1, 4]) // 'ell'
```

If you need to apply an arbitrary function, stored in a variable `f`, to arbitrary arguments, it is simpler to use the expression `f(...args)` instead of `f.apply(null, args)`. But if the variable `f` holds a *method*, then you have no choice. You cannot call `obj.f(...args)` and must use `f.apply(obj, args)`.

 NOTE: Before JavaScript had the `super` keyword, you had to use `bind`, `call`, or `apply` to invoke a superclass constructor—see Exercise 16.

11.12 Proxies

A proxy is an entity that appears to its user as if it were an object, but that intercepts property access, prototype access, and method invocations. When intercepted, these actions can do arbitrary work.

For example, an ORM (object-relational mapper) might support method names such as

```
const result = orm.findEmployeeById(42)
```

where `Employee` matches a database table. But if there is no matching table, the method would produce an error.

Here, `orm` is a proxy object that intercepts all method invocations. When invoked with a method whose name is `find...ById`, the intercepting code extracts the table name from the method name and makes a database lookup.

This is a powerful concept that can be used for very dynamic and powerful effects. Examples are:

* Automatic logging of property access or mutation
* Controlling property access, such as validation or protection of sensitive data
* Dynamic properties, for example DOM elements or database columns
* Making remote calls as if they were local

To construct a proxy, provide two objects:

* The *target* is the object whose operations we want to control.

- The *handler* is an object with *trap functions* that are invoked when the proxy is being manipulated.

There are thirteen possible trap functions, shown in Table 11-3.

Let us start with a simple example, where we log property reads and writes to an object obj. In the handler, we set two trap functions.

```
const obj = { name: 'Harry Smith', salary: 100000 }
const logHandler = {
  get(target, key, receiver) {
    const result = target[key]
    console.log(`get ${key.toString()} as ${result}`)
    return result
  },
  set(target, key, value, receiver) {
    console.log(`set ${key.toString()} to ${value}`)
    target[key] = value
    return true
  }
}
const proxy = new Proxy(obj, logHandler)
```

In the get and set functions, the target parameter is the target object of the proxy (here, obj). The receiver is the object whose property was accessed. That is the proxy object unless it is in the prototype chain of another object.

Now we must give the proxy, not the original object, to any code that we want to monitor.

Suppose someone changes the salary:

```
proxy.salary = 200000
```

Then a message is generated:

```
set salary to 200000
```

Operations that are not trapped are passed to the target. In our example, calling

```
delete proxy.salary
```

will delete the salary field from the target.

The JavaScript API provides one useful proxy implementation that allows you to hand a proxied object to code that you trust, and then revoke access because you don't trust what might happen later.

Obtain the proxy as:

```
const target = . . .
const p = Proxy.revocable(target, {})
```

Table 11-3 Trap Functions

Name	Description
`get(target, key, receiver)`	`receiver[key]`, `receiver.key`
`set(target, key, value, receiver)`	`receiver[key] = value`, `receiver.key = value`
`deleteProperty(target, key)`	`delete proxy[key]`, `delete proxy.key`
`has(target, key)`	`key in target`
`getPrototypeOf(target)`	`Object.getPrototypeOf(proxy)`
`setPrototypeOf(target, proto)`	`Object.setPrototypeOf(proxy, proto)`
`isExtensible(target)`	`Object.isExtensible(proxy)`
`preventExtensions(target)`	`Object.preventExtensions(proxy)`
`getOwnPropertyDescriptor(target, key)`	`Object.getOwnPropertyDescriptor(proxy, key)`, `Object.keys(proxy)`
`ownKeys(target)`	`Object.keys(proxy)`, `Object.getOwnProperty(Names|Symbols)(proxy)`
`defineProperty(target, key, descriptor)`	`Object.defineProperty(proxy, key, descriptor)`
`apply(target, thisArg, args)`	`thisArg.proxy(...args)`, `proxy(...args)`, `proxy.apply(thisArg, args)`, `proxy.call(thisArg, ...args)`
`construct(target, args, newTarget)`	`new proxy(args)`, or invocation through `super`

The `Proxy.revocable` function returns an object with a property `proxy`, the proxied object, and a `revoke` method that revokes all access to the proxy.

Hand the proxy to the code that you trust. All operations access the target object.

After you call

```
p.revoke() // p.proxy is no longer usable
```

all operations on the proxy throw an exception.

You are required to supply a handler for intercepting traps. If you are happy with the default behavior, supply an empty object. See Exercise 24 for an example with a nontrivial handler.

11.13 The Reflect Class

The Reflect class implements the thirteen trap operations from Table 11-3.

You can call the corresponding Reflect functions instead of implementing their actions manually:

```
const logHandler = {
  get(target, key, receiver) {
    console.log(`get ${key.toString()}`)
    return Reflect.get(target, key, receiver)
      // Instead of return target[key]
  },
  set(target, key, value, receiver) {
    console.log(`set ${key.toString()}`)
    return Reflect.set(target, key, value, receiver)
      // Instead of target[key] = value; return true
  }
}
```

Now suppose we want to log *all* trappable operations. Note that the code looks the same for each handler function, except for the function name. Instead of writing many almost identical handler functions, you can write a second proxy that traps the getter for the function name:

```
const getHandler = {
  get(target, trapKey, receiver) {
    return (...args) => {
      console.log(`Trapping ${trapKey}`)
      return Reflect[trapKey](...args);
    }
  }
}

const logEverythingHandler = new Proxy({}, getHandler)

const proxy = new Proxy(obj, logEverythingHandler)
```

To understand what is happening, let us look at a specific scenario.

1. The proxy user sets a property:

   ```
   proxy.name = 'Fred'
   ```

2. The appropriate method of the logEverythingHandler is invoked:

   ```
   logEverythingHandler.set(obj, 'name', 'Fred', proxy)
   ```

3. To make this call, the virtual machine must locate the set method of logEverythingHandler.

4. Since logEverythingHandler is itself a proxy, the get method of that proxy's handler is invoked:

```
getHandler.get({}, 'set', logEverythingHandler)
```

5. That call returns a function

```
(...args) => { console.log(`Trapping set`); return Reflect.set(...args) }
```

as the value of `logEverythingHandler.set`.

6. Now the function call that was started in step 2 can proceed. The function is invoked with arguments `(obj, 'name', 'Fred', proxy)`.

7. A console message is printed, followed by the call

```
Reflect.set(obj, 'name', 'Fred', proxy)
```

8. This call causes `obj.name` to be set to `'Fred'`.

If you want to log the arguments to the trap functions (which include the target and proxy), you have to be very careful to avoid infinite recursion. One way to do this is to keep a map of known objects that are printed by name, instead of calling `toString` which would cause further trap calls.

```
const knownObjects = new WeakMap()

const stringify = x => {
  if (knownObjects.has(x))
    return knownObjects.get(x)
  else
    return JSON.stringify(x)
}

const logEverything = (name, obj) => {
  knownObjects.set(obj, name)
  const getHandler = {
    get(target, trapKey, receiver) {
      return (...args) => {
        console.log(`Trapping ${trapKey}(${args.map(stringify)})`)
        return Reflect[trapKey](...args);
      }
    }
  }

  const result = new Proxy(obj, new Proxy({}, getHandler))
  knownObjects.set(result, `proxy of ${name}`)
  return result
}
```

Now you can call:

```
const fred = { name: 'Fred' }
const proxyOfFred = logEverything('fred', fred)
proxyOfFred.age = 42
```

You will see the following logging statements:

```
Trapping set(fred,age,42,proxy of fred)
Trapping getOwnPropertyDescriptor(fred,age)
Trapping defineProperty(fred,"age",{"value":42,
  "writable":true,"enumerable":true,"configurable":true})
```

The `Reflect` class was designed for use with proxies, but three of its methods are useful on their own because they are a bit more convenient than their classic counterparts:

1. `Reflect.deleteProperty` returns a `boolean` to tell whether the deletion was successful. The `delete` operator doesn't.

2. `Reflect.defineProperty` returns a `boolean` to indicate whether the definition succeeded. `Object.defineProperty` throws an exception upon failure.

3. `Reflect.apply(f, thisArg, args)` is guaranteed to call `Function.prototype.apply`, but `f.apply(thisArg, args)` might not since the `apply` property can be redefined.

11.14 Proxy Invariants

When you implement proxy operations, the virtual machine checks that they do not yield nonsense values. For example:

- `construct` must return an object.
- `getOwnPropertyDescriptor` must return a descriptor object or `undefined`.
- `getPrototypeOf` must return an object or `null`.

In addition, the virtual machine carries out consistency checks for proxy operations. A proxy must respect certain aspects of its target, including:

- Nonwritable target properties
- Nonconfigurable target properties
- Nonextensible targets

The ECMAScript specification describes "invariants" that a proxy must fulfill. For example, the description of the `get` operation on proxies includes this requirement: "The value reported (by `get`) for a property must be the same as the value of the corresponding target object property if the target object property is a nonwritable, nonconfigurable own data property."

Similarly, if a target property is not configurable, then `has` cannot hide it. If a target is not extensible, then the `getPrototypeOf` operation must yield the actual prototype, and `has` and `getOwnPropertyDescriptor` must report the actual properties.

These invariants make sense when a proxy augments an existing object without adding any properties of its own. Unfortunately, they force us to lie about the properties that the proxy adds. Consider an array-like object that stores a range of values, say the integers between 10 and 99. There is no need to store the values. We can compute them dynamically. That's what proxies are good at. Here is a function that creates such a range proxy:

```
const createRange = (start, end) => {
  const isIndex = key =>
    typeof key === 'string' && /^[0-9]+$/.test(key) && parseInt(key) < end - start

  return new Proxy({}, {
    get: (target, key, receiver) => {
      if (isIndex(key)) {
        return start + parseInt(key)
      } else {
        return Reflect.get(target, key, receiver)
      }
    }
  })
}
```

The `get` trap produces range values on demand:

```
const range = createRange(10, 100)
console.log(range[10]) // 20
```

However, we can't yet iterate over the keys:

```
console.log(Object.keys(range)) // []
```

That is not surprising. We first need to define the `ownKeys` trap:

```
ownKeys: target => {
  const result = Reflect.ownKeys(target)
  for (let i = 0; i < end - start; i++)
    result.push(String(i))
  return result
}
```

Unfortunately, even after adding the `ownKeys` trap to the handler, `Object.keys(range)` yields an empty array.

To fix this, we need to provide property descriptors for the index properties:

```
getOwnPropertyDescriptor: (target, key) => {
  if (isIndex(key)) {
    return {
      value: start + Number(key),
      writable: false,
      enumerable: true,
      configurable: true // Not what we actually want
    }
  } else {
```

```
        return Reflect.getOwnPropertyDescriptor(target, key)
    }
}
```

Now `Object.keys` yields an array containing `'10'` to `'99'`. However, there is a fly in the ointment. The index properties must be configurable. Otherwise, the invariant rules kick in. You cannot report a nonconfigurable property that isn't already present in the target. (Our target is an empty object.) We don't actually want index properties to be configurable, but our hands are tied. If we want to prohibit deletion or reconfiguration of index properties, we need to provide additional traps—see Exercise 27.

As you can see, implementing dynamic properties in proxies is not for the faint of heart. Whenever possible, situate properties in the proxy target. For example, the range proxy should have a `length` property and a `toString` method. Just add those to the target object and don't handle them in the traps—see Exercise 28.

Exercises

1. Why is the `Symbol.toPrimitive` method for the `Percent` class in Section 11.2, "Customization with Symbol Properties" (page 223), unsatisfactory? Try adding and multiplying percent values. Why can't you provide a fix that works both for percent arithmetic and string concatenation?

2. A "glob pattern" is a pattern for matching file names. In its simplest form, `*` matches any sequence of characters other than the / path separator, and `?` matches a single character. Implement a class `Glob`. Using well-known symbols, enable the use of glob pattern for the string methods `match`, `matchAll`, `replace`, `search`, and `split`.

3. As described in Table 11-1, you can change the behavior of `x instanceof y` by ensuring that `y` has a well-known symbol property. Make it so that `x instanceof Natural` checks whether `x` is an integer ≥ 0, and `x instanceof Range(a, b)` checks if `x` is an integer in the given range. I am not saying this is a good idea, but it is interesting that it can be done.

4. Define a class `Person` so that for it and any subclasses, the `toString` method returns [object *Classname*].

5. Look at the output of the following calls and explain the results:

```
Object.getOwnPropertyDescriptors([1,2,3])
Object.getOwnPropertyDescriptors([1,2,3].constructor)
Object.getOwnPropertyDescriptors([1,2,3].prototype)
```

6. Suppose you seal an object by calling `Object.seal(obj)`. Trying to set a nonexistent property throws an exception in strict mode. But you can still read nonexistent properties without an exception. Write a function `reallySeal` so that reading or writing nonexistent properties on the returned object throws an exception. Hint: Proxies.

7. Google for "JavaScript object clone" and review a few blog articles and StackOverflow answers. How many of them work correctly with shared mutable state and circular references?

8. Write a function `freezeCompletely` that freezes an object and recursively all of its property values. Handle cyclic dependencies.

9. Using `Object.getOwnPropertyDescriptors`, find all properties of the array [1, 2, 3], the `Array` function, and of `Array.prototype`. Why do all three have a `length` property?

10. Construct a new string object as `new String('Fred')` and set its prototype to `Array.prototype`. Which methods can you successfully apply to the object? Start by trying `map` and `reverse`.

11. The `new.target` expression, introduced in the note at the end of Section 11.10, "Function Properties" (page 235), is set to the constructor function when an object is constructed with the `new` operator. Make use of this feature by designing an abstract class `Person` that cannot be instantiated with `new`. However, allow instantiation of concrete subclasses such as `Employee`.

12. How can one enforce abstract classes with the `constructor` property of the prototype instead of the technique of the preceding exercise? Which is more robust?

13. The `new.target` expression is `undefined` if a function is called without `new`. What is an easier way of determining this situation in strict mode?

14. Explore the `name` property of functions. What is it set to when the function is defined with a name? Without a name but assigned to a local variable? What about anonymous functions that are passed as arguments or returned as function results? What about arrow expressions?

15. In Section 11.11, "Binding Arguments and Invoking Methods" (page 236), you saw that `call` is necessary to invoke a method from a different class. Provide a similar example for `bind`.

16. In this exercise, you will explore how JavaScript programmers had to implement inheritance before the `extends` and `super` keywords. You are given a constructor function

```
function Employee(name, salary) {
  this.name = name
  this.salary = salary
}
```

Methods are added to the prototype.

```
Employee.prototype.raiseSalary = function(percent) {
  this.salary *= 1 + percent / 100
}
```

Now implement a `Manager` subclass without using the `extends` and `super` keywords. Use `Object.setPrototypeOf` to set the prototype of `Manager.prototype`. In the `Manager` constructor, you need to invoke the `Employee` constructor on the *existing* this object instead of creating a new one. Use the `bind` method described in Section 11.11, "Binding Arguments and Invoking Methods" (page 236).

17. Attempting to solve the preceding exercise, Fritzi sets

    ```
    Manager.prototype = Employee.prototype
    ```

    instead of using `Object.setPrototypeOf`. What are the unhappy results of this decision?

18. As noted at the end of Section 11.8, "Accessing and Updating the Prototype" (page 231), `Array.prototype` is actually an array. Verify this with `Array.isArray`. Why is `[] instanceof Array` false? What happens to arrays if you add elements to the `Array.prototype` array?

19. Use the logging proxy from Section 11.12, "Proxies" (page 237), to monitor reading and writing of array elements. What happens when you read or write an element? The `length` property? What happens if you inspect the proxy object in the console by typing its name?

20. Isn't it annoying when one misspells the name of a property or method? Using a proxy, implement autocorrect. Pick the closest existing name. You need to use some measure of closeness for strings, such as the number of common characters or the Levenshtein edit distance.

21. It is possible to change the behavior of objects, arrays, or strings by overriding methods of the `Object`, `Array`, or `String` class. Implement a proxy that disallows such overrides.

22. An expression `obj.prop1.prop2.prop3` will throw an exception if any of the intermediate properties yield `null` or `undefined`. Let's solve that nuisance with proxies. First, define a safe object that returns itself when looking up any property. Next, define a function so that `safe(obj)` is a proxy for `obj` that returns the safe object when looking up any property whose

value is `null` or `undefined`. Extra credit if you can extend this technique to method calls so that `safe(obj).m1().m2().m3()` doesn't throw an exception if any of the intermediate methods return `null` or `undefined`.

23. Create a proxy that supports an XPath-like syntax for finding elements in an HTML or XML document.

```
const root = makeRootProxy(document)
const firstItemInSecondList = root.html.body.ul[2].li[1]
```

24. Make a revocable proxy, as described in Section 11.12, "Proxies" (page 237), that makes all properties read-only until access is revoked entirely.

25. In Section 11.14, "Proxy Invariants" (page 242), the `getOwnPropertyDescriptor` trap returns a descriptor for index properties whose `configurable` attribute is `true`. What happens if you set it to `false`?

26. Debug the `ownKeys` trap in Section 11.14, "Proxy Invariants" (page 242), by logging the calls to the {} target, using the `logEverything` method of Section 11.13, "The `Reflect` Class" (page 240). Also place a logging call into the `getOwnPropertyDescriptor` trap. Now read through Section 9.5.11 of the ECMAScript 2020 standard. Does the implementation follow the algorithm of the standard?

27. Add traps to the range proxy in Section 11.14, "Proxy Invariants" (page 242) to prevent deleting or modifying the index properties. Also add a `has` trap.

28. Add a `length` property and a `toString` method to the range proxy in Section 11.14, "Proxy Invariants" (page 242). Add it to the proxy target and don't provide special handling in the traps. Provide appropriate attributes.

29. The range proxy in Section 11.14, "Proxy Invariants" (page 242), is instantiated by calling the `createRange` function. Use a constructor function so that a user can call `new Range(10, 100)` and get a proxy instance that looks as if it was an instance of a `Range` class.

30. Continue the preceding exercise so that the `Range` class extends `Array`. Be sure to set the `Symbol.species` property, as described in Section 11.2.3, "Species" (page 225).

Iterators and Generators

Topics in This Chapter

Chapter 12

In this short chapter, you will learn how to implement iterators that can be used in the `for of` loop and array spreads. You will be able to work with iterators in your own code.

Implementing an iterator can be a bit tedious, but generators greatly simplify this task. A generator is a function that can yield multiple values, suspending after each value is produced and resuming when the next value is requested. Generators are also the building blocks of callback-free asynchronous programming.

All of the material in this chapter is at an advanced level.

12.1 Iterable Values

Perhaps the most common use of iterable values in JavaScript is the `for of` loop. For example, arrays are iterable. The loop

```
for (const element of [1, 2, 7, 9])
```

iterates over the elements of the given array. Strings are also iterable, and the loop

```
for (const ch of 'Hello')
```

iterates over the code points of the given string.

The following values are iterable:

- Arrays and strings
- Sets and maps
- The objects returned by the keys, values, and entries methods of arrays, typed arrays, sets, and maps (but not Object)
- DOM data structures such as the one returned by the call document .querySelectorAll('div')

In general, a value is iterable if it has a method with key Symbol.iterator that yields an iterator object:

```
const helloIter = 'Hello'[Symbol.iterator]()
```

An iterator object has a next method that yields an object containing the next value and an indicator whether the iteration is finished:

```
helloIter.next() // Yields { value: 'H', done: false }
helloIter.next() // Yields { value: 'e', done: false }
. . .
helloIter.next() // Yields { value: 'o', done: false }
helloIter.next() // Yields { value: undefined, done: true }
```

In a loop

```
for (const v of iterable)
```

an iterator object is obtained by calling iterable[Symbol.iterator](). The next method of that object is invoked in each loop iteration. Each time, it yields an object { value: . . ., done: . . . }. As long as done is false, the variable v is set to the object's value property. Once done is true, the for of loop exits.

Here is a list of situations in which iterables are used in JavaScript:

- As already discussed, in a loop for (const v of iterable)
- In an array spread: [...iterable]
- With array destructuring: [first, second, third] = iterable
- With the function Array.from(iterable)
- With set and map constructors: new Set(iterable)
- With the yield* directive that you will see later in this chapter
- In any place where a programmer makes use of the iterator constructed by calling the function that is returned from iterable[Symbol.iterator]()

12.2 Implementing an Iterable

In this section, you will see how to create iterable objects that can appear in for of loops, array spreads, and so on.

It is best to work through a concrete example first. Let us implement an iterable Range class whose iterator yields values between two given bounds.

```
class Range {
  constructor(start, end) {
    this.start = start
    this.end = end
  }
  . . .
}
```

If we have a Range instance, it should be usable in a for of loop:

```
for (const element of new Range(10, 20))
  console.log(element) // Prints 10 11 . . . 19
```

An iterable object must have a method with name Symbol.iterator. Since the method name is not a string, it is enclosed in brackets:

```
class Range {
  . . .
  [Symbol.iterator]() { . . . }
}
```

That method returns an object with a next method. We define a second class to produce those objects.

```
class RangeIterator {
  constructor(current, last) {
    this.current = current
    this.last = last
  }
  next() { . . . }
}

class Range {
  . . .
  [Symbol.iterator]() { return new RangeIterator(this.start, this.end) }
}
```

The next method returns objects of the form { value: . . ., done: . . . }, like this:

```
next() {
  . . .
  if (. . .) {
    return { value: some value, done: false }
  } else {
    return { value: undefined, done: true }
  }
}
```

If you like, you can omit done: false and value: undefined.

In our example:

```
class RangeIterator {
  . . .
  next() {
    if (this.current < this.last) {
      const result = { value: this.current }
      this.current++
      return result
    } else {
      return { done: true }
    }
  }
}
```

By explicitly defining two classes, it becomes obvious that the Symbol.iterator method yields an instance of a different class with a next method.

Alternatively, you can create the iterator objects on the fly:

```
class Range {
  constructor(start, end) {
    this.start = start
    this.end = end
  }
  [Symbol.iterator]() {
    let current = this.start
    let last = this.end
    return {
      next() {
        if (current < last) {
          const result = { value: current }
          current++
          return result
        } else {
          return { done: true }
        }
      }
    }
  }
}
```

The Symbol.iterator method yields an object with a next method, which yields the { value: current } and { done: true } objects.

This is more compact but perhaps not quite as easy to read.

12.3 Closeable Iterators

If an iterator object has a method called return (!), it is *closeable*. The return method is called when the iteration is terminated prematurely. For example, suppose lines(filename) is an iterable over the lines of a file. Now consider this function:

```
const find = (filename, target) => {
  for (line of lines(filename)) {
    if (line.contains(target)) {
      return line // iterator.return() called
    }
  } // iterator.return() not called
}
```

The return method of the iterator is called when the loop is abruptly exited through a return, throw, break, or labeled continue statement. In this example, the iterator's return method is called if a line contains the target string.

If no line contains the target string, the for of loop returns normally, and the return method is not called.

If you use an iterator and manually call next on it, and if you abandon it before having received done: true, then you should call iterator.return().

Of course, you should never call next after return.

Implementing a closeable iterator is a bit unpleasant because you need to put the closing logic in two places: the call to return and the branch of the next method that detects the absence of further values.

Here is a skeleton implementation of a function that yields an iterable over the lines of a file. Exercise 6 asks you to flesh out the details.

```
const lines = filename => {
  const file = . . . // Open the file
  return {
    [Symbol.iterator]: () => ({
      next: () => {
        if (done) {
          . . . // Close the file
          return { done: true }
        } else {
          const line = . . . // Read a line
          return { value: line }
        }
      },
      ['return']: () => {
        . . . // Close the file
        return { done: true } // Must return an object
      }
    })
  }
}
```

12.4 Generators

In the previous sections, you saw how to implement an iterator whose `next` method produces one value at a time. The implementation can be tedious. The iterator needs to remember some amount of state between successive calls to `next`. Even the case of a simple range was not trivial. Unfortunately, you can't just use a loop:

```
for (let i = start; i < end; i++)
    . . .
```

That doesn't work because the values are produced all together, not one at a time.

However, in a *generator function*, you can do just that:

```
function* rangeGenerator(start, end) {
  for (let i = start; i < end; i++)
    yield i
}
```

The `yield` keyword produces a value, but it does not exit the function. The function is suspended after each yielded value. When the next value is required, the function continues after the `yield` statement and eventually yields another value.

The `*` symbol tags this function as a generator function. Unlike a regular function that can produce only one result when it returns, a generator function produces a result each time the `yield` statement is executed.

When you invoke a generator function, the function body does not yet start executing. Instead, you obtain an iterator object:

```
const rangeIter = rangeGenerator(10, 20)
```

Like any iterator, the `rangeIter` object has a `next` method. When you call `next` for the first time, the generator function body runs until it reaches a `yield` statement. Then the `next` method returns an object { value: *yielded value*, done: false }.

```
let nextResult = rangeIter.next() // { value: 10, done: false }
```

From now on, each time the `next` method is invoked, execution of the generator function resumes at the last `yield` statement and continues until another `yield` statement is reached.

```
nextResult = rangeIter.next() // { value: 11, done: false }
    . . .
nextResult = rangeIter.next() // { value: 19, done: false }
```

When the generator function returns, the `next` method returns { value: *returned value*, done: true } to indicate that the iteration is complete.

```
nextResult = rangeIter.next() // { value: undefined, done: true }
```

If at any time the generator function code throws an exception, the call to `next` terminates with that exception.

 NOTE: In JavaScript, `yield` is shallow—you can only yield inside the generator function, not in a function that the generator function calls.

A generator function can be a named or anonymous function:

```
function* myGenerator(. . .) { . . . }
const myGenerator = function* (. . .) { . . . }
```

If an object property or a method is a generator function, prefix it with an asterisk:

```
const myObject = { * myGenerator(. . .) { . . . }, . . . }
  // Syntactic sugar for myGenerator: function* (. . .) { . . . }

class MyClass {
  * myGenerator(. . .) { . . . }
  . . .
}
```

Arrow functions cannot be generators.

You can place an invocation of a generator function everywhere an iterable is accepted—in `for of` statements, array spreads, and so on:

```
[...rangeGenerator(10, 15)] // The array [10, 11, 12, 13, 14]
```

12.5 Nested Yield

Suppose we want to iterate over all elements of an array. Of course, an array is already iterable, but let's provide a generator anyway. The implementation is straightforward:

```
function* arrayGenerator(arr) {
  for (const element of arr)
    yield element
}
```

What if `arr` is [1, [2, 3, 4], 5], with an element that is itself an array? In this case, we would like to flatten out the traversal and yield the elements 1, 2, 3, 4, and 5 in turn. A first attempt might be:

```
function* flatArrayGenerator(arr) {
  for (const element of arr)
    if (Array.isArray(element)) {
      arrayGenerator(element) // Error—does not yield any elements
    } else {
      yield element
    }
}
```

However, this approach does not work. The call

```
arrayGenerator(element)
```

does not execute the body of the arrayGenerator generator function. It merely obtains and discards the iterator. The call

```
const result = [...flatArrayGenerator([1, [2, 3, 4], 5])]
```

sets result to the array [1, 5].

If you want to obtain all values of a generator inside a generator function, you need to use a yield* statement:

```
function* flatArrayGenerator(arr) {
  for (const element of arr)
    if (Array.isArray(element)) {
      yield* arrayGenerator(element) // Yields the generated elements one at a time
    } else {
      yield element
    }
}
```

Now the call

```
const result = [...flatArrayGenerator([1, [2, 3, 4], 5])]
```

yields the flattened array [1, 2, 3, 4, 5].

However, if the array is deeply nested, the result is still not correct: flatArrayGenerator([1, [2, [3, 4], 5], 6]) yields the values 1, 2, [3, 4], 5, and 6.

The remedy is simple—call flatArrayGenerator recursively:

```
function* flatArrayGenerator(arr) {
  for (const element of arr)
    if (Array.isArray(element)) {
      yield* flatArrayGenerator(element)
    } else {
      yield element
    }
}
```

The point of this example is that yield* overcomes a limitation of generator functions in JavaScript. Every yield statement must be in the generator function itself. It cannot be in a function that is called from a generator function. The `yield*` statement takes care of the situation where one generator function calls another, splicing in the yielded values of the invoked generator.

The `yield*` statement also splices in the values of an iterable, yielding one value in each call to `next`. That means we could have simply defined our `arrayGenerator` as:

```
function* arrayGenerator(arr) {
  yield* arr
}
```

 NOTE: A generator function can return a value when it is finished, in addition to yielding values:

```
function* arrayGenerator(arr) {
  for (const element of arr)
    yield element
  return arr.length
}
```

The return value is included with the last iteration result, when the `done` property is `true`. When iterating over the yielded values, the return value is ignored. But you can capture it as the value of a `yield*` expression inside another generator function:

```
function* elementsFollowedByLength(arr) {
  const len = yield* arrayGenerator(arr);
  yield len;
}
```

12.6 Generators as Consumers

Up to this point, we used generators to produce a sequence of values. Generators can also consume values. When calling `next` with an argument, it becomes the value of the `yield` expression:

```
function* sumGenerator() {
  let sum = 0
  while (true) {
    let nextValue = yield sum
    sum += nextValue
  }
}
```

Here, the value of the `yield sum` expression is stored in the `nextValue` variable and added to the sum. There is a two-way communication:

- The generator receives values from the caller of the `next` method and accumulates them.

- The generator sends the current sum to the caller of the next method.

 CAUTION: You need an initial call to next in order to get to the first yield statement. Then you can start calling next with values that are consumed by the generator.

When calling the method named return (!), the generator is shut down, and further calls to next yield { value: undefined, done: true }.

Here is a complete sequence of calls to the iterator:

```
const accum = sumGenerator()
accum.next() // Advance to first yield
let result = accum.next(3) // Returns { value: 3, done: false }
result = accum.next(4) // Returns { value: 7, done: false }
result = accum.next(5) // Returns { value: 12, done: false }
accum.return() // Shuts down and returns { value: undefined, done: true }
```

Calling throw(error) on the iterator object causes the error to be thrown in the pending yield expression. If the generator function catches the error and progresses to a yield or return statement, the throw method returns a { value: . . ., done: . . . } object. If the generator function terminates because the error was not caught, or because another error was thrown, then the throw method throws that error.

In other words, throw is exactly like next, except that it causes the yield expression to throw an error instead of yielding a value.

To demonstrate throw, consider the following variation of the sum generator:

```
function* sumGenerator() {
  let sum = 0
  while (true) {
    try {
      let nextValue = yield sum
      sum += nextValue
    } catch {
      sum = 0
    }
  }
}
```

Calling throw resets the accumulated value:

```
const accum = sumGenerator()
accum.next() // Advance to first yield
let result = accum.next(3)
result = accum.next(4)
result = accum.next(5)
accum.throw() // Returns { value: 0, done; false }
```

If you call `throw` before the first `yield` expression was reached, the generator is shut down and the error is thrown by the call to the `throw` method.

12.7 Generators and Asynchronous Processing

Having read the preceding section, you may wonder why you would ever want a generator that accumulates values. There are much easier ways of computing a sum. Such generators become far more interesting with asynchronous programming.

When you read data from a web page, the data is not available instantly. As you saw in Chapter 9, a JavaScript program has a single thread of execution. If you wait for something to happen, your program can do nothing else. Therefore, web requests are asynchronous. You receive a callback when the requested data is available. As an example, here we obtain a true random number, using the `XMLHttpRequest` class that is available in web browsers (but not Node.js):

```
const url = 'https://www.random.org/integers/?num=1&min=1&max=1000000000\
&col=1&base=10&format=plain&rnd=new'
const req = new XMLHttpRequest();
req.open('GET', url)
req.addEventListener('load', () => console.log(req.response)) // Callback
req.send()
```

Let's put this into a function. The function has a handler function as parameter that is invoked when the random number has been received:

```
const trueRandom = handler => {
  const url = 'https://www.random.org/integers/?num=1&min=1&max=1000000000\
&col=1&base=10&format=plain&rnd=new'
  const req = new XMLHttpRequest();
  req.open('GET', url)
  req.addEventListener('load', () => handler(parseInt(req.response)))
  req.send()
}
```

Now we can get a random integer easily:

```
trueRandom(receivedValue => console.log(receivedValue))
```

But suppose we want to add three such random numbers. Then we need to make three calls and compute the sum when all answers are ready. This is not for the faint of heart:

```
trueRandom(first =>
  trueRandom(second =>
    trueRandom(third => console.log(first + second + third))))
```

Of course, as you have seen in Chapter 9, you can use promises and the async/await syntax to deal with this situation. Promises are actually built upon generators. This section gives you a brief outline of how generators can help with asynchronous processing.

Let us use a generator to provide the illusion of synchronous calls. We will shortly define a function nextTrueRandom that delivers a random integer into a generator. Here is the generator:

```
function* main() {
  const first = yield nextTrueRandom()
  const second = yield nextTrueRandom()
  const third = yield nextTrueRandom()
  console.log(first + second + third)
}
```

Launching the generator yields an iterator:

```
const iter = main()
```

That is the iterator into which we will feed values as they become available:

```
const nextTrueRandom = () => {
  trueRandom(receivedValue => iter.next(receivedValue))
}
```

Just one thing remains to be done. The iteration needs to start:

```
iter.next() // Kick it off
```

Now the main function starts executing. It calls nextTrueRandom and then suspends in the yield expression until someone calls next on the iterator.

That call to next doesn't happen until the asynchronous data is available. And this is where generators get interesting. They allow us to suspend a calculation and continue it later when a value is available. Eventually, the value is obtained, and the nextTrueRandom function calls iter.next(receivedValue). That value is stored in first.

Then execution suspends again in the second yield expression, and so on. Eventually we have all three values and can compute their sum.

For a brief period, after generators were added in ES7, they were touted as a solution for avoiding asynchronous callbacks. However, as you have seen, the setup is not very intuitive. It is much easier to use promises and the async/await syntax of Chapter 9. Value-consuming generators were an important stepping stone towards promises, but they are not commonly used by application programmers.

12.8 Async Generators and Iterators

A generator function yields values that you can retrieve with an iterator. Each time you call iter.next(), the generator runs until the next yield statement and then suspends itself.

An *async generator* is similar to a generator function, but you are allowed to use the await operator inside the body. Conceptually, an async generator produces a sequence of values in the future.

To declare an async generator, use both the async keyword and the * that denotes a generator function:

```
async function* loadHanafudaImages(month) {
  for (let i = 1; i <= 4; i++) {
    const img = await loadImage(`hanafuda/${month}-${i}.png`)
    yield img
  }
}
```

When you call an async generator, you get an iterator. However, when you call next on the iterator, the next value may not yet be available. It may not even be known whether the iteration still continues. Therefore, next returns a promise for a { value: . . ., done: . . . } object.

Of course, you can retrieve the promised values from the iterator, but that is tedious—see Exercise 16. It is easier to use a special form of the for loop, the for await of loop:

```
for await (const img of loadHanafudaImages(month)) {
  imgdiv.appendChild(img)
}
```

The for await of loop must be inside an async function because it invokes the await operator on each generated promise.

If any of the promises is rejected, the for await of loop throws an exception, and the iteration terminates.

The for await of loop works with any *async iterable*. An async iterable has a property with key Symbol.asyncIterator whose value is a function yielding an *async iterator*. An async iterator has a next method yielding promises for { value: . . ., done: . . . } objects. Async generators are the most convenient mechanism for producing async iterables, but you can also implement them by hand—see Exercise 17.

CAUTION: Async iterables are *not iterables*. They do not work with the `for of` loop, spreads, or destructuring. For example, you cannot do this:

```
const results = [...loadHanafudaImages(month)]
    // Error, not an array of promises
for (const p of loadHanafudaImages(month)) p.then(imgdiv.appendChild(img))
    // Error, not a loop over the promises
```

 NOTE: On the other hand, the `for await of` loop works with regular iterables. It simply does the same as the `for of` loop.

Here is an example of an async iterable that produces a range of numbers with a delay between them:

```
class TimedRange {
  constructor(start, end, delay) {
    this.start = start
    this.end = end
    this.delay = delay
  }

  async *[Symbol.asyncIterator]() {
    for (let current = this.start; current < this.end; current++) {
      yield await produceAfterDelay(current, this.delay)
    }
  }
}
```

The implementation of the iterator function is straightforward, thanks to the `await` and `yield` syntax. Simply wait until the next value is available, and then yield it.

You can consume the results in a `for await of` loop:

```
let r = new TimedRange(1, 10, 1000)
for await (const e of r) console.log(e)
```

Let us conclude with a more realistic example. Many APIs have a `page` parameter that allows fetching of successive pages of data, for example:

```
https://chroniclingamerica.loc.gov/search/titles/results/
    ?terms=michigan&format=json&page=5
```

Here we page through the results of such a query:

```
async function* loadResults(url) {
  let page = 0
  try {
    while (true) {
      page++
      const response = await fetch(`${url}&page=${page}`)
      yield await response.json()
    }
  } catch {
    // End iteration
  }
}
```

If we call the generator from a for async of loop, we traverse all responses. By itself, that is not so exciting. We could have done that traversal in an async function, without using a generator.

However, one can use this generator as a building block for other useful functions. Normally, an API uses paging because it is expected that the client will stop after having found a satisfactory result. Here is how to implement such a search, stopping as soon as the callback returns true:

```
const findResult = async (queryURL, callback) => {
  for await (const result of loadResults(queryURL)) {
    if (callback(result)) return result
  }
  return undefined
}
```

Note two things. First, the findResult function is not a generator but merely an async function. By putting the hard part of a computation into an async generator, it can be consumed by any async function. Moreover, crucially, the fetching of the pages is lazy. As soon as a match is found, the findResult function exits, abandoning the generator without fetching further pages.

Exercises

1. Implement a function that receives an iterable value and prints every other element.

2. Implement a function that receives an iterable value and returns another iterable value that yields every other element.

3. Implement an iterable value that yields an infinite number of die tosses, random integers between 1 and 6. Write it in a single line:

```
const dieTosses = { . . . }
```

4. Write a function `dieTosses(n)` that returns an iterable yielding `n` random integers between `1` and `6`.

5. What is wrong with this implementation of a `Range` iterator?

```
class Range {
  constructor(start, end) {
    this.start = start
    this.end = end
  }
  [Symbol.iterator]() {
    let current = this.start
    return {
      next() {
        current++
        return current <= this.end ? { value: current - 1 } : { done: true }
      }
    }
  }
}
```

6. Complete the implementation of the file iterator in Section 12.3, "Closeable Iterators" (page 252). Use the `openSync`, `readSync`, and `closeSync` methods of the Node.js `fs` module (https://nodejs.org/api/fs.html). Note that you need to close the file in both the `next` and the `return` functions. You can avoid the code duplication by calling `return` from `next`.

7. Change the `arrayGenerator` function of Section 12.5, "Nested Yield" (page 255), so that for array elements that are strings, each character is yielded separately.

8. Enhance the preceding exercise so that the values of any iterable array element are yielded separately.

9. Using a generator, produce a tree iterator that visits the nodes of a tree one at a time. If you are familiar with the DOM API, visit the nodes of a DOM document. Otherwise, make your own tree class.

10. Using a generator and Heap's algorithm (https://en.wikipedia.org/wiki/Heap%27s_algorithm), produce an iterator that yields all permutations of an array. For example, if the array has values [1, 2, 3], your iterator should produce [1, 2, 3], [1, 3, 2], [2, 3, 1], [2, 1, 3], [3, 1, 2], and [3, 2, 1] (not necessarily in this order).

11. How can you make the `return` method of a generator object return a value? Would you ever want to?

12. Section 12.6, "Generators as Consumers" (page 257), lists a number of different scenarios for the behavior of the `throw` method. Make a table that

summarizes each scenario and the expected behavior. Provide brief programs to demonstrate the behavior in each scenario.

13. Write a function `trueRandomSum(n, handler)` that computes the sum of `n` random numbers and passes it to the given handler. Use a generator, following Section 12.6, "Generators as Consumers" (page 257).

14. Repeat the preceding exercise without using a generator.

15. Consider this `async` function:

```
const putTwoImages = async (url1, url2, element) => {
  const img1 = await loadImage(url1)
  element.appendChild(img1)
  const img2 = await loadImage(url2)
  element.appendChild(img2)
  return element
}
```

And now consider this generator function yielding promises:

```
function* putTwoImagesGen(url1, url2, element) {
  const img1 = yield loadImage(url1)
  element.appendChild(img1)
  const img2 = yield loadImage(url2)
  element.appendChild(img2)
  return element
}
```

This is essentially the transformation that the JavaScript compiler does for any `async` function. Now fill in the ___ to complete a function `genToPromise` that takes an arbitrary generator yielding promises and turns it into a `Promise`:

```
const genToPromise = gen => {
  const iter = gen()
  const nextPromise = arg => {
    const result = ___
    if (result.done) {
      return Promise.resolve(___)
    } else {
      return Promise.resolve(___).then(___)
    }
  }

  return nextPromise()
}
```

16. Use the iterator returned from the `loadHanafudaImages` generator function in Section 12.8, "Async Generators and Iterators" (page 261), to add all images to a DOM element. Do not use a `for await of` loop.

17. Implement the `TimedRange` class from Section 12.8, "Async Generators and Iterators" (page 261), without using a generator function. Produce the promise-yielding iterator by hand.

18. One plausible use of the `for await of` loop is with `Promise.all`. Suppose you have an array of image URLs. Turn them into an array of promises:

    ```
    const imgPromises = urls.map(loadImage)
    ```

    Run them in parallel, await the resulting promise, and iterate over the responses. Which of the four loops below run without errors? Which one should you use?

    ```
    for (const img of Promise.all(imgPromises)) element.appendChild(img)
    for await (const img of Promise.all(imgPromises)) element.appendChild(img)
    for (const img of await Promise.all(imgPromises)) element.appendChild(img)
    for await (const img of await Promise.all(imgPromises)) element.appendChild(img)
    ```

19. Which of these loops run without errors? For those that do, how does their behavior differ from those of the preceding exercise?

    ```
    for (const p of urls.map(loadImage))
      p.then(img => element.appendChild(img))
    for (const p of urls.map(async url => await loadImage(url)))
      element.appendChild(await p)
    for await (const img of urls.map(url => await loadImage(url)))
      element.appendChild(img)
    for (const img of await urls.map(loadImage))
      element.appendChild(img)
    for await (const img of await urls.map(loadImage))
      element.appendChild(img)
    ```

20. Some APIs (such as the GitHub API described at `https://developer.github.com/v3/guides/traversing-with-pagination`) yield paged results with a slightly different mechanism than that of the example in Section 12.8, "Async Generators and Iterators" (page 261). The `Link` header of each response contains a URL to navigate to the next result. You can retrieve it as:

    ```
    let nextURL
      = response.headers.get('Link').match(/<(?<next>.*?)>; rel="next"/).groups.next;
    ```

    Adapt the `loadResults` generator function to this mechanism.

    Extra credit if you can demystify the regular expression.

An Introduction to TypeScript

Topics in This Chapter

Chapter 13

TypeScript is a superset of JavaScript that adds compile-time typing. You annotate variables and functions with their expected types, and TypeScript reports an error whenever your code violates the type rules. Generally, that is a good thing. It is far less costly to fix compile-time errors than to debug a misbehaving program. Moreover, when you provide type information, your development tools can give you better support with autocompletion and refactoring.

This chapter contains a concise introduction into the main features of TypeScript. As with the rest of the book, I focus on modern features and mention legacy constructs only in passing. The aim of this chapter is to give you sufficient information so you can decide whether to use TypeScript on top of JavaScript.

Why wouldn't everyone want to use TypeScript? Unlike ECMAScript, which is governed by a standards committee composed of many companies, TypeScript is produced by a single vendor, Microsoft. Unlike ECMAScript, where standards documents describe the correct behavior in mind-numbing detail, the TypeScript documentation is sketchy and inconclusive. TypeScript is—just like JavaScript—sometimes messy and inconsistent, giving you another potential source of grief and confusion. TypeScript evolves on a different schedule than ECMAScript, so there is yet another moving part. And, finally, you have yet another part in your tool chain that can act up.

You will have to weigh the advantages and drawbacks. This chapter will give you a flavor of TypeScript so you can make an informed decision.

 TIP: If, after reading this chapter, you come to the conclusion that you want static type checking but you aren't sure about TypeScript, check out Flow (`https://flow.org`) and see if you prefer its type system, syntax, and tooling.

13.1 Type Annotations

Consider the following JavaScript function computing the average of two numbers:

```
const average = (x, y) => (x + y) / 2
```

What happens when you call

```
const result = average('3', '4')
```

Here, `'3'` and `'4'` are concatenated to `'34'`, which is then converted to the number 34 and divided by 2, yielding 17. That is surely not what you intended.

In situations like that, JavaScript provides no error messages. The program silently computes the wrong result and keeps running. In all likelihood, something will eventually go wrong elsewhere.

In TypeScript, you annotate parameters, like this:

```
const average = (x: number, y: number) => (x + y) / 2
```

Now it is clear that the `average` function is intended to compute the average of two *numbers*. If you call

```
const result = average('3', '4') // TypeScript: Compile-time error
```

the TypeScript compiler reports an error.

That is the promise of TypeScript: You provide type annotations, and TypeScript detects type errors before your program runs. Therefore, you spend far less time with the debugger.

In this example, the annotation process is very straightforward. Let us consider a more complex example. Suppose you want to allow an argument that is either a number or an array of numbers. In TypeScript, you express this with a *union type* `number | number[]`. Here, we want to replace a target value, or multiple target values, with another value:

```
const replace = (arr: number[], target: number | number[], replacement: number) => {
  for (let i = 0; i < arr.length; i++) {
    if (Array.isArray(target) && target.includes(arr[i])
        || !Array.isArray(target) && target === arr[i]) {
      arr[i] = replacement
    }
  }
}
```

TypeScript can now check whether your calls are correct:

```
const a = [11, 12, 13, 14, 15, 16]
replace(a, 13, 0) // OK
replace(a, [13, 14], 0) // OK
replace(a, 13, 14, 0) // Error
```

 CAUTION: TypeScript knows about the types of the JavaScript library methods, but as I write this, the online playground is misconfigured and doesn't recognize the `includes` method of the `Array` class. Hopefully this will be fixed by the time you read this book. If not, replace `target.includes(arr[i])` with `target.indexOf(arr[i]) >= 0`.

 NOTE: In these examples, I used arrow functions. The annotations work in exactly the same way with the `function` keyword:

```
function average(x: number, y: number) { return (x + y) / 2 }
```

To use TypeScript effectively, you need to learn how to express types such as "array of type T" and "type T or type U" in the TypeScript syntax. This is simple in many common situations. However, type descriptions can get fairly complex, and there are situations where you need to intervene in the type-checking process. All real-world type systems are like that. You need to expend a certain amount of upfront effort before you can reap the reward—error detection at compile time.

13.2 Running TypeScript

The easiest way to experiment with TypeScript is the "playground" at https://www.typescriptlang.org/play. Simply type in your code and run it. If you mouse over a value, its type is displayed. Errors are shown as wiggly underlines—see Figure 13-1.

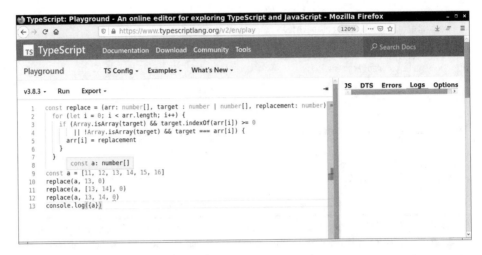

Figure 13-1 The TypeScript playground

Visual Studio Code (https://code.visualstudio.com/) has excellent support for TypeScript, as do other editors and integrated development environments.

To work with TypeScript on the command line, install it with the npm package manager. Here is the command for a global installation:

```
npm install -g typescript
```

In this chapter, I will always assume that TypeScript operates in the *strict mode* and targets the latest version of ECMAScript. Similar to plain JavaScript, TypeScript's strict mode outlaws "sloppy" legacy behavior. To activate these settings, include a file tsconfig.json in your project directory with the following contents:

```
{
  "compilerOptions": {
    "target": "ES2020",
    "strict": true,
    "sourceMap": true
  },
  "filesGlob": [
    "*.ts"
  ]
}
```

To compile TypeScript files to JavaScript, run

```
tsc
```

in the directory that contains TypeScript files and `tsconfig.json`. Each TypeScript file is translated to JavaScript. You can run the resulting files with `node`.

To start up a REPL, run

```
ts-node
```

in a directory with a `tsconfig.json` file, or

```
ts-node -O '{ "target": "es2020", "strict": true }'
```

in any directory.

13.3 Type Terminology

Let us step back and think about types. A type describes a set of values that have something in common. In TypeScript, the `number` type consists of all values that are JavaScript numbers: regular numbers such as `0`, `3.141592653589793`, and so on, as well as `Infinity`, `-Infinity`, and `NaN`. We say that all these values are *instances* of the `number` type. However, the value `'one'` is not.

As you saw already, the type `number[]` denotes arrays of numbers. The value `[0, 3.141592653589793, NaN]` is an instance of the `number[]` type, but the value `[0, 'one']` is not.

A type such as `number[]` is called a *composite* type. You can form arrays of any type: `number[]`, `string[]`, and so on. Union types are another example of composite types. The union type

```
number | number[]
```

is composed of two simpler types: `number` and `number[]`.

In contrast, types that are not composed of simpler types are *primitive*. TypeScript has primitive types `number`, `string`, `boolean`, as well as a few others that you will encounter in the following section.

Composite types can get complex. You can use a *type alias* to make them easier to read and reuse. Suppose you like to write functions that accept either a single number or an array. Simply define a type alias:

```
type Numbers = number | number[]
```

Use the alias as a shortcut for the type:

```
const replace = (arr: number[], target: Numbers, replacement: number) => . . .
```

NOTE: The `typeof` operator yields the value of a variable or property. You can use that type to declare another variable of the same type:

```
let values = [1, 7, 2, 9]
let moreValues: typeof values = []
  // typeof values is the same as number[]
let anotherElement: typeof values[0] = 42
  // typeof values[0] is the same as number
```

13.4 Primitive Types

Every JavaScript primitive type is also a primitive type in TypeScript. That is, TypeScript has primitive types `number`, `boolean`, `string`, `symbol`, `null`, and `undefined`.

The `undefined` type has one instance—the value `undefined`. Similarly, the value `null` is the sole instance of the `null` type. You won't want to use these types by themselves, but they are very useful in union types. An instance of the type

```
string | undefined
```

is either a string or the `undefined` value.

The `void` type can only be used as the return type of a function. It denotes the fact that the function returns no value (see Exercise 2).

The `never` type denotes the fact that a function won't ever return because it always throws an exception. Since you don't normally write such functions, it is very unlikely that you will use the `never` type for a type annotation. Section 13.13.6, "Conditional Types" (page 303), has another application of the `never` type.

The `unknown` type denotes any JavaScript value at all. You can convert any value to `unknown`, but a value of type `unknown` is not compatible with any other type. This makes sense for parameter types of very generic functions (such as `console.log`), or when you need to interface with external JavaScript code. There is an even looser type `any`. Any conversion to *or from* the `any` type is allowed. You should minimize the use of the `any` type because it effectively turns off type checking.

A literal value denotes another type with a single instance—that same value. For example, the string literal `'Mon'` is a TypeScript type. That type has just one value—the string `'Mon'`. By itself, such a type isn't very useful, but you can form a union type, such as

```
'Mon' | 'Tue' | 'Wed' | 'Thu' | 'Fri' | 'Sat' | 'Sun'
```

This is a type with seven instances—the names of the weekdays.

With a type like this, you will usually want to use a type alias:

```
type Weekday = 'Mon' | 'Tue' | 'Wed' | 'Thu' | 'Fri' | 'Sat' | 'Sun'
```

Now you can annotate a variable as Weekday:

```
let w: Weekday = 'Mon' // OK
w = 'Mo' // Error
```

A type such as Weekday describes a finite set of values. The values can be literals of any type:

```
type Falsish = false | 0 | 0n | null | undefined | '' | []
```

NOTE: If you want constants with nicer names, TypeScript lets you define an enumerated type. Here is a simple example:

```
enum Weekday { MON, TUE, WED, THU, FRI, SAT, SUN }
```

You can refer to these constants as Weekday.MON, Weekday.TUE, and so on. These are synonyms for the numbers 0, 1, 2, 3, 4, 5, and 6. You can also assign values:

```
enum Color { RED = 4, GREEN = 2, BLUE = 1 }
```

String values are OK too:

```
enum Quarter { Q1 = 'Winter', Q2 = 'Spring', Q3 = 'Summer', Q4 = 'Fall' }
```

13.5 Composite Types

TypeScript provides several ways of building more complex types out of simpler ones. This section describes all of them.

Given any type, there is an array type:

```
number[] // Array of number
string[] // Array of string
number[][] // Array of number[]
```

These types describe arrays whose elements all have the same type. For example, a number[] array can only hold numbers, not a mixture of numbers and strings.

Of course, JavaScript programmers often use arrays whose elements have mixed types, such as [404, 'not found']. In TypeScript, you describe such an array as an instance of a *tuple type* [number, string]. A tuple type is a list of types enclosed in brackets. It denotes fixed-length arrays whose elements have the specified types. In our example, the value [404, 'not found'] is an instance of the tuple type [number, string], but ['not found', 404] or [404, 'error', 'not found'] are not.

> **NOTE:** The type for an array that starts out with a number and a string and then has other elements is
>
> `[string, number, ...unknown[]]`

Just as a tuple type describes the element types of arrays, an *object type* defines the property names and types of objects. Here is an example of such a type:

```
{ x: number, y: number }
```

You can use a type alias to make this declaration easier to reuse:

```
type Point = { x: number, y: number }
```

Now you can define functions whose parameters are `Point` instances:

```
const distanceFromOrigin = (p: Point) => Math.sqrt(Math.pow(p.x, 2) + Math.pow(p.y, 2))
```

A *function type* describes the parameter and return types of a function. For example,

```
(arg1: number, arg2: number) => number
```

is the type of all functions with two `number` parameters and a `number` return value.

The `Math.pow` function is an instance of this type, but `Math.sqrt` is not, since it only has one parameter.

> **NOTE:** In JavaScript, you must provide names with the parameter types of a function type, such as `arg1` and `arg2` in the preceding example. These names are ignored, with one exception. A method is indicated by naming the first parameter `this`—see Section 13.8.2, "The Instance Type of a Class" (page 285). In all other cases, I will use `arg1`, `arg2`, and so on in a function type so you can see right away that it is a type, not an actual function. For a rest parameter, I will use `rest`.

You have already seen union types. The values of the union type *T | U* are the instances of *T* or *U*. For example, an instance of

```
number | string
```

is either a number or a string, and

```
(number | string)[]
```

describes arrays whose elements are numbers or strings.

An *intersection type T & U* has instances that combine the requirements of *T* and *U*. Here is an example:

```
Point & { color: string }
```

To be an instance of this type, an object must have numeric x and y properties (which makes it a Point) as well as a string-valued color property.

13.6 Type Inference

Consider a call to our average function:

```
const average = (x: number, y: number) => (x + y) / 2
. . .
const a = 3
const b = 4
let result = average(a, b)
```

Only the function parameters require a type annotation. The type of the other variables is *inferred*. From the initialization, TypeScript can tell that a and b must have type number. By analyzing the code of the average function, TypeScript infers that the return type is also number, and so is the type of result.

Generally, type inference works well, but sometimes you have to help TypeScript along.

The initial value of a variable may not suffice to determine the type that you intend. For example, suppose you declare a type for error codes.

```
type ErrorCode = [number, string]
```

Now you want to declare a variable of that type. This declaration does not suffice:

```
let code = [404, 'not found']
```

TypeScript infers the type (number | string)[] from the right-hand side: arrays of arbitrary length where each element can be a number or string. That is a much more general type than ErrorCode.

 TIP: To see the inferred type, use a development environment that displays type information. Figure 13-2 shows how Visual Studio Code displays inferred types.

The remedy is to use a type annotation with the variable:

```
let code: ErrorCode = [404, 'not found']
```

You face the same problem when a function returns a value whose type is ambiguous, such as the following:

Figure 13-2 Type information in Visual Studio Code

```
const root = (x: number) => {
  if (x >= 0) return Math.sqrt(x)
  else return [404, 'not found']
}
```

The inferred return type is number | (number | string)[]. If you want number | ErrorCode, put a return type annotation behind the parameter list:

```
const root = (x: number): number | ErrorCode => {
  if (x >= 0) return Math.sqrt(x)
  else return [404, 'not found']
}
```

Here is the same function with the function syntax:

```
function root(x: number): number | ErrorCode {
  if (x >= 0) return Math.sqrt(x)
    else return [404, 'not found']
}
```

A type annotation is also needed when you initialize a variable with undefined:

```
let result = undefined
```

Without an annotation, TypeScript infers the type any. (It would be pointless to infer the type undefined—then the variable could never change.) Therefore, you should specify the intended type:

```
let result: number | undefined = undefined
```

Later, you can store a number in `result`, but not a string:

```
result = 3 // OK
result = '3' // Error
```

Sometimes you know more about the type of an expression than TypeScript can infer. For example, you might have just received a JSON object and you know its type. Then use a *type assertion*:

```
let target = JSON.parse(response) as Point
```

A type assertion is similar to a cast in Java or C#, but no exception occurs if the value doesn't actually conform to the target type.

When you process union types, TypeScript follows the decision flow to ensure that a value is of the correct type in each branch. Consider this example:

```
const less = (x: number | number[] | string | Date | null) => {
  if (typeof x === 'number')
    return x - 1;
  else if (Array.isArray(x))
    return x.splice(0, 1)
  else if (x instanceof Date)
    return new Date(x.getTime() - 1000)
  else if (x === null)
    return x
  else
    return x.substring(1)
}
```

TypeScript understands the `typeof`, `instanceof`, and `in` operators, the `Array.isArray` function, and tests for `null` and `undefined`. Therefore, the type of `x` is inferred as `number`, `number[]`, `Date`, and `null` in the first four branches. In the fifth branch, only the `string` alternative remains, and TypeScript allows the call to `substring`.

However, sometimes this inference doesn't work. Here is an example:

```
const more = (values: number[] | string[]) => {
  if (array.length > 0 && typeof x[0] === 'number') // Error—not a valid type guard
    return values.map(x => x + 1)
  else
    return values.map(x => x + x)
}
```

TypeScript can't analyze the condition. It is simply too complex.

In such a situation, you can provide a custom *type guard function*. Its special role is indicated by the return type:

```
const isNumberArray = (array: unknown[]): array is number[] =>
  array.length > 0 && typeof array[0] === 'number'
```

The return type array is number[] indicates that this function returns a boolean and can be used to test whether the array argument has type number[]. Here is how to use the function:

```
const more = (values: number[] | string[]) => {
  if (isNumberArray(values))
    return values.map(x => x + 1)
  else
    return values.map(x => x + x)
}
```

Here is the same type guard with the function syntax:

```
function isNumberArray(array: unknown[]): array is number[] {
  return array.length > 0 && typeof array[0] === 'number'
}
```

13.7 Subtypes

Some types, for example number and string, have no relationship with each other. A number variable cannot hold a string variable, nor can a string variable hold a number value. But other types are related. For example, a variable with type number | string *can* hold a number value.

We say that number is a *subtype* of number | string, and number | string is a *supertype* of number and string. A subtype has more constraints than its supertypes. A variable of the supertype can hold values of the subtype, but not the other way around.

In the following sections, we will examine the subtype relationship in more detail.

13.7.1 The Substitution Rule

Consider again the object type

```
type Point = { x: number, y: number }
```

The object { x: 3, y: 4 } is clearly an instance of Point. What about

```
const bluePoint = { x: 3, y: 4, color: 'blue' }
```

Is it also an instance of Point? After all, it has x and y properties whose values are numbers.

In TypeScript, the answer is "no." The bluePoint object is an instance of the type

```
{ x: number, y: number, color: string }
```

For convenience, let us give a name to that type:

```
type ColoredPoint = { x: number, y: number, color: string }
```

The `ColoredPoint` type is a subtype of `Point`, and `Point` is a supertype of `ColoredPoint`. A subtype imposes all the requirements of the supertype, and then some.

Whenever a value of a given type is expected, you can supply a subtype instance. This is sometimes called the *substitution rule*.

For example, here we pass a `ColoredPoint` object to a function with a `Point` parameter:

```
const distanceFromOrigin = (p: Point) => Math.sqrt(Math.pow(p.x, 2) + Math.pow(p.y, 2))
const result = distanceFromOrigin(bluePoint) // OK
```

The `distanceFromOrigin` function expects a `Point`, and it is happy to accept a `ColoredPoint`. And why shouldn't it be? The function needs to access numeric `x` and `y` properties, and those are certainly present.

 NOTE: As you just saw, the type of a variable need not be exactly the same as the type of the value to which it refers. In this example, the parameter `p` has type `Point`, but the value to which it refers has type `ColoredPoint`. When you have a variable of a given type, you can be assured that the referenced value belongs to that type *or a subtype*.

The substitution rule has one exception in TypeScript. You cannot substitute an *object literal* of a subtype. The call

```
const result = distanceFromOrigin({ x: 3, y: 4, color: 'blue' }) // Error
```

fails at compile time. This is called an *excess property check*.

The same check is carried out when you assign an object literal to a typed variable:

```
let p: Point = { x: 3, y: 4 }
p = { x: 0, y: 0, color: 'red' } // Error—excess property blue
```

You will see the rationale for this check in the following section.

It is easy enough to bypass an excess property check. Just introduce another variable:

```
const redOrigin = { x: 0, y: 0, color: 'red' }
p = redOrigin // OK—p can hold a subtype value
```

13.7.2 Optional and Excess Properties

When you have an object of type `Point`, you can't read any properties other than `x` and `y`. After all, there is no guarantee that such properties exist.

```
let p: Point = . . .
console.log(p.color) // Error—no such property
```

That makes sense. It is exactly the kind of check that a type system should provide.

What about writing to such a property?

```
p.color = 'blue' // Error—no such property
```

From a type-theoretical point of view, this would be safe. The variable p would still refer to a value that belongs to a subtype of Point. But TypeScript prohibits setting "excess properties."

If you want properties that are present with some but not all objects of a type, use *optional properties*. A property marked with ? is permitted but not required. Here is an example:

```
type MaybeColoredPoint = {
  x: number,
  y: number,
  color?: string
}
```

Now the following statements are OK:

```
let p: MaybeColoredPoint = { x: 0, y: 0 } // OK—color optional
p.color = 'red' // OK—can set optional property
p = { x: 3, y: 4, color: 'blue' } // OK—can use literal with optional property
```

Excess property checks are meant to catch typos with optional properties. Consider a function for plotting a point:

```
const plot = (p: MaybeColoredPoint) => . . .
```

The following call fails:

```
const result = plot({ x: 3, y: 4, colour: 'blue' })
  // Error—excess property colour
```

Note the British spelling of colour. The MaybeColoredPoint class has no colour property, and TypeScript catches the error. If the compiler had followed the substitution rule without the excess property check, the function would have plotted a point with no color.

13.7.3 Array and Object Type Variance

Is an array of colored points more specialized than an array of points? It certainly seems to. Indeed, in TypeScript, the ColoredPoint[] type is a subtype of Point[]. In general, if S is a subtype of T, then the array type S[] is a subtype of *T*[]. We say that arrays are *covariant* in TypeScript since the array types vary in the same direction as the element types.

However, this relationship is actually *unsound*. It is possible to write TypeScript programs that compile without errors but create errors at runtime. Consider this example:

```
const coloredPoints: ColoredPoint[] = [{ x: 3, y: 4, color: 'blue' },
                                       { x: 0, y: 0, color: 'red' }]
const points: Point[] = coloredPoints // OK for points to hold a subtype value
```

We can add a plain Point via the points variable:

```
points.push({ x: 4, y: 3 }) // OK to add a Point to a Point[]
```

But coloredPoints and points *refer to the same array*. Reading the added point with the coloredPoints variable causes a runtime error:

```
console.log(coloredPoints[2].color.length)
    // Error—cannot read property 'length' of undefined
```

The value coloredPoints[2].color is undefined, which should not be possible for a ColoredPoint. The type system has a blind spot.

This was a conscious choice by the language designers. Theoretically, only immutable arrays should be covariant, and mutable arrays should be *invariant*. That is, there should be no subtype relationship between mutable arrays of different types. However, invariant arrays would be inconvenient. In this case, TypeScript, as well as Java and C#, made the decision to give up on complete type safety for the sake of convenience.

Covariance is also used for object types. To determine whether one object type is a subtype of another, we look at the subtype relationships of the matching properties. Let us look at two types that share a single property:

```
type Colored = { color: string }
type MaybeColored = { color: string | undefined }
```

In this case, string is a subtype of string | undefined, and therefore Colored is a subtype of MaybeColored.

In general, if *S* is a subtype of *T*, then the object type { *p*: *S* } is a subtype of { *p*: *T* }. If there are multiple properties, all of them must vary in the same direction.

As with arrays, covariance for objects is unsound—see Exercise 11.

In this section, you have seen how array and object types vary with their component types. For variance of function types, see Section 13.12.3, "Function Type Variance" (page 293), and for generic variance, Section 13.13.5, "Generic Type Variance" (page 302).

13.8 Classes

The following sections cover how classes work in TypeScript. First, we go over the syntactical differences between classes in JavaScript and TypeScript. Then you will see how classes are related to types.

13.8.1 Declaring Classes

The TypeScript syntax for classes is similar to that of JavaScript. Of course, you provide type annotations for constructor and method parameters. You also need to specify the types of the instance fields. One way is to list the fields with type annotations, like this:

```
class Point {
  x: number
  y: number

  constructor(x: number, y: number) {
    this.x = x
    this.y = y
  }

  distance(other: Point) {
    return Math.sqrt(Math.pow(this.x - other.x, 2) + Math.pow(this.y - other.y, 2))
  }

  toString() { return `(${this.x}, ${this.y})` }

  static origin = new Point(0, 0)
}
```

Alternatively, you can provide initial values from which TypeScript can infer the type:

```
class Point {
  x = 0
  y = 0
  . . .
}
```

 NOTE: This syntax corresponds to the field syntax that is a stage 3 proposal in JavaScript.

You can make the instance fields private. TypeScript supports the syntax for private features that is currently at stage 3 in JavaScript.

```
class Point {
  #x: number
  #y: number

  constructor(x: number, y: number) {
    this.#x = x
    this.#y = y
  }

  distance(other: Point) {
    return Math.sqrt(Math.pow(this.#x - other.#x, 2) + Math.pow(this.#y - other.#y, 2))
  }

  toString() { return `(${this.#x}, ${this.#y})` }

  static origin = new Point(0, 0)
}
```

 NOTE: TypeScript also supports `private` and `protected` modifiers for instance fields and methods. These modifiers work just like in Java or C++. They come from a time where JavaScript did not have a syntax for private variables and methods. I do not discuss those modifiers in this chapter.

 NOTE: You can declare instance fields as `readonly`:

```
class Point {
  readonly x: number
  readonly y: number
  . . .
}
```

A `readonly` property cannot be changed after its initial assignment.

```
const p = new Point(3, 4)
p.x = 0 // Error—cannot change readonly property
```

Note that `readonly` is applied to *properties*, whereas `const` applies to *variables*.

13.8.2 The Instance Type of a Class

The instances of a class have a TypeScript type that contains every public property and method. For example, consider the `Point` class with public fields from the preceding sections. Its instances have the type

```
{
  x: number,
  y: number,
  distance: (this: Point, arg1: Point) => number
  toString: (this: Point) => string
}
```

Note that the constructor and static members are not a part of the instance type.

You can indicate a method by naming the first parameter this, as in the preceding example. Alternatively, you can use the following compact notation:

```
{
  x: number,
  y: number,
  distance(arg1: Point): number
  toString(): string
}
```

Getter and setter methods in classes give rise to properties in TypeScript types. For example, if you define

```
get x() { return this.#x }
set x(x: number) { this.#x = x }
get y() { return this.#y }
set y(y: number) { this.#y = y }
```

for the Point class with private instance fields in the preceding section, then the TypeScript type has properties x and y of type number.

If you only provide a getter, the property is readonly.

 CAUTION: If you only provide a setter and no getter, reading from the property is permitted and returns undefined.

13.8.3 The Static Type of a Class

As noted in the preceding section, the constructor and static members are not part of the instance type of a class. Instead, they belong to the static type.

The static type of our sample Point class is

```
{
  new (x: number, y: number): Point
  origin: Point
}
```

The syntax for specifying a constructor is similar to that for a method, but you use new in place of the method name.

You don't usually have to worry about the static type (but see Section 13.13.4, "Erasure," page 300). Nevertheless, it is a common cause of confusion. Consider this code snippet:

```
const a = new Point(3, 4)
const b: typeof a = new Point(0, 0) // OK
const ctor: typeof Point = new Point(0, 0) // Error
```

Since a is an instance of Point, typeof a is the instance type of the Point class. But what is typeof Point? Here, Point is the constructor function. After all, that's all a class is in JavaScript—a constructor function. Its type is the static type of the class. You can initialize ctor as

```
const ctor: typeof Point = Point
```

Then you can call new ctor(3, 4) or access ctor.origin.

13.9 Structural Typing

The TypeScript type system uses *structural typing*. Two types are the same if they have the same structure. For example,

```
type ErrorCode = [number, string]
```

and

```
type LineItem = [number, string]
```

are the same type. The names of the types are irrelevant. You can freely copy values between the two types:

```
let code: ErrorCode = [404, 'Not found']
let items: LineItem[] = [[2, 'Blackwell Toaster']]
items[1] = code
```

This sounds potentially dangerous, but it is certainly no worse than what programmers do every day with plain JavaScript. And in practice, with object types, it is quite unlikely that two types have exactly the same structure. If we use object types in our example, we might arrive at these types:

```
type ErrorCode = { code: number, description: string }
type LineItem = { quantity: number, description: string }
```

They are different since the property names don't match.

Structural typing is very different from the "nominal" type systems in Java, C#, or C++, where the names of the type matter. But in JavaScript, what matters are the capabilities of an object, not the name of its type.

To illustrate the difference, consider this JavaScript function:

```
const act = x => { x.walk(); x.quack(); }
```

Obviously, in JavaScript, the function works with any x that has methods walk and quack.

In TypeScript, you can accurately reflect this behavior with a type:

```
const act = (x: { walk(): void, quack(): void }) => { x.walk(); x.quack(); }
```

You may have a class Duck that provides these methods:

```
class Duck {
  constructor(. . .) { . . . }
  walk(): void { . . . }
  quack(): void { . . . }
}
```

That's swell. You can pass a Duck instance to the act function:

```
const donald = new Duck(. . .)
act(donald)
```

But now suppose you have another object—not an instance of this class, but still with walk and quack methods:

```
const daffy = { walk: function () { . . . }, quack: function () { . . . } };
```

You can equally well pass this object to the act function. This phenomenon is called "duck typing," after the proverbial saying: "If it walks like a duck and quacks like a duck, it must be a duck."

The structural typing in TypeScript formalizes this approach. Using the structure of the type, TypeScript can check at compile time that each value has the needed capabilities. The type names don't matter at all.

13.10 Interfaces

Consider an object type to describe objects that have an ID method:

```
type Identifiable = {
  id(): string
}
```

Using this type, you can define a function that finds an element by ID:

```
const findById = (elements: Identifiable[], id: string) => {
  for (const e of elements) if (e.id() === id) return e;
  return undefined;
}
```

To make sure that a class is a subtype of this type, you can define the class with an implements clause:

```
class Person implements Identifiable {
  #name: string
  #id: string
  constructor(name: string, id: string) { this.#name = name; this.#id = id; }
  id() { return this.#id }
}
```

Now TypeScript checks that your class really provides an `id` method with the correct types.

NOTE: That is all that the `implements` clause does. If you omit the clause, `Person` is still a subtype of `Identifiable`, because of structural typing.

There is an alternate syntax for object types that looks more familiar to Java and C# programmers:

```
interface Identifiable {
  id(): string
}
```

In older versions of TypeScript, object types were more limited than interfaces. Nowadays, you can use either.

There are a couple of minor differences. One interface can extend another:

```
interface Employable extends Identifiable {
  salary(): number
}
```

With type declarations, you use an intersection type instead:

```
type Employable = Identifiable & {
  salary(): number
}
```

Interfaces, unlike object types, can be defined in fragments. You can have

```
interface Employable {
  id(): string
}
```

followed elsewhere by

```
interface Employable {
  salary(): number
}
```

The fragments are merged together. This merging is not done for `type` declarations. It is debatable whether this is a useful feature.

NOTE: In TypeScript, an interface can extend a class. It then picks up all properties of the instance type of the class. For example,

```
interface Point3D extends Point { z: number }
```

has the fields and methods of `Point`, as well as the `z` property.

Instead of such an interface, you can use an intersection type

```
type Point3D = Point & { z: number }
```

 ## 13.11 Indexed Properties

Sometimes, you want to use objects with arbitrary properties. In TypeScript, you need to use an *index signature* to let the type checker know that arbitrary properties are OK. Here is the syntax:

```
type Dictionary = {
  creator: string,
  [arg: string]: string | string[]
}
```

The variable name of the index argument (here, `arg`) is immaterial, but you must supply a name.

Each `Dictionary` instance has a `creator` property and any number of other properties whose values are strings or string arrays.

```
const dict: Dictionary = { creator: 'Pierre' }
dict.hello = ['bonjour', 'salut', 'allô']
let str = 'world'
dict[str] = 'monde'
```

 CAUTION: The types of explicitly provided properties must be subtypes of the index type. The following would be an error:

```
type Dictionary = {
  created: Date, // Error—not a string or string[]
  [arg: string]: string | string[]
}
```

There would be no way to check that an assignment to `dict[str]` is correct with an arbitrary value for `str`.

You can also describe array-like types with integer index values:

```
type ShoppingList = {
  created: Date,
  [arg: number] : string
}

const list: ShoppingList = {
  created: new Date()
}
list[0] = 'eggs'
list[1] = 'ham'
```

13.12 Complex Function Parameters

In the following sections, you will see how to provide annotations for more optional, default, rest, and destructured parameters. Then we turn to "overloading"—specifying multiple parameter and return types for a single function.

13.12.1 Optional, Default, and Rest Parameters

Consider the JavaScript function

```
const average = (x, y) => (x + y) / 2 // JavaScript
```

In JavaScript, you have to worry about the fact that someone might call `average(3)`, which would evaluate to `(3 + undefined) / 2`, or `NaN`. In TypeScript, that's not an issue. You cannot call a function without supplying all of the required arguments.

However, JavaScript programmers often provide optional parameters. In our `average` function, the second parameter can be optional:

```
const average = (x, y) => y === undefined ? x : (x + y) / 2 // JavaScript
```

In TypeScript, you tag optional parameters with a ?, like this:

```
const average = (x: number, y?: number) => y === undefined ? x : (x + y) / 2
  // TypeScript
```

Optional parameters must come after the required parameters.

As in JavaScript, you can provide default parameters in TypeScript:

```
const average = (x = 0, y = x) => (x + y) / 2  // TypeScript
```

Here, the parameter types are inferred from the types of the defaults.

Rest parameters work exactly like in JavaScript. You annotate a rest parameter as an array:

```
const average = (first = 0, ...following: number[]) => {
  let sum = first
  for (const value of following) { sum += value }
  return sum / (1 + following.length)
}
```

The type of this function is

```
(arg1: number, ...arg2: number[]) => number
```

13.12.2 Destructuring Parameters

In Chapter 3, we looked at functions that are called with a "configuration object," like this:

```
const result = mkString(elements,
  { separator: ', ', leftDelimiter: '(', rightDelimiter: ')' })
```

When implementing the function, you can, of course, have a parameter for the configuration object:

```
const mkString = (values, config) =>
  config.leftDelimiter + values.join(config.separator) + config.rightDelimiter
```

Or you can use destructuring to declare three parameter variables:

```
const mkString = (values, { separator, leftDelimiter, rightDelimiter }) =>
  leftDelimiter + values.join(separator) + rightDelimiter
```

In TypeScript, you need to add types. However, the obvious way does not work:

```
const mkString = (values: unknown[], { // TypeScript
    separator: string,
    leftDelimiter: string, // Error—duplicate identifier
    rightDelimiter: string // Error—duplicate identifier
  }) => leftDelimiter + values.join(separator) + rightDelimiter
```

The syntax for TypeScript type annotations is in conflict with the destructuring syntax. In JavaScript (and therefore, in TypeScript), you can add variable names after the property names:

```
const mkString = (values, { // JavaScript
    separator: sep,
    leftDelimiter: left,
    rightDelimiter: right
}) => left + values.join(sep) + right
```

To correctly specify the types, add a type annotation to the entire configuration object:

```
const mkString = (values: unknown[], // TypeScript
    { separator, leftDelimiter, rightDelimiter }
    : { separator: string, leftDelimiter: string, rightDelimiter: string })
=> leftDelimiter + values.join(separator) + rightDelimiter
```

In Chapter 3, we also provided default arguments for each option. Here is the function with the defaults:

```
const mkString = (values: unknown[], // TypeScript
    { separator = ',', leftDelimiter = '[', rightDelimiter = ']' }
    : { separator?: string, leftDelimiter?: string, rightDelimiter?: string })
=> leftDelimiter + values.join(separator) + rightDelimiter
```

Note that with the defaults, the type changes slightly—each property is now optional.

13.12.3 Function Type Variance

In Section 13.7.3, "Array and Object Type Variance" (page 282), you saw that arrays are covariant. Replacing the element type with a subtype yields an array subtype. For example, if Employee is a subtype of Person, then Employee[] is a subtype of Person[].

Similarly, object types are covariant in the property types. The type { partner: Employee } is a subtype of { partner: Person }.

In this section, we examine subtype relationships between function types.

Function types are *contravariant* in their parameter types. If you replace a parameter type with a *supertype*, you get a subtype. For example, the type

```
type PersonConsumer = (arg1: Person) => void
```

is a subtype of

```
type EmployeeConsumer = (arg1: Employee) => void
```

That means, an `EmployeeConsumer` variable can hold a `PersonConsumer` value:

```
const pc: PersonConsumer = (p: Person) => { console.log(`a person named ${p.name}`) }
const ec: EmployeeConsumer = pc
  // OK for ec to hold subtype value
```

This assignment is sound because pf can surely accept `Employee` instances. After all, it is prepared to handle more general `Person` instances.

With the return type, we have covariance. For example,

```
type EmployeeProducer = (arg1: string) => Employee
```

is a subtype of

```
type PersonProducer = (arg1: string) => Person
```

The following assignment is sound:

```
const ep: EmployeeProducer = (name: string) => ({ name, salary: 0 })
const pp: PersonProducer = ep
  // OK for pp to hold subtype value
```

Calling pp('Fred') surely produces a `Person` instance.

If you drop the last parameter type from a function type, you obtain a subtype. For example,

```
(arg1: number) => number
```

is a subtype of

```
(arg1: number, arg2: number) => number
```

To see why, consider the assignment

```
const g = (x: number) => 2 * x
  // Type (arg1: number) => number
const f: (arg1: number, arg2: number) => number = g
  // OK for f to hold subtype value
```

It is safe to call f with two arguments. The second argument is simply ignored.

Similarly, if you make a parameter optional, you obtain a subtype:

```
const g = (x: number, y?: number) => y === undefined ? x : (x + y) / 2
  // Type (arg1: number, arg2?: number) => number
const f: (arg1: number, arg2: number) => number = g
  // OK for f to hold subtype value
```

Again, it is safe to call f with two arguments.

Finally, if you add a rest parameter, you get a subtype.

```
let g = (x: number, y: number, ...following: number[]) => Math.max(x, y, ...following)
  // Type: (arg1: number, arg2: number, ...rest: number[]) => number
let f: (arg1: number, arg2: number) => number = g
  // OK for f to hold subtype value
```

Once again, calling f with two parameters is fine.

Table 13-1 gives a summary of all subtype rules that were covered so far.

Table 13–1 Forming Subtypes

Action	Supertype A variable of this type...	Subtype ...can hold a value of this type
Replace array element type with subtype	Person[]	Employee[]
Replace object property type with subtype	{ partner: Person }	{ partner: Employee }
Add object property	{ x: number, y: number }	{ x: number, y: number, color: string }
Replace function parameter type with *supertype*	(arg1: Employee) => void	(arg1: Person) => void
Replace function return type with subtype	(arg1: string) => Person	(arg1: string) => Employee
Drop the last parameter	(arg1: number, arg2: number) => number	(arg1: number) => number
Make the last parameter optional	(arg1: number, arg2: number) => number	(arg1: number, arg2?: number) => number
Add a rest parameter	(arg1: number) => number	(arg1: number, ...rest: number[]) => number

13.12.4 Overloads

In JavaScript, it is common to write functions that can be called flexibly. For example, this JavaScript function counts how many times a letter occurs in a string:

```
function count(str, c) { return str.length - str.replace(c, '').length }
```

What if we have an array of strings? In JavaScript, it is easy to extend the behavior:

```
function count(str, c) {
  if (Array.isArray(str)) {
    let sum = 0
    for (const s of str) {
      sum += s.length - s.replace(c, '').length
    }
```

```
    return sum
  } else {
    return str.length - str.replace(c, '').length
  }
}
```

In TypeScript, we need to provide a type for this function. That is not too hard: `str` is either a string or an array of strings:

```
function count(str: string | string[], c: string) { . . . }
```

This works because in either case, the return type is `number`. That is, the function has type

```
(str: string | string[], c: string) => number
```

But what if the return type differs depending on the argument types? Let's say we remove the characters instead of counting them:

```
function remove(str, c) { // JavaScript
  if (Array.isArray(str))
    return str.map(s => s.replace(c, ''))
  else
    return str.replace(c, '')
}
```

Now the return type is either `string` or `string[]`.

But it is not optimal to use the union type `string | string[]` as the return type. In an expression

```
const result = remove(['Fred', 'Barney'], 'e')
```

we would like `result` to be typed as `string[]`, not the union type.

You can achieve this by *overloading* the function. JavaScript doesn't actually allow you to overload functions in the traditional sense—that is, implement separate functions with the same name but different parameter types. Instead, you list the declarations that you wish you could implement separately, followed by the one implementation:

```
function remove(str: string, c: string): string
function remove(str: string[], c: string): string[]
function remove(str: string | string[], c: string) {
  if (Array.isArray(str))
    return str.map(s => s.replace(c, ''))
  else
    return str.replace(c, '')
}
```

With arrow functions, the syntax is a little different. Annotate the type of the variable that will hold the function, like this:

```
const remove: {
  (arg1: string, arg2: string): string
  (arg1: string[], arg2: string): string[]
} = (str: any, c: string) => {
  if (Array.isArray(str))
    return str.map(s => s.replace(c, ''))
  else
    return str.replace(c, '')
}
```

> **CAUTION:** Perhaps for historical reasons, the syntax of this overload annotation does not use the arrow syntax for function types. Instead, the syntax is reminiscent of an `interface` declaration.
>
> Also, the type checking is not as good with arrow functions. The parameter `str` must be declared with type `any`, not `string | string[]`. With `function` declarations, TypeScript works harder and checks the execution paths of the function, guaranteeing that `string` arguments yield `string` results, but `string[]` arguments return `string[]` values.

Overloaded methods use a syntax that is similar to functions:

```
class Remover {
  c: string
  constructor(c: string) { this.c = c }

  removeFrom(str: string): string
  removeFrom(str: string[]): string[]
  removeFrom(str: string | string[]) {
    if (Array.isArray(str))
      return str.map(s => s.replace(this.c, ''))
    else
      return str.replace(this.c, '')
  }
}
```

13.13 Generic Programming

A declaration of a class, type, or function is *generic* when it uses *type parameters* for types that are not yet specified and can be filled in later. For example, in TypeScript, the standard `Set<T>` type has a type parameter `T`, allowing you to form sets of any type, such as `Set<string>` or `Set<Point>`. The following sections show you how to work with generics in TypeScript.

13.13.1 Generic Classes and Types

Here is a simple example of a generic class. Its instances hold key/value pairs:

```
class Entry<K, V> {
  key: K
  value: V
  constructor(key: K, second: V) {
    this.key = key
    this.value = value
  }
}
```

As you can see, the type parameters K and V are specified inside angle brackets after the name of the class. In the definitions of fields and the constructor, the type parameters are used as types.

You *instantiate* the generic class by substituting types for the type variables. For example, Entry<string, number> is an ordinary class with fields of type string and number.

A *generic type* is a type with one or more type parameters, such as

```
type Pair<T> = { first: T, second: T }
```

 NOTE: You can specify a default for a type parameter, such as

```
type Pair<T = any> = { first: T, second: T }
```

Then the type Pair is the same as Pair<any>.

TypeScript provides generic forms of the Set, Map, and WeakMap classes that you saw in Chapter 7. You simply provide the types of the elements:

```
const salaries = new Map<Person, number>()
```

Types can also be inferred from the constructor arguments. For example, this map is typed as a Map<string, number>:

```
const weekdays = new Map(
  [['Mon', 0], ['Tue', 1], ['Wed', 2], ['Thu', 3], ['Fri', 4], ['Sat', 5], ['Sun', 6]])
```

 NOTE: The generic Array<T> class is exactly the same as the type T[].

13.13.2 Generic Functions

Just like a generic class is a class with type parameters, a *generic function* is a function with type parameters. Here is an example of a function with one type parameter. The function counts how many times a target value is present in an array.

```
function count<T>(arr: T[], target: T) {
  let count = 0
  for (let e of arr) if (e === target) count++
  return count
}
```

Using a type parameter ensures that the array type is the same as the target type.

```
let digits = [3, 1, 4, 1, 5, 9, 2, 6, 5, 3, 5]
let result = count(digits, 5) // OK
result = count(digits, 'Fred') // Type error
```

The type parameters of a generic function are always placed before the opening parenthesis that starts the list of function parameters. A generic arrow function looks like this:

```
const count = <T>(arr: T[], target: T) => {
  let count = 0
  for (let e of arr) if (e === target) count++
  return count
}
```

The type of this function is

```
<T> (arg1: T[], arg2: T) => number
```

When calling a generic function, you do not need to specify the type parameters. They are inferred from the argument types. For example, in the call `count(digits, 5)`, the type of `digits` is `number[]`, and TypeScript can infer that `T` should be `number`.

You can, if you like, supply the type explicitly, before the arguments, like this:

```
count<number>(digits, 4)
```

You occasionally need to do this if TypeScript doesn't infer the types that you intended. You will see an example in the following section.

13.13.3 Type Bounds

Sometimes, the type parameters of a generic class or function need to fulfill certain requirements. You express these requirements with a *type bound*.

Consider this function that yields the tail—all but the first element—of its argument:

```
const tail = <T>(values: T) => values.slice(1) // Error
```

This approach cannot work since TypeScript doesn't know whether values has a slice method. Let's use a type bound:

```
const tail = <T extends { slice(from: number, to?: number): T }>(values: T) =>
  values.slice(1) // OK
```

The type bound ensures that the call values.slice(1) is valid. Note that the extends keyword in a type bound actually means "subtype"—the TypeScript designers just used the existing extends keyword instead of coming up with another keyword or symbol.

Now we can call

```
let result = tail([1, 7, 2, 9]) // Sets result to [7, 2, 9]
```

or

```
let greeting = 'Hello'
console.log(tail(greeting)) // Displays ello
```

Of course, we can give a name to the type that is used as a bound:

```
type Sliceable<T> = { slice(from: number, to?: number): T }
const tail = <T extends Sliceable<T>>(values: T) => values.slice(1)
```

For example, the type number[] is a subtype of Sliceable<number[]> since the slice method returns a number[] instance. Similarly, string is a subtype of Sliceable<string>.

 CAUTION: If you try out the call

```
console.log(tail('Hello')) // Error
```

compilation fails with an error—the type 'Hello' is not a subtype of Sliceable<'Hello'>. The problem is that 'Hello' is both an instance of the literal type 'Hello' and the type string. TypeScript chooses the literal type as the most specific one, and typechecking fails. To overcome this problem, explicitly instantiate the template function:

```
console.log(tail<string>('Hello')) // OK
```

or use a type assertion:

```
console.log(tail('Hello' as string))
```

13.13.4 Erasure

When TypeScript code is translated to plain JavaScript, all types are erased. As a consequence, the call

```
let newlyCreated = new T()
```

is illegal. At runtime, there is no T.

To construct objects of arbitrary types, you need to use the constructor function. Here is an example:

```
const fill = <T>(ctor: { new() : T }, n: number) => {
  let result: T[] = []
  for (let i = 0; i < n; i++)
    result.push(new ctor())
  return result
}
```

Note the type of ctor—a function that can be called with new and yields a value of type T. That is a constructor. This particular constructor has no arguments.

When calling the fill function, you provide the name of a class:

```
const dates = fill(Date, 10)
```

The expression Date is the constructor function. In JavaScript, a class is just "syntactic sugar" for a constructor function with a prototype.

Similarly, you cannot make a generic instanceof check. The following will not work:

```
const filter = <T>(values: unknown[]) => {
  let result: T[] = []
  for (const v of values)
    if (v instanceof T) // Error
      result.push(v)
  return result
}
```

The remedy is, again, to pass the constructor:

```
const filter = <T>(values: unknown[], ctor: new (...args: any[]) => T) => {
  let result: T[] = []
  for (const v of values)
    if (v instanceof ctor) // OK—right-hand side of instanceof is a constructor
      result.push(v)
  return result
}
```

Here is a sample call:

```
const pointsOnly = filter([3, 4, new Point(3, 4), Point.origin], Point)
```

Note that in this case, the constructor accepts arbitrary arguments.

 CAUTION: The instanceof test only works with a *class*. There is no way of testing at runtime whether a value is an instance of a type or interface.

13.13.5 Generic Type Variance

Consider a generic type such as

```
type Pair<T> = { first: T, second: T }
```

Now suppose you have a type `Person` and a subtype `Employee`. What is the appropriate relationship between `Pair<Person>` and `Pair<Employee>`?

Type theory provides three possibilities for a type variable. It can be covariant (that is, the generic type varies in the same direction), contravariant (with subtype relationships flipped), and invariant (with no subtype relationships between the generic types).

In Java, type variables are always invariant, but you can express relationships with wildcards such as `Pair<? extends Person>`. In C#, you can choose the variance of type parameters: `Entry<out K, in V>`. TypeScript does not have any comparable mechanism.

Instead, when deciding whether a generic type instance is a subtype of another, TypeScript simply substitutes the actual types and then compares the resulting nongeneric types.

For example, when comparing `Pair<Person>` and `Pair<Employee>`, substituting the types `Person` and `Employee` yields

```
{ first: Person, second: Person }
```

and the subtype

```
{ first: Employee, second: Employee }
```

As a result, the `Pair<T>` type is covariant in `T`. This is unsound (see Exercise 15). However, as discussed in Section 13.7.3, "Array and Object Type Variance" (page 282), this unsoundness is a conscious design decision.

Let us look at another example that illustrates contravariance:

```
type Formatter<T> = (arg1: T) => string
```

To compare `Formatter<Person>` and `Formatter<Employee>`, plug in the types, then compare

```
(arg1: Person) => string
```

and

```
(arg1: Employee) => string
```

Since function parameter types are contravariant, so is the type variable `T` of `Formatter<T>`. This behavior is sound.

13.13.6 Conditional Types

A conditional type has the form *T* extends *U* ? *V* : *W*, where *T*, *U*, *V*, and *W* are types or type variables. Here is an example:

```
type ExtractArray<T> = T extends any[] ? T : never
```

If T is an array, then ExtractArray<T> is T itself. Otherwise, it is never, the type that has no instances.

By itself, this type isn't very useful. But it can be used to filter out types from unions:

```
type Data = string | string[] | number | number[]
type ArrayData = ExtractArray<Data> // The type string[] | number[]
```

For the string and number alternatives, ExtractArray yields never, which is simply dropped.

Now suppose you want to have just the element type. The following doesn't quite work:

```
type ArrayOf<T> = T extends U[] ? U : never // Error—U not defined
```

Instead, use the infer keyword:

```
type ArrayOf<T> = T extends (infer U)[] ? U : never
```

Here, we check whether T extends X[] for some X, and if so, bind U to X. When applied to a union type, the non-arrays are dropped and the arrays replaced by their element type. For example, ArrayOf<Data> is number | string.

13.13.7 Mapped Types

Another way to specify indexes is with *mapped types*. Given a union type of string, integer, or symbol literals, you can define indexes like this:

```
type Point = {
  [propname in 'x'|'y']: number
}
```

This Point type has two properties x and y, both of type number.

 CAUTION: This notation is similar to the syntax for indexed properties (see Section 13.11, "Indexed Properties," page 290). However, a mapped type has only one mapping, and it cannot have additional properties.

This example is not very useful. Mapped types are intended for transforming existing types. Given an Employee type, you can make all properties readonly:

```
type ReadonlyEmployee = {
  readonly [propname in keyof Employee]: Employee[propname]
}
```

There are two pieces of new syntax here:

- The type keyof T is the union type of all property names in T. That is 'name' | 'salary' | . . . in this example.

- The type $T[p]$ is the type of the property with name p. For example, Employee['name'] is the type string.

Mapped types really shine with generics. The TypeScript library defines the following utility type:

```
type Readonly<T> = {
  readonly [propname in keyof T]: T[propname]
}
```

This type marks all properties of T as readonly.

 TIP: By using Readonly with a parameter type, you can assure callers that the parameter is not mutated.

```
const distanceFromOrigin = (p: Readonly<Point>) =>
  Math.sqrt(Math.pow(p.x, 2) + Math.pow(p.y, 2))
```

Another example is the Pick utility type that lets you pick a subset of properties, like this:

```
let str: Pick<string, 'length' | 'substring'> = 'Fred'
  // Can only apply length and substring to str
```

The type is defined as follows:

```
type Pick<T, K extends keyof T> = {
  [propname in K]: T[propname]
};
```

Note that extends means "subtype." The type keyof string is the union of all string property names. A subtype is a subset of those names.

You can also remove a modifier:

```
type Writable<T> = {
  -readonly [propname in keyof T]: T[propname]
}
```

To add or remove the ? modifier, use ? or -?:

```
type AllRequired<T> = {
  [propname in keyof T]-?: T[propname]
}
```

Exercises

1. What do the following types describe?

   ```
   (number | string)[]
   number[] | string[]
   [[number, string]]
   [number, string, ...:number[]]
   [number, string, ...:(number | string)[]]
   [number, ...: string[]] | [string, ...: number[]]
   ```

2. Investigate the difference between functions with return type `void` and return type `undefined`. Can a function returning `void` have any `return` statements? How about returning `undefined` or `null`? Must a function with return type `undefined` have a `return` statement, or can it implicitly return `undefined`?

3. List all types of the functions of the `Math` class.

4. What is the difference between the types `object`, `Object`, and `{}`?

5. Describe the difference between the types

   ```
   type MaybeColoredPoint = {
     x: number,
     y: number,
     color?: string
   }
   ```

   and

   ```
   type PerhapsColoredPoint = {
     x: number,
     y: number,
     color: string | undefined
   }
   ```

6. Given the type

   ```
   type Weekday = 'Mon' | 'Tue' | 'Wed' | 'Thu' | 'Fri' | 'Sat' | 'Sun'
   ```

   is `Weekday` a subtype of `string` or the other way around?

7. What is the subtype relationship between `number[]` and `unknown[]`? Between `{ x: number, y: number }` and `{ x: number | undefined, y: number | undefined }`? Between `{ x: number, y: number }` and `{ x: number, y: number, z: number }`?

8. What is the subtype relationship between `(arg: number) => void` and `(arg: number | undefined) => void`? Between `() => unknown` and `() => number`? Between `() => number` and `(number) => void`?

9. What is the subtype relationship between `(arg1: number) => number` and `(arg1: number, arg2?: number) => number`?

10. Implement the function

```
const act = (x: { bark(): void } | { meow(): void }) => . . .
```

that invokes either `bark` or `meow` on `x`. Use the `in` operator to distinguish between the alternatives.

11. Show that object covariance is unsound. Use the types

```
type Colored = { color: string }
type MaybeColored = { color: string | undefined }
```

As with arrays in Section 13.7.3, "Array and Object Type Variance" (page 282), define two variables, one of each type, both referring to the same value. Create a situation that shows a hole in the type checker by modifying the `color` property of one of the variables and reading the property with the other variable.

12. In Section 13.11, "Indexed Properties" (page 290), you saw that it is impossible to declare

```
type Dictionary = {
  created: Date, // Error—not a string or string[]
  [arg: string]: string | string[]
}
```

Can you overcome this problem with an intersection type?

13. Consider this type from Section 13.11, "Indexed Properties" (page 290):

```
type ShoppingList = {
  created: Date,
  [arg: number] : string
}
```

Why does the following code fail?

```
const list: ShoppingList = {
  created: new Date()
}
list[0] = 'eggs'
const more = ['ham', 'hash browns']
for (let i in arr)
  list[i + 1] = arr[i]
```

Why does this code not fail?

```
for (let i in arr)
  list[i] = arr[i]
```

14. Give an example of supertype/subtype pairs for each of the rows of Table 13-1 that is different from those given in the table. For each pair, demonstrate that a supertype variable can hold a subtype instance.

15. The generic `Pair<T>` class from Section 13.13.5, "Generic Type Variance" (page 302), is covariant in `T`. Show that this is unsound. As with arrays in Section 13.7.3, "Array and Object Type Variance" (page 282), define two variables, one of type `Pair<Person>` and of type `Pair<Employee>`, both referring to the same value. Mutate the value through one of the variables so that you can produce a runtime error by reading from the other variable.

16. Complete the generic function

    ```
    const last = <. . .> (values: T)  => values[values.length - 1]
    ```

    so that you can call:

    ```
    const str = 'Hello'
    console.log(last(str))
    console.log(last([1, 2, 3]))
    console.log(last(new Int32Array(1024)))
    ```

    Hint: Require that `T` has a `length` property and an indexed property. What is the return type of the indexed property?

Index

Learn Scala & Java Quickly

- Get started quickly with Scala's interpreter, syntax, tools, and unique idioms

- Master core language features

- Become familiar with object-oriented programming in Scala

- Use Scala for real-world programming tasks

- Use modules to simplify the development of well-performing complex systems

- Express actions more concisely with lambda expressions

- Leverage modern concurrent programming based on cooperating tasks

informit.com/horstmann

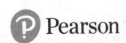

Credits